Holly Instone | Eloise Maniglia | Amelia Doyle | Camille Foltyn | Steph Se— ONTARIO
Elizabeth | Cristy Guillermo | Marissa Thill | Jinade Garside | Rebecca Ke—
| Sarita Doell | Sarah Codyre | Eve O'Brien | Charles Baksh | Rico Blankespoor | Marissa Bailey | Shaina
Ensing | Maryem Mangera | Teighan Sinclair | Lucy New | Meg Trenham | Chantelle Alberts | Inez
MacIntosh | Ashleigh Kail | Jess Rood | Liliya Tsacheva | Ornella Saitta | Kristoff— —lie | Alana
Quinn | Izzie Rowey | Aisha Akhtar | Sara Vieira | Meg Gainsford | Rea— —— | Azayah
Campbell | Marie Tintinger | Emma Farmer | Deanna Gonfal— —— Jeffries
Mathilde Bernard | Joseph McQueen | Immy Gray | Pri— —— Sobetsk
| Lolita Minasova | Lina Hellberg | Caroline Stump | No— —orran
Sukii Sahota | Sophia Kormind | Sinéad Fitzgibbon | Dan— —Schat—
| Helena Hollins | Eliza Burdass | Morgan Jai | Hannah G— —rry Sharp
| Emily Jenkinson | Aimee Fitzpatrick | Doireann McInerne— —nnon | Rebecca Bet—
| Sarah Lawrence | Olivia Coombs | Andrea Zinck | Paig— —na Oliveira | Clara Gregger
Catherine Smallbone | Jessica Jeppesen | Lauren Macfarlane —ophie Roiter | Lindsay McCafferty | André
Zink | Julia Hedemann | Ruta Buzo | Mia Turco | Summer Henthorn | Millie Turton | Dana Chapin | Lydia
Dale | Ariah Hills | Rika Kulschewski | Greer Thomson | Katie Small | Nathan Jariwala | Jeanny Ong | Reina
Enrique | Adina Shaw | Zoe Stins | Daša Janičijevič | Patrycja Zelezniak | Maysa Marres | Ludivine Lavigne
| Jeanette Andersen | Nicola Haire | Brydie Clark | Matthew Goldsworthy | Gemma Albin | Stina Teesaar
Brontë Grosvenor | Jema Walsh | Phoebe Warn | Nathan van der Heijden | Nicola Barker | Syazana Gonzaga
| Melanie Kowalewski | Jaye Henderson | Rena Santiago | Noora Airaksinen | Megan Cabl | Casey Rowe
Sophie Wrench | Zabtq Pez | Craig Brownlee | Judy Huynh | Eilidh Rayfield | Danika Shanhun | Sarah Miles
| Shristy Roy | Lexi H | Natacha Orford | Cristina Loan Ballestin | Ulrika Nordström | Jordan Goldie | Sarah
Mcdonald | Seren Timothy | Brielle Tilley | Sofia Larsson | Katrein Eder | Monique Pavleska | Chloe Bater
Rebecca McGuinness | Emma Busby | Emily Cribbs | Lili Hristovski | Dan Teodorescu | Kayleigh William—
| Grace Wheatley | Linda Snoek | Emma Towers | Faith Verderose | Jennifer Stringer | Alina Volzhanskaya
| Paige Louise | Martina Vella | Ana Duff | Caroline Abbott | Christina§ Sanchez | Chantelle Hodges | Laure—
Bussey | Daniela Cernicchiaro | Laura Goudie | Isabella Lewandowski | Lydia Hawkins | Maja Baškovč
Jonathan Mendes | Ashleigh Chilton | Arianna Testi | Megan Town | Charlie Andrews | Amadia Iuhas
Yasmin Larni | Cara Tate | Célestine Maurey | Sarah Waters | Pernille Liu Lofthus | Dominika Wrzos | Crysta—
Nicole | Aisling Maher | Rachel Babbage | Rhiannon Bealey | Melissa Carson | Grace Nagle | Raniya Dass
Akane Irifune | Megan Carro-Lemay | Ane Høgsberg | Keean Yap | Amar Marouf | Jane T. | Stacie Jackson
| Holly Aspinall | XY Leung | Jasmine Casidy | Kimmy Weedon | Hasna Mahmood | Alessandra Wilkinson
Smith | Rachel Nell | Mette Scheuer Larsen | Yerkem Sembayeva | Sophia Guddemi | Svea Nöll | Sabrina
Stroj | Laura Zecha | Renee Bardōt | Pauline Huet | Maria Simensen | Curtis Coady | Siqiao Zeng | Poppy
Borges-Wilby | Abbey McFadden | Aimon Polidano | Emily McPhee | Brayden Peeters | Jessica Gayle
Miriam Meller | Matilda Hamara | Emily Hough | Catherine Baldwin | Katie Iverach | Josi Lucke | Swetha
Ilangovan | Amy Davis | Freyja Björnsdottir | Michelle Hoowin | Denise Mäkinen | Courtney Collier | Josipa
Babic | Vigdis Knudsen Moe | Alysha Devine | Evie Kent | Selma Serdarevic | Laura Minns | Mali Ealand
Lynn de Veer | Trudie Walker | Domenica Furina | Rósa Egholm | Antonia Araouzou | Eva Noa Albers van
der Linden | Ilya Kim | Laura Killeen | Eliza Sharpe | Lisa Breiteig | Elizabeth Nabwire | Ellen Pannell
Vannessa Chew | Nicole Brock | Sanchana Jadhav | Yara Edward | Kristen Constantinou | Daisy Hudson
Amy Fredella | Ashley Disley | Maddie Gill | Gemma Bell | Natalie Jane Cupac | Anna Bondesson | Paula
Kennedy | Harri Hughes | Zoha Kamran | Robin Sterrenburg | Polina Zarnitskaya | Roxy Boettge | Courtney
Yule | Hattie Frakes | Vera Kulish | Sophie Szibbat | Tatyana Trifanova | Maryam Sheikh | Caitlin Matthews
| Rebecca Klein | Beth Allen | Margarida Rito | Danielle Schmidt | Pavel Alam | Charlotte Angelvin |
Hannah M | Gemma C | Helin Kurisoo | Bessie Fairweather | Aymanne Z | Sulistiya Sunaryo | Morwenna
Hope | Shona Ferguson | Ffion Hopley | Laura Slater | Cassie Heyden | Tia Lowe | Caitlin Crothers | Hollie
Minney | Carly Strange | Ahmad Fawaz | Abeerah Haseeb | Gracey Ponifasio | Hannah Vallee | Kristin
Sundal | Holly Edmondson | Chelsea Mirrin | Brandon Stubbs | Maddy Yeomans | Olivia Latham-Duut
Alex Bool | Kay Ineson | Maddie Binding | Masha Nazarova | Fraser Bootman | Holly MacDonald | Agnieszka
From space | Victoria Cliff | Kylie Burton | Melissa Ciappara | Demi Alexandra | Darci Buck | Joyce Palgrave
| Charlotte Turland | Alicia Lichtenstern | Miriam Goa | Amy Bunting | Rachel Luke | Lucy Palmer | Nicole
O' Connor | Rob Connett | Danielle Fernandes | Caitlin Manalo | Kathleen Maggs | Lara van Haaps | Rhea
Shah | Kimberley Pham | Sam Graham | Mark Shtafinskyi | Sofie Roenning | Jing Sheng Li | Dina Linda
Milberga | Georgie Farr | Amy Gallimore | Katie Harlow | Amber Shelton | Katie Patchett | Tanushree Sikda—
| Adéle Heiberg | Mia Manthorp | Yvonne Keeley | Emilia Kariuki | Samantha Lugowski | Jennifer Maniciat
| Rebecca Barnwell | Regina Gonsalves | Cassie Webster | Annika Hanau | Ashlyn Carroll | Charlotte Leigh
| Jessica Purnell | Preeya Lakhani | Courtney Dove | Ryan Cotter | Erin Jayne | Agnieszka Kulus | Maria
Traczyk | Louise Ballantyne | Kaytie Extance | Laura Culkin | Amelia H—

FEB - - 2018

147 THINGS

Jim Chapman

147 THINGS

My user's guide to the universe,
from black holes to belly buttons

SIDGWICK & JACKSON

First published 2017 by Sidgwick & Jackson
an imprint of Pan Macmillan
20 New Wharf Road, London N1 9RR
Associated companies throughout the world
www.panmacmillan.com

ISBN 978-1-5098-5415-8

9 8 7 6 5 4 3 2 1

A CIP catalogue record for this book is available from the British Library.

Printed and bound by CPI Group (UK) Ltd, Croydon, CR0 4YY

Visit **www.panmacmillan.com** to read more about all our books
and to buy them. You will also find features, author interviews and
news of any author events, and you can sign up for e-newsletters
so that you're always first to hear about our new releases.

For Brian

Contents

Introduction

Since the dawn of time there have been many important questions. Are we alone in the universe? Is there anything after death? What is the meaning of life? Which dinosaur had the biggest penis?*

My name's Jim Chapman and at any one time I would say that about 90 per cent of my brain is made up of an entirely random jumble of facts, stats and notions.

Want to know whether the chicken or the egg came first? I'm your guy.

Interested in how far back in time you could go to kidnap a baby that would be able to deal with twenty-first-century life? Step this way.

Whether it be how this planet went from dust, rocks and water swirling in space to a place where your phone knows more than you ever will, how the first ever living organism came into being, or why on earth I have nipples that I don't need, my thirst for knowledge is nigh on unquenchable. My wife, Tanya, bears the brunt of most of this, as I come running into a room brandishing a fact like an excitable child who wants to show you his new toy but won't let you actually touch it. If she's not available, I'll tell the nearest thing with ears (usually my dog, Martha) and for a moment I'll feel very smug, safe in

---

* The slightly underwhelming answer is that we don't know for sure. We need bones for fossils to survive and, despite the slang name, there aren't any in this particular part of the body. Birds and reptiles are the closest living relatives to dinosaurs and their genitalia-size to body-size ratio varies quite a lot. The best guess is that a forty-foot-long *Tyrannosaurus rex* would likely have had a penis length of between ten inches and twelve feet. So now you know. Makes that scene in *Jurassic Park* take on a whole new meaning, doesn't it?

the knowledge that I am, without doubt, the smartest human to have ever existed. Then I'm off to replace what I just discovered with some other nugget of information that is equally as non-essential to my life, but super interesting nonetheless.

What would happen if you found yourself in the vacuum of space in nothing but your underwear? What is it about the way we communicate on the internet that can make people so rude? Were cave men and women into fashion? What is it about the modern world that makes so many people feel so anxious? Why the bloody hell can't horses vomit?

The truth is, I barely get by as a functional member of society, but I do know a lot of weird things. I'm fascinated by this stuff because it throws into perspective just how wondrous life is. The sheer unlikelihood that any of it exists at all, that we are all made of atoms born in distant stars, that you're reading marks made by shooting oil and salt onto mashed up trees and you can understand them.* That you are you, that I am me and we know what that means, that we can communicate to each other using language. Every day I discover something that makes me feel either minuscule or so overwhelmingly rare that I struggle to comprehend it, and both of those feelings excite me. In a world in which we're so focused on now, and so often worried, it bears repeating that we are exceedingly lucky to exist at all. Not just to be living, but to be this version of you that lives right here and right now. You are just about the most unlikely thing in the entire universe and that should be celebrated, at least with a decent-sized high five (if you have nobody near enough to touch, do it in your head under the promise that, should our paths cross, I will gladly high your five at a moment's notice).

It's easy to get deadened to the astonishing things around us in today's world and I wanted to write something that was

---

* Or on liquid crystals, or through ionized gas, or microcapsules full of clear fluid, or beamed direct into your brain unit or whatever new way of reading they've invented whenever you're reading this.

full of marvels, something that helps you to realize how exceptional, how fascinating and how bloody strange it all is.

I also know, because the people who have found me via social media often tell me, that for lots of us, very often, it all feels a bit much. Every generation thinks it's the first to experience the hot mess of adolescence and adulthood, but for those of us who've come of age in the glare of the internet, we really have had to deal with an intensity to certain experiences that no previous generation has. I love my job and I love the new ways of communicating, creating and connecting that technology provides, but it would be silly to ignore the stories, the studies and the research into how our constantly switched-on world is impacting on us.

One of my favourite facts is that canned food was invented in 1810, but nobody thought of inventing the can opener until 1858, which means that for nearly fifty years, people must have been bashing cans against rocks and hoping for the best. Comparatively, the internet is a pre-teen and social media is in its infancy, and so sometimes it feels as if we're at the stage of throwing the tin against anything hard and seeing if food comes out.

Much to my dismay, it dawned on me recently that I am an actual real-life human adult and I remember a time when it took forty-five minutes to send an email. I grew up without much access to the web and fell into my job at a very strange and exciting time. As such, I found myself in a fairly unique position; I was just the right age to witness and embrace the changeover from Encyclopaedia Britannica to Wikipedia, and have made my career from that odd and totally world-altering shift.

Doing what I do means that I have met a lot of people – some of whom know me via my job, some of whom haven't got a bloody clue who I am – and, almost without exception, the humans that live today are among the most intelligent, interested, funny and surprising people you could ever hope to come across. I wanted to write a book that they would all find interesting. Of course, I am a complete over-sharer, so there are lots of stories about my life in here too, because these are things that have either helped me to not die, or have made existing that little bit more manageable (or because there's just a really funny anecdote about me waxing my dangly bits and I couldn't leave it out).

This isn't going to be a book that begins with me being born (because the creation of the universe and life in general is marginally more important than my existence – marginally, mind) but you will find out lots of things you probably won't already know from my outpouring online. I'll share them with you because I think the thing that happened is interesting and/or because I'm a moron and learned whatever lesson it taught me the hard way, and I'd like to save you the pain of making the same mistakes (again, I refer to the waxing of my genitals).

I should point out that the only thing that qualifies me to do this is curiosity. I'm not a scientist, or a psychologist, or an expert in much,* but pretty much everything fascinates me. There's also a list at the end of the book of places you can go to find out about any subjects that might especially interest or affect you.

I have a YouTube channel, as well as the other usual suspects when it comes to social media; I'm a presenter; I do a bit of modelling here and there; I write for magazines and you might hear my voice on the radio once in a while. Of all my siblings, I'm the only one with a degree (and half a masters, but for some reason there is no award for this. I push for 'halfster'), which apparently makes me 'The Smart One'. Personally, I don't believe a word of that; both my twin brother and my two sisters are already accomplished authors, talented individuals and general overachievers. One thing I do know for sure how to do is appreciate when I'm out of my depth and when it's time to call in an expert. So, throughout this book I'll introduce you to a range of geniuses and remarkably interesting boffins.

_____

* Though I do know bloody loads about Harry Potter.

From the science of heartbreak to what would really happen if you fell into a volcano, from being addicted to our phones to why having a dog in your house is so weird when you really think about it, and from finding your purpose to coping strategies and the end of the world, I'll cover the entire contents of my brain, and some of the suggestions that have come from yours, too.

These are the 147 Things that I know. The entire content of my noggin. Some are deep and important, and they've had a massive impact on me. Others are ridiculous and seem inconsequential, but they all have their place in my life, and it wouldn't surprise me if they find a place in yours, too. Because here's the first thing I know: most of the time the world feels like it's in complete chaos – things are constantly changing, the traffic is terrible and I'm usually running late to whatever thing I'm supposed to be at – but regardless of train strikes, traffic jams, the impending apocalypse, or the bottom of your shopping bag ripping open, being alive is really bloody brilliant.

Whatever age you are, it always feels like the generation above you are better at being adults. My nan celebrated her ninety-third birthday recently and still tells me that she feels the age that I am now. I'm approaching thirty and will not hesitate to tell you that I'm totally unqualified for the mortgage that I am currently paying and the dog I am responsible for. I'm married, for Christ's sake. I'm an actual adult, yet I'm adamant that I'm sixteen years old. I can remember when I was growing up, waiting for the moment I'd suddenly have figured it all out. That moment has yet to come for me, and if my ninety-three-year-old nan is still waiting for it, I'm not convinced it ever will. But you know what? The more I think about it, the more I think that life would be dull if we knew how to do it all properly. Where's the challenge in an existence that you're totally prepared for? What can you learn if you already know everything? If you feel like you're bullshitting your way through life, join the club – there are about 7 billion of us waiting for you there. Look at the bigger picture to give yourself some perspective.

Therein lies the magic; stepping back and remembering that I'm one of 7 billion hairless apes spinning through a universe so large that it's impossible to comprehend can actually make my day-to-day seem a bit less stressful. If I'm ever cursing my luck about something, remembering the fact that every one of my long line of ancestors stretching back to the beginning of humankind managed to reproduce before dying makes me feel pretty lucky (all of us exist because they literally got lucky). If ever I'm scared that things are changing too fast, it makes me feel a little less freaked out to remember that every year a very large percentage of the atoms that make up our bodies are replaced, that change is the only constant and that if I didn't change, I'd die.

I'm going to share everything I know and I'm pretty confident that, ironically, by the time I get it all down on paper, my brain will be nothing more than a useless lump of pink scrambled egg whose only remaining purpose will be to perform the basic tasks required to keep a human body going. But I have a lot of good stuff to share with you so I'll take one for the team.

Without further ado, here it is, my guide to the universe, my 147 Things.

Thing 1:
The chances of you being alive right now to read this book are about 1 in $10^{2,685,000}$

Before we get going, let's just take a moment to appreciate the sheer scale of this insanity.

When I sat down to write this book, I fully intended to type out the number above in full. I wanted to demonstrate the vastness of the figure and what a miracle your existence is. But then I took a moment to think about it and, upon reflection, it occurred to me that wasting my time and yours by typing a single '1' followed by 2,685,000 zeroes wouldn't improve anyone's life. Despite that, I did actually have a crack at it and quickly changed my mind. After only one full page of zeroes (and the initial 1) at font size twelve, I had only used up 2,814 characters. With 2,682,187 remaining, I made myself a peppermint tea and worked out just how many pages it would take to complete the statistic. It turns out it's a little over 954. With that in mind, just take my word for it when I say that you are indeed a unique and beautiful snowflake and if anyone ever tries to tell you any different, you now have $10^{2,685,000}$ reasons why they are wrong.

It was a clever chap by the name of Ali Binazir who did the maths and came up with a pretty hefty equation that worked out the probability of you. Here are some of the most amazing bits:

The chances of your parents meeting in the first place were about 1 in 20,000 and the odds of them having a child would vary according to time and place, but work out at somewhere around 1 in 2,000. Following so far? These numbers are pretty big, but at this point you are not so astronomically rare that my brain wants to dribble from my nose. But wait, because now we get to your folks engaging in intercourse, having sex, making love, bumping uglies, doing the no-pants dance (as much as you won't want to think about it, it's very likely that they did do this at least once, and I bet they enjoyed it too and made loads of noise) and the moment of your conception. At this point, the numbers suddenly skyrocket. In his lifetime, the average male will produce around 525 billion sperm cells, somewhere in the region of 80 million of which are set free with every ejaculation, while women are born with roughly 2 million eggs. The probability of the sperm that made half of you meeting the egg that made the other half was roughly 1 in 400 quadrillion (for your reference, here is what that number looks like: 400,000,000,000,000,000).

Of course, you didn't happen in isolation and everything you just read relates only to the generation that directly created you. When you think bigger and trace it back over millennia, accounting for you, your parents, grandparents and all their parents as far back as possible, the odds of them meeting and tolerating each other long enough to touch their bits together, then the combined odds against the long line of ancestors who made you existing are so huge that it makes me feel sick.[*]

If you're still not convinced that you are a miracle, picture this: in the observable universe,[†] there are 10 billion galaxies (or possibly 2 trillion as of the end of 2016 – I mean, who's counting?), each with an estimated 100 billion stars. That makes a billion trillion – or one sextillion – stars in the universe. A

---

[*] It also pretty quickly becomes more people than have ever existed, which is another story, but let's just say that it's a certainty that in the not too distant past, more than kissing cousins was *definitely* a thing.

[†] Observable Universe. The first thing I always think when I hear this is that there must also be an unobservable universe. Right? What's going on there then? The simple answer is nobody knows. There's all sorts of complex maths

YOU ARE RARER THAN A HEN WITH TEETH EATING A FOUR LEAF CLOVER WITH A SNOWFLAKE ON IT

involved but the basic principle is that we can only see things that are close enough to us that light emitted since the big bang has reached us. So, beyond the bit we know about, all 93 billion light years of it, there is a massively bigger part we just can't see. In theory. It would be a fair assumption that past that point is just more universe, but really there could be anything – plasma monkeys, planets made entirely of peanut butter, more Kardashian sisters.

billion trillion looks like this: 1,000,000,000,000,000,000,000,000. When written down, all of the stars we can see in the universe don't even take up a whole line of this book, but the probability of you existing takes up 954 pages. If that's not enough, the number of atoms in the known universe that make up those stars and the planets and everything else that has ever existed and ever will exist is estimated to be 10^{80}. That's 100,000, 000,000,000,000,000,000,000,000,000,000,000,000,000, 000,000,000,000,000,000,000,000,000,000,000,000,000 and it's not even a scratch on you.

Sometimes the world has a way of making you feel ordinary, when the truth is, according to maths and according to physics and according to biology, you are among the rarest and most special things within it.

Now that's out the way, let's get on with things.

Thing 2:
Curiosity killed the cat
(and hurt my testicles)

Having only just said it's brilliant to be curious and full of wonder, I'd like to begin with a cautionary tale. It's important to remember that you can't un-know stuff. You'll have eaten the apple from the tree of knowledge, or taken the red pill, or walked in on your parents as they were 'play fighting'. I know that many of the things that help me find perspective freak other people out. For example, when I told my wife that the chances of her existing were 1 in $10^{2,685,000}$ she said, 'I don't understand what you're going on about and it scares me to think about that.' Regardless, it's only fair to be up front about the things that I have learned, even if you can't sugar-coat them.

To illustrate this, I want to begin with the story of the time I 'accidentally' stuck a wax strip to my undercarriage and spent the next two hours in excruciating pain. Note the use of inverted commas around the word 'accidentally'. I suppose, technically, I put it there on purpose, but only because I had a spare one and I was curious to see if it would work and if it would cause as much pain as I anticipated. (It didn't work and it caused a whole lot more pain that I had anticipated.)*

Once a month or so, I will have a bit of a body blitz from top to bottom; I'll give my beard an extra thorough tidy and get rid of those sparse necky bits, pluck any long, unwanted eyebrow hairs, I'll cut my toenails, trim my armpits, give my chest hair a once over and have a crack at the other area you tend to have significant growth. Most of the time I will do any body-hair trimming with a trimmer that reaches all the intimate areas of a man's body without too much difficulty, but on this occasion I had spotted a few rogue hairs on my shoulders which needed to be dealt with. There are some parts of my body that I would rather have hair-free and my shoulders are two of them, so I put the trimmer down and reached for the wax strips.

As you can probably appreciate, this hour or so in the bathroom to give my body the once over is not one of the most dignified of my life, so I like to do it when my wife isn't around. She doesn't knock before entering a room and I prefer to engage in the sort of positions necessary for efficient hair removal without an audience, in an effort to maintain at least a modicum of mystery about me. In this instance, she had popped to the shops and we were going to meet later for lunch.

Anyway, it's not like my shoulders had a particularly dense growth and a few minutes later they were as smooth as a baby's bottom. A little pink, but free of any fluff. However, I was left with a dilemma; the wax strips I was using were the type that come in a pair, stuck together. To use them, you peel them apart and you end up with two sticky bits. My shoulders only needed

---

* This is what I believe the scientific community call 'an experiment'.

five and five is an odd number, meaning I was left with the sixth strip.

I've always been a curious soul, so with the rest of my being already at optimal hair length and my reluctance to waste the spare, I figured, 'What the hell, I'll try anything once,' and stuck the sixth strip to my testicles. Hindsight is a wonderful thing and it took me all of about 3.7 seconds after application and the initial 'Is it secure?' tug to realize that what I had done may have been a slight error in judgement. You might not know this, but when waxing, ideally you want a taut, plump surface so that when you tear the strip away the skin stays put while the wax and any hairs caught in it are removed. To be clear: I learned this fact later.

I took a deep breath, pulled myself as taut as possible with one hand, took the wax strip with the other, closed my eyes and yanked. The strip released about a centimetre as the force of my pull took my testes from my grasp and everything that I had tried to keep firm quickly relaxed and simply moved with the strip. Needless to say, the pain was excruciating and was made much, much worse by the knowledge that I still had nearly an entire adhesive strip to remove and would have to endure for a lot longer.

Another tug, another yelp, lots more eye watering, only very minimal movement with the wax and the panic begins to set in. What if I can't get it off? I would definitely not call my wife for help. I couldn't let her see me like this. I would have to divorce her afterwards out of sympathy for putting her through such an ordeal. Did I have any male friends I felt comfortable enough to be naked and vulnerable with, and who I trusted not to film it and put the footage online immediately? Maybe my mum? No way, what a ludicrous idea. The fear talking. Just suck it up and have another go.

After the third go I very nearly did call my mum, but then I remembered the little oily sheets you get in the box with the wax strips that you use to melt away any excess after successful hair removal. The issue was that this most definitely did not fall under the category of successful hair removal. It was catastrophic and had barely removed any hair at all. Regardless, I opened up the first of the sachets, removed the sheet and went to work. Really, these sheets are supposed to be used to remove nothing more than a little waxy residue and they were totally inadequate for the thick coating I had glued to me.

By this point, I can honestly say that any semblance of a human personality had burnt away and I was the purest expression of my animal self. I felt like those creatures that gnaw their own legs off to escape from a trap, though in my circumstances that was definitely not going to be an option (my head couldn't reach, or I might have tried). However, an hour later, after much experimentation, including with my wife's various kinds of oily make-up remover, I was sat shaking on the edge of the bath holding a defiantly hairless wax strip. I concluded that:

1. Having a curious mind is a brilliant thing, but I can now see what happened to the cat.

2. There are some things man is just not meant to know.

3. Waxing your testicles is a terrible idea.

HOW DID WE GET HERE?

Thing 3:
Make the most of planet Earth; it's only going to exist for a billion more years

The traditional way to begin one of those 'Jim Chapman: My Story' books would be to talk about me being born. But this isn't really *my* story and I'm a morbid soul so I thought I'd begin with how everything is going to die.

So, before we go any further, I'm going to give a brief history of the entire universe up to now. I reckon this should take me about 24 pages in total, but do bear with me. It's genuinely fascinating and might put into perspective the stuff about kissing and puberty that is yet to come.*

Most of us take the Sun for granted. If we pay it attention at all, it's either grumbling that it's come up as we pull the duvet back over our head in the morning, moaning there's not enough of it in the summer, or doing that very British thing of announcing after one day of sunshine that now it's 'too hot, I mean, I like it hot, but this is too hot'. But without it, not only would there be no life on Earth, there would be no anything.

It's kind of ironic that the basis of every single thing we know of on Earth is made up of stars that died a long time ago, yet (assuming us humans don't blow the planet up in the next billion years, which is a very big assumption) it's our closest star that will ultimately destroy it all.

The Sun, as I'm sure you are already aware, is a burning ball

---

* That said, there's a good story about my first kiss if you skip to page 135.

of hydrogen and helium gas (with small amounts of other bits and bobs) 149,600,000 km away in space. If the Sun was the circle below, then Earth would be this full stop.

It's fair to say it's quite big, and it's held together by the same gravity that allows the planets in the solar system to orbit around it. We love the Sun because, without it, Earth would be cold and barren and dead (and it would be very hard to get a tan), but it's already tolerated us for four fifths of the time it's willing to and, in about a billion years or so, it'll throw its toys out of the pram in a cataclysmic grump.

A billion years, you say? That's ages. A billion years ago we were all just sludge and now we have aeroplanes and iPads and emojis (and Kimojis). In another billion years, think what we could do.

Well, yes, you're right to an extent. But it will happen. It's non-negotiable. Now I don't know about you, but I can still remember lying awake at night trying to get my head around the fact that I would definitely die. When I think about the Sun dying, I get a similar feeling.*

---

* However, on the plus side, matter and energy can't be destroyed or created, but can only change form. You are made from the universe and the universe will go on being made from you long after your consciousness stops being aware of it. You are and will always be a tiny but important part of the greatest show there is. The best explanation for dying I ever heard was that we go back to where we were before we were born.

So how will this happen, Jim?

The Sun emits more energy in one second than has been used in the entirety of mankind's history via a process called fusion, which transforms hydrogen into helium and a little light and heat. Once our star has exhausted the hydrogen in its core, fusion stops and the outward pressure of the reaction means the Sun is no longer strong enough to resist the force of gravity, so it caves in on itself. The entire mass of the star is squeezed into an increasingly small spot where the heat and pressure become so great that all of the helium created by the initial reaction actually transforms into carbon. The energy from this is so great that it sticks two fingers up to gravity and starts to swell.

Our adorable little home planet is situated smack bang in the middle of what is known as the habitable zone. We're not so far from the Sun that we freeze to death and not so close that everything we know and love combusts and turns to ashes. However, when the Sun expands, the habitable zone in our solar system is going to get a lot less habitable.

It's estimated that the Sun will still exist for another 5 billion years or so after that, but it won't go quietly and we're all screwed well before it finally kicks the celestial bucket. As it expands it will become a red giant, and swallow Mercury and Venus and most likely Earth too. The good news is that there is a possibility that it won't grow large enough to actually engulf us. The bad news is that it makes absolutely no difference either way because we'll be much too close to it and therefore much too dead long before it touched us.

The best estimates give a life expectancy for Earth of somewhere around the billion-year mark. Bearing in mind that this planet was only created about 4.5 billion years ago, it's less than you might have hoped for. Still, a billion years should probably be plenty of time to find another star with another suitable planet in another habitable zone for us to get cosy on – after all, there are about 60 billion potential home worlds in the Milky

Way alone. Then again, some estimates make a compelling case that human beings will be extinct in the next 100 years because of the rate we are using up our resources, destroying the planet and killing one another. We just about invented aeroplanes and iPads and emojis (and Kimojis) the first time around. I really don't fancy our chances if we have to start again.

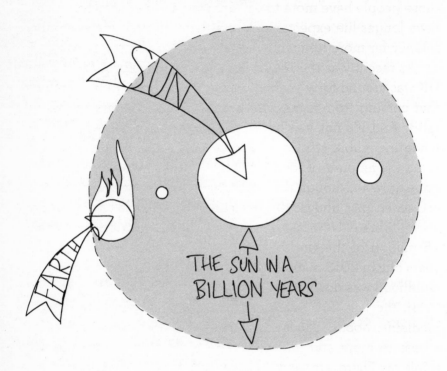

THE SUN IN A BILLION YEARS

A brief Interlude to cheer you up

At this point I imagine you're thinking, *Oh great, thanks, Jim. I bought your book as a fun read and so far we've had your testicles in extreme close-up and the death of everything.*

Fair point. Here're three quick things to turn that frown upside down . . .

Thing 4:
Things are definitely getting better

Fewer people than ever before in human history are dying; those people have more to eat, are staying in education longer, have longer life expectancies and their children are surviving infancy far more frequently.[*]

As recently as the 1840s, the average life expectancy in the UK was around forty years old. Now it's eighty, with the bulk of that coming from a massive improvement in infant mortality rates. And it's not just here – all countries in the world have made incredible strides on life expectancy. Over the last fifty years the amount of food available for the average person has gone up, even though the population has doubled. In 1800, it's estimated just under 90 per cent of the people of the world were illiterate. Now it's under 20 per cent. In 1990, more than 7.5 million of the world's children died before they were five years old; in 2013, a study found the number of people dying in childhood was down to 3.7 million.

In the last 200 years, whether it's clean air, clean water, medicine, books, education, light – more of humankind has access to more and more of pretty much everything you can think of. There are seven Harry Potter films, and they're all bloody fantastic.

This isn't to say that there aren't awful things happening all over the planet, or that you shouldn't feel sad sometimes. And it most certainly isn't to say that you should sit back and put your feet up: job done, humanity has reached its apex. We can always do better and should absolutely aim for zero starvation and 100 per cent education in a world where nobody gets sick.

---

[*] All of the data I'm using here comes from different bits of the brilliant website ourworldindata.org, which you should check out if you're interested in this sort of thing.

And I'm certainly not ignoring the very real problems that we face from our growing population and climate change. But, on balance, despite the news headlines telling us how terrible everything is, the fundamental story of humanity is probably a good news story. Well done, humans, give yourselves a pat on the back.

On a personal level, having been on a trip to Sierra Leone with Comic Relief while writing this book, I can say that I was ultimately left with a tremendous sense of optimism that the massive challenges people are facing will be overcome. I spent some time in a slum community and met a bunch of the young men who were playing football on a tatty rectangle of dusty earth with a knackered old ball. They lived in abject poverty and I just assumed they would be desperate and angry and sad. I was naive to assume that, because the contentment they had from food, shelter and clean water made me realize how much I focus on completely non-essential things. There was nothing else for them to buy or own other than the essentials and so all that mattered was making sure there was enough to eat, enough to drink, a place to sleep and plenty of friends for a kick about.

Though there was sadness and struggle, it was impossible to come away feeling anything other than optimism. You and I are part of the most adaptable, resourceful and imaginative species on the planet and that's something to feel good about.

Thing 5:
Doing your good deed for the day will make you feel great

Pick a point in our modern history and the chances are that there was something big happening: the Magna Carta, two world wars, a cold war, Syrian refugees, Trump as president. Living in a world of instability and massive change can lead to a general feeling of uncertainty, add that to the mountain of stuff that we live with on a day-to-day basis, such as running late for work, your boss being a complete dick, not having enough money to make ends meet or getting bullied at school, and you have a recipe for feeling powerless and generally a bit rubbish. Here's a way to take the edge off: study after study has shown that helping others actually makes you feel better. Giving to charity triggers your mesolimbic system, which deals with rewards in your brain and also sets off chemicals that make you feel good. There have also been studies that show people who volunteer and give to charity have higher self-esteem, stronger friendships, have a more optimistic outlook on life and feel more peaceful, purposeful and generally like they can change the world. Obviously, you shouldn't now beat yourself up if you're not currently doing this stuff – that certainly won't help – but it is worth bearing in mind that sometimes when you give a little you literally do get a little.

Thing 6:
The giant panda is no longer an endangered species

OK, there are still only 2,000 of them in the wild and they're still listed as 'vulnerable', but they are no longer endangered and that has to make you feel pretty good. They're also frickin' adorable when they sneeze. Google it.

OK, that's enough of the warm and fuzzy stuff, back to our whistle-stop tour of the birth and death (mainly death) of the universe.

Thing 7:
The world was no fun 4.5 billion years ago (let's not go back there)

It's a common thing for people to say that life was better in the old days. But it's worth remembering that for most of its existence the universe hasn't been a particularly welcoming place for life.

Let's go back, right to the beginning.

In the beginning, everything that became the universe was crunched into an almost infinitely small point called a singularity. There is no before. In fact, it's kind of freaky to get your head around where it is, since space and time didn't exist yet.* Then, 13.8 billion years ago, it expanded with a speed and scale that just isn't possible to think about. Inside the first second, gravity and every other force in the universe came into existence.

One minute into the big bang, the temperature of the rapidly expanding universe (it's about a million billion miles big at this stage) was about 10 billion degrees. Over the next 10 billion years, things got a bit less hostile and 5 billion years ago our sun was born, surrounded by a cloud of gas and debris that

---

* It's OK if you can't get your head around this. I mean, time didn't even exist. So how long was the singularity there for before it exploded? Forever? For no time at all? Did it just pop into existence the very same instance it went 'pop'? There are scientists whose whole careers are spent picking apart the first trillionth of a second after the big bang. It's entirely mental and I can totally see the attraction of the 'work your arse off for six days, rest on the seventh' model.

over the next hundred million years would slowly begin to form the planets, moons and asteroids in our solar system.

So, to recap, it took a long time for Earth to exist (about 9 billion years from the birth of the universe) and for most of that time it was impossible for life to exist.

I really don't think we all appreciate having a planet as much as we should. And even when we got one, I'm not sure Earth was keen on the idea of having life on it, at least to begin with. It was a pretty hostile hunk of rock back then. The atmosphere consisted mostly of methane, ammonia, hydrogen and carbon dioxide – basically farts and bleach.

If you decided to hop in your time machine (which doesn't exist, so you couldn't) to take the dog out for a brisk stroll back then, you'd both die horrifying deaths before you'd even checked to make sure you were carrying poo bags. Then your corpses would quickly be cooked because, without oxygen to provide an ozone layer, UV radiation from the Sun utterly ravaged the surface of Earth.* It was stuffy, to say the least.

Somewhere between 3 and 4 billion years ago, life began. I can't imagine it was a particularly thrilling existence for those beings. Then again, seeing as this life consisted entirely of single-celled organisms, I can't imagine they had much of a clue.

History is a little hazy on the details, as 4 billion years is a long time and nearly all of the rock that would contain fossil records has worn away or melted back into the Earth's core. There is evidence, though, of at least one type of bacteria that was a complete game-changer.

This bacteria was called cyanobacteria and it was different from all of its bacteria friends. Basically, if Pixar made a film called *The Cells*, this would be the hero (if Pixar do make this film now, I want royalties). Rather than getting its energy from chemicals in the environment, this little guy got big and strong

---

* At this stage in the book, my editor wanted to put something accessible and welcoming. Nonsense, I said. Let's kill and cook an imaginary dog.

PLANET EARTH, 4.5 BILLION YEARS AGO

from the Sun's rays. It was the first organism to photosynthesize. (You may remember from school that photosynthesis is the process by which some living things harness light energy from the Sun's rays, which they then transform into the chemical energy that allows them to live and grow, or you may not.) The thing with photosynthesis is that it has a pretty nasty byproduct that would have massive implications on the world's climate and all life that was yet to come: oxygen.

Today, most life forms are big fans of oxygen; we humans, for example, very much enjoy breathing it, as does pretty much every complex organism that springs to mind.

However, before plucky little Cy, most of the world's life was anaerobic: it was intolerant to oxygen (which makes sense, seeing as there was hardly any of it around). Life forms gained energy from other gases or various chemicals found in their environments and were happy as clams to live in their toasty surroundings. Carbon dioxide, water vapour and methane are all greenhouse gases and they made up much of the air back then. Again, you probably learned this in school, but just in case: a greenhouse gas is one that effectively insulates the planet, allowing less of the Sun's energy to reflect off the surface of Earth and escape back into space. You know when you get into bed and it's really cold so you shove your entire body under the duvet and get warm really quick, but if you stay there too long you overheat? Imagine that but for an entire planet.

However, oxygen is greedy; it chemically reacts with pretty much everything and it completely changed the face of the planet. As the cyanobacteria gobbled up the carbon dioxide and released oxygen, the greenhouse effect lessened and the world got cooler as it grew an ozone layer.

At this point, it's worth giving an honorary mention to all those single-celled organisms that didn't like oxygen (which, remember, is pretty much *all* other life), because they died. RIP, little guys. Ultimately oxygen is great for us and the majority of other modern life, but it was less good for everything else.

About 541 million years ago though, there was a massive explosion of pretty much all of the complex life we know about. Life lives, then it dies, and the bodies of those once-living things – whether they are single-cell organisms or our earliest ancestors – are either eaten by bacteria or bigger things, or they fall to the floor. Over time, more and more dead things fell to the bottom of the ocean and were buried under generation after generation after generation of other dead things, as well as rock and general detritus (tonnes of poo, presumably; it's got to go somewhere).

Then, between 225 million and 65 million years ago, the dinosaurs got a go. Primates overlap for the last few years of the dinosaurs' bit (which must have been terrifying for the primates). Shortly after (in a planetary timescale, at least), 'dry-nosed' primates appear, and for the next 60 million years it's basically ape central, until about 2.5 million years ago, when you get our earliest relatives starting to appear. Fast forward to

200,000 years ago, and *Homo sapiens* arrives, then at some point in the next 100,000 years, we appear – *Homo sapiens sapiens*.

Then, for the next forty-odd thousand years, it's like a greatest hits compilation of cool-sounding ancient stuff – including Cro-Magnon, Neolithic, Mesopotamians, Minoans, Bronze Age, Ancient Egypt, Ancient Greece, Roman, Persian, the Han Dynasty – as we basically learn how to do EVERY-THING. Then there's the Middle Ages, which mainly consisted of poor people being taxed more than they could afford while royalty killed one another to be in charge, then there's early modern, and finally modern history.*

So that's basically everything. However, all the time this was going on, all the single-celled organisms were still lying there. And seeing as all life is carbon-based, all the carbon that made up these organisms was buried along with them. Over the eons and under the immense heat and pressure of all that was going on below and above this buried carbon, it reformed, altered and transformed into oil. Sometimes plant life that had sunk to the bottom of swamps got similar treatment and transformed into coal.

It took hundreds of millions of years for all of this to occur. Then, only in the last few thousand years, every once in a while, a group of people would work out that you could burn it.†

It wasn't until the 1800s that we went a bit oil crazy and decided to see if we could burn all of it.

Of course, when you burn carbon you release all that carbon dioxide, which goes about blanketing the Earth and heating it up just like it did all those millennia ago.

Despite our intelligence and the fact that we can trace life back 4 billion years and we are fully aware of what we are doing,

---

* That's the one that goes: War, Revolution, War, Revolution, Man on the Moon, War, War, Boaty McBoatface, Trump.

† I like to imagine all of the trial and error it took to see which stuff burnt. These stones? No. These ones? No. These ones? Yes. Water? No. Sand? No. This gloopy dirty water? Yes, that burns like a bastard.

we are still burning these fossil fuels and releasing the carbon dioxide that was safely stored away, under the crust of the planet. In just the few short centuries since humankind discovered fossil fuels, we have single-handedly sent the entire planet well on its way back to an atmosphere that is entirely unsuitable for most living things as we know them.

Can you imagine how annoying that must be for the universe? It spends 13.7 billion years going from absolutely nothing to absolutely everything by way of the big bang, it spends considerable time and effort making us a planet we can live on, and we manage to balls it up in about 200 years.

Today's plant life still soaks up carbon dioxide and releases oxygen, which should mitigate some of the extra CO_2 and keep our climate somewhat balanced. The trouble is that we seem discontented with only burning old life, and choose to deforest on a massive scale as well. With fewer trees around to inhale the spare carbon dioxide, it has nowhere to go, and continues to add to the global warming we are inflicting on the planet. According to the WWF, somewhere between 46–58,000 square miles of forest is destroyed each year to make room for agriculture and/or for the timber the trees provide. Not only does the absence of plant life mean that there is nothing to take up the carbon dioxide, but the act of deforestation itself and whatever springs up in the place of the forest usually pumps out even more of the stuff. It's estimated that 15 per cent of all greenhouse gas is emitted in just such circumstances.

Which brings us right up to seven years ago, of course, when I made the decision to start using some of that burnt carbon (transformed into electricity) to talk to a camera and post those chats on the internet. I was twenty-two years old and had heard about this new thing people were doing called YouTube. I decided to try it out by posting a video about my experiences at a music festival.

More recently still, I thought it would be a good idea to spend hours a day sitting at my laptop, writing a book, for which I did research on the effects of burning carbon-based fuels and resolved to install solar panels on my roof to make a start on using a renewable system.

It's not immediately obvious, but keeping the internet running requires data centres that need energy to function and to remain cool. Even reading one of my tweets or watching one of my videos has an impact – it's estimated that every ten minutes of online video consumed generates around 1g of carbon dioxide. It's not a huge amount, but when you consider that nearly the entire population is using the internet for myriad purposes, it soon mounts up to about 2 per cent of global emissions, and growing.

At the risk of getting all preachy (which is something I always want to avoid, even though I am passionate about this topic), what we have is finite and what we do has an impact. The crux is this: although we are all the most important things, right in the centre of our own worlds, the actual world takes the brunt of our decisions and at some point it will have had enough and suffocate us all.

It's basically just good party etiquette – don't turn up and think it's all about you, don't drink your host's booze and help yourself to their food, and don't leave a trail of destruction after you or you'll be asked to leave and won't be invited back.

Bottom line: pretty much the entirety of the past sucked. We didn't have electric lights, the internet or Netflix. I love living in a world where all those things exist and I'm definitely not saying that we should all move to a commune in the woods, but the problem is real and it is immediate. Until we adopt renewable energy on a global level, the future of our species (and a lot of life on Earth) will die in a hot mess. OK, now that's out the way, let's get on with thinking about what this all means to us.

While I was thinking about writing the beginning of this book, I was reading lots about human history and evolution, and you know what I found really odd? Pets.

Thing 8:
Having a pet is really weird when you think about it

Imagine if you went to someone's house and when you went to use the toilet, they had a small tiger shark in their bath. Surely you'd have some questions? So why is it completely normal for us to have 'slightly less dangerous' wolves and 'a little bit smaller but will still claw your hand to ribbons' wildcats around us? I've been fascinated with wildlife since I was tiny. I've been on safari and I'm a huge fan of David Attenborough, but the fact that we have brought some of those animals into our homes is very weird when you think about it.

If you witnessed somebody taking their pet giraffe for a walk or playing fetch with their penguin in the park, you'd have a few questions. We've essentially created man's best friend from wild wolves. They sleep in our beds, lick our faces, take up all the room on the sofa, fart continuously and snore louder than you'd think possible, and it has become so normal that we don't even consider how strange it is.

We've had domesticated dogs by our side for at least 20,000 years; they began as wolves that we slowly altered over countless generations by picking those with the bits that best suited our needs and breeding them with others. If we were looking for a dog with long legs, we'd find a couple with the lengthiest pins around and mate them. If we wanted the friendliest pooch we could muster, we'd go find a couple of well-mannered hounds, play some Barry White, maybe throw in a plate of spaghetti, *Lady and the Tramp*-style, and wait for the most affectionate puppies in the world to pop out. Selective mating like this is how we shaped so many different breeds of dog, the majority of which now look as little like a wolf as they do a horse. But the right canine and the right human will fit together beautifully and their bond will be all but unbreakable.

I'm not sure why, but children and animals tend to really like me. Adults are less fussed, but the fact that babies enjoy staring at my face, toddlers like to give me cheeky grins and most animals will single me out for cuddles makes me very happy.*

We had a family dog when I was younger, but my mum accidentally ran her over and couldn't face the idea of getting another pet that she might unintentionally murder. It took us years of nagging to finally convince her that it's not about the inevitable loss, but the love they bring to your life while they're around. We also told her that, with any luck, the dog would outlive her and it would no doubt eat her face for sustenance until her body was finally discovered. For some reason, Mum considered this to be something that lived in the 'against' column in the dog-getting equation, but eventually she caved and we got a miniature schnauzer called Babs. We quickly fell in love, but before too long I moved out of my mum's and had a dog-shaped hole in my life.

I'm very paternal and feel a need to nurture things, so I've always wanted my own dog but was never settled enough to get one. When Tan and I left my mother's place to begin on our own, we moved house pretty much every year for half a decade. We went from a rented place in Norwich to buying our own one, then on to London where we rented various spots for a number of years before finally buying the home we live in now. When we finally committed to our current house, it seemed that all the stars aligned. It was big enough for a dog, near enough to a park for walks, had a tiny garden for poops and the carpet was all threadbare and gross and perfect for house training!

I always wanted a big dog that could run for miles and get up on its hind legs to give me a hug. Instead, I ended up with the complete opposite: a teeny, tiny miniature dachshund.

---

* I'm choosing to take that as a compliment. Animals and babies are clearly wise.

Considering they're already a small breed of dog, mine is particularly minuscule. She just never really grew. She's utterly pathetic and would last less than five minutes in the wild before being eaten by a cat. Her legs are pointless, she's slow, it took an eternity to get her house trained, she barks like her life depends on it whenever the doorbell rings and she's stubborn. But she's wedged herself, well and truly, into the centre of my universe.

Considering my dog looks like a prawn that somebody dropped in some hair, she's the cutest little toerag you could ever meet and has a lot of gumption. People often say that small dogs have the biggest personalities and, in Martha's case, this is very true. She rules the local park with an iron paw and takes zero shit from any of the other canines (although she does smell them a whole lot and has a particular affinity for foxes). She has even been known to chase off a few great danes that didn't want to play her game of 'you chase me and I'll roll over'. One of her favourite pastimes is to lick inside my nostrils, as deep as her little tongue can go, which is in fact much deeper than you'd think. I'm pretty sure she licked the base of my brain once. She knows the basics: sit, stay, lie down, roll over, paw, and if you have a treat in your hand, she's very eager to please.

All dog owners think their dog is the best (although, weirdly, mine actually is), but here's some evidence as to what you're missing out on if you don't already have one in your life:

- Having a fluff bag to tell your problems to, play with, stroke or just be around relieves stress and lowers blood pressure

- Dogs need walks, which means you have an obligation to get out of the house, get some fresh air and get some exercise

- You also meet lots of people on the way, because other dog walkers always say hi and if your dog is

particularly cute or adventurous they will break the ice
for you. So they're great if you're looking for new
friendly faces, acquaintances, enduring friendships or
perhaps the love of your life

- There's some evidence to suggest that dogs may even
  be able to sniff out some forms of cancer, although
  they sniff absolutely everything (and I mean
  everything), so don't worry unduly if yours has a thing
  for a specific part of your body

A pup is not just for Christmas though, they require a lot
of time and are a huge responsibility. They can be expensive
to keep but when you get in after a long day and you see how
unconditionally excited they are to see you, it's totally worth it.*

---

* Like anyone else who's ever owned a dog, I've often wondered what goes on in
her brain. Luckily scientists have now trained dogs to lie still in a brain scanner,
so we know that the bits of their brains connected to positive feelings are active
when they smell their owner. So, although they almost certainly don't think
exactly like us, we know they definitely do like us.

Ultimately, greet your dog every day with the wonder you would reserve for a shark in the bath.

Thing 9:
Every other species is fine being naked, so why do we wear clothes?*

Every once in a while I put my dog in a cute little outfit (she always wriggles out), but other than that, animals don't wear clothes. So why is one of the world's biggest industries devoted to us humans covering our wobbly bits in the most stylish way possible? Why don't we all just let it hang out in the office, or on public transport, or when having a few drinks with friends?

According to lice, we have been wearing clothes for at least 170,000 years. David Reed from the Florida Museum of Natural History is not a lice whisperer, but a very clever man who, using the obvious deduction that clothing lice couldn't have existed before clothing (because, as their name would suggest, they live in it), traced them back to when they first arrived on the scene. DNA tests confirmed that they diverged from their nearest relative, head lice, around 170,000 years ago, which means we've been wearing clothes much longer than previously thought.

People often make the assumption that we wear clothes to protect ourselves from the cold, and they would be right – after all, we have much less hair to insulate us than a polar bear† – but

---

* Except for Donald Duck. He wears a top and nothing on the bottom half. Odd fellow. Clearly the same rules do not apply to talking birds (most parrots don't wear anything at all).

† Apologies if anyone gets a waxing flashback here.

warmth is just one reason; way back when we first started covering up, to the best of our knowledge, humans were all still in Africa and staying warm was not a concern. A more likely reason to get dressed up in a climate like that was to protect our skin from the Sun's ultraviolet rays or for adornment purposes, to display an individual's social status.

So, we wear clothes to symbolize our social standing and to protect ourselves from the environment, but I still wouldn't choose to be naked, even if the temperature was perfect and showing where you land on the social hierarchy wasn't necessary. Back to my dog; she is naked all the time, she even poops when I'm watching her, but I have far too much modesty and I would be much too embarrassed to even consider getting my kit off with other people present. Surprise surprise, once again it boils down to our mega brains.

Embarrassment is a relatively new emotion to the world and it seems to be specific to humans. It's a feeling that requires other people to observe your behaviour to make it possible. I can quite happily walk around my house totally starkers because, in the absence of society, I know that I have no standards to keep up. We only get embarrassed when we break little social rules in front of other people who also follow those same rules. We all want to avoid the negative feeling that comes when we make a tit of ourselves, so we try not to do it. People with damage to certain parts of the pre-frontal cortex often have less self-awareness and can also feel less embarrassment. It makes loads of sense that embarrassment would evolve this way, because with everyone following the same rules, we can cooperate, tend to trust one another more and weed out those people that don't play well with others. It's a very efficient way of keeping us in line.

Basically, every society today, even those that don't wear many clothes anywhere else, all cover their junk. So, at some point in our shared history, it clearly became socially unacceptable to wander around with your dilly-dangle out.

One suggestion for why is that there's a lot going on in that

36

region of the body, some of it not particularly hygienic, some of it pretty distracting, so it's probably best to keep your leaky bits safely covered up.

Also, a common behaviour that occurs during courtship in a lot of the animal kingdom is 'refusal'. If you've ever watched a wildlife programme, you'll know exactly what this is. One animal (usually the male) tries to impress another (usually the female) by fighting off any rivals, or displaying something big or colourful. When the female has picked her mate, she will display herself to let him know that the game is afoot. But she will often stop displaying as he approaches in a kind of 'you gotta do better than that, stud' manoeuvre, to test his commitment. If he really thinks the juice is worth the squeeze, he will persist and the female is more likely to know that he means business. This is refusal in practice.

For us, it seems to be that our clothing is both alluring and refusing. By wearing certain things, we can accentuate our best bits and appear more attractive. We can show our social standing by wearing a nice watch, or designer labels, but our clothes are also a barrier to the good stuff. Only when both parties are satisfied that they have made a good choice (or they have drunk enough to make that choice irrelevant) do the clothes come off and the real fun begins. Also, by this point embarrassment is much less of an issue because you're in it together.

So, it turns out that there's a reason you have that dream when you have to give an important talk and you forget to wear clothes. Forgetting your clothes would break social rules, you'd have limited options for refusal and you'd be so very embarrassed.

Clothes I get, but fashion is still weird

I'm very passionate about the fashion industry, so when I gush about it, occasionally the response I get is that it's vacuous and doesn't actually mean anything real. But I couldn't disagree more. Granted, from time to time you may come across a small number of 'fashion wankers' (these are easily recognized as people who take it all far too seriously, will judge you for wearing anything that costs less than a small house in Manchester, whose day has often been an 'utter disaster' based on their skinny decaf macchiato with almond milk tasting like they used cashew milk and who usually enjoy a double air-kiss with the required 'mwah' noises), but overall it's an exciting, creative and vibrant community. And as always with this stuff, I think it's the things we don't *need* to do but do anyway that are most interesting. We don't need to make music, or paint, or tell stories. But we do, because to experience them is special. I think the process through which the essential need to cover our bodies from the elements has become an art form is actually really important.

What I think's especially exciting within the last few years is that men are beginning to be more open to the idea of expressing themselves through their clothes. In Britain, menswear is actually the fastest growing bit of the whole fashion industry.

Not long ago it would have taken a brave man to openly admit that he actively takes pride in his appearance; now though, it's almost expected and encouraged for a man to take pride in the way he looks. Men didn't start buying more clothes because designers suddenly found the magic formula for what guys want; it's an effect of an overarching attitude shift in the way men perceive themselves and others. Fashion just happens to be an easily accessible route to this, while also providing the opportunity to express your tastes, style and show what makes you unique. What's exciting to me is the buyer has complete control: he picks what to buy and he decides what to wear those purchases with.

To me, this feels like a positive step towards a world where we are all entitled to celebrate our differences whether they relate to sexuality, race and gender, or to how much facial hair you have, what colour you like to wear, or how skinny you like your jeans to be.

Which isn't to say that we should put tailoring above clean water in our list of priorities, or that the fit of your jeans is going to lead to the culmination of your being, just that it often gets a rough press and I think we should give it a bit of credit.

Stereotypes are being torn down as people are recognized as much more than the sum of their parts and much more than the groups they belong to or the places they live. People are being seen as the individuals they are and fashion is one of the easiest and most direct ways of displaying that individuality.

Thing 10:
We are the (very)
new kids on the block

OK, so now the big subjects like the creation of everything, pets and clothes are out of the way, let's move on to the tiny, inconsequential portion of the universe's history that has involved us humans. It's tempting to think that everything out there was created just for our benefit, but when you crunch the numbers it just doesn't add up.

Carl Sagan, the brilliant science author, once suggested that we should think about the history of the universe as one year, beginning at midnight on 1 January. The oldest galaxies form on 22 January. Our solar system forms on 2 September. Early life on Earth appears on about 14 September. The dinosaurs arrive on Christmas Day. Primitive humans arrive at about 22.30 on New Year's Eve. The entirety of human history has happened in the last fifteen seconds.

By extension, it's incredible how little of human history has involved the things that now utterly shape our lives. There's debate as to exact dates, but most people agree that the length of time there have been what is known as anatomically modern humans is around about 200,000 years.

Now, let's think about the time since then as one day, beginning at midnight.

At about 3.30 a.m. we started wearing clothes. By about 9 a.m. we'd learned to control fire. At 5 p.m., we migrated out of Africa and became what is known as 'behaviourally modern'. Just before 7.30 at night, the oldest cave paintings we've ever found appear. At about 11 p.m., we started to cultivate wheat. The Bronze Age gets going at about 11.25. Socrates, Plato and Aristotle pop by at about quarter to midnight. About three and a half minutes later, the Roman Empire forms and hangs around for another three and a half minutes. At about ten to midnight, the Middle Ages start.

Shakespeare was born about three minutes ago.

The Second World War ended thirty-one seconds ago.

The iPhone has been around for about four seconds. Instagram about three seconds.

No wonder we're still trying to work things out.

It's important to keep in mind, whenever the modern world feels full on, that everything we do involves us trying to solve new problems with old brains. Brains that have spent a huge amount of time becoming good at overcoming issues in an environment we no longer find ourselves in. When life gets on top of us, we have a tendency to think that the issue lies with our brains, that it's our minds that are in the wrong. Actually, we're giving it a bloody good go with hardware that is out of date.

I also thought about 40 pages in would probably be the point people might be feeling a bit distracted and checking their phones, so I just want to say that's completely normal and explain why.

40

THE
HUMAN
BRAIN

Thing 11:
Eat more, think less

We can now basically run our entire lives from our smart-phones; we can book dinner, hail a cab, tweet, write emails, text friends, play games, order our groceries, post a snapchat, take photos, add meetings to our calendars, tweet again and browse the internet, all while listening to music or watching a video. Our tech is designed to make our existence more streamlined, but actually it can overindulge and distract us when we are supposed to be focusing on something else. And we love it.

We're wired to enjoy novelty and so when we're supposed to be writing that important email but decide to quickly send that text first, or google something, or check to see if any of your friends have liked your latest Instagram post, we get a little hit of dopamine (an important neurotransmitter that plays a big part in feeling pleasure). This rewards us for staying off-task and doing things that are less than effective for the job you're meant to be focused on. If we stayed on topic and completed what we were supposed to do in the first place, we would get a much bigger, much more satisfying reward from our brain, but instead we often choose instant gratification and go for lots of little hits via the many apps we turn to. Although we live in a time where our phones are more capable than the most power-ful computer of the generation previous, we still have the brains of cavemen.

In fact, to emphasize this point, I kept track of the extra nonsense that I got up to while writing just the paragraph above, and I think I have a problem.

- I replied to three emails

- Looked at watches online

- Sent a tweet

- Checked my Instagram

- Posted two (nearly three, but I didn't like the last one) snapchats

- Read two whatsapps and replied to one of them

It took me an eternity to write those 162 words and I imagine that if I hadn't been keeping track and making myself feel guilty, I would probably have been distracted even more.

I don't know about you, but when I have too many jobs to do and have to start multitasking, I start to feel a little stressed.

Actually, I do know about you, because unless you're an anomaly, research has shown that we are not very good at doing more than one thing at a time. Smart guy and neuroscientist Earl Miller says that rather than our brains being able to competently handle multiple challenges at once, like your laptop, we tend to rapidly swap between them and make our own heads hurt. I certainly know that my thoughts get a bit 'swampy', as I call it. I struggle to focus on the tasks at hand and waste a lot of my time saying 'What was I just doing?' to myself as I switch from one thing to the next.

Based on what I just discovered, I think I'm guiltier of this than most; I can't ignore my phone if there is a little red number next to any of the app icons. I hate leaving texts unread or not replying to emails. I just find it too distracting. I'm too curious about what's behind those notifications, and guess what? Not only does this make you less efficient at getting any one of those individual jobs done, but it can also temporarily make you dumber. A study by psychologist Glenn Wilson found that giving someone a task to perform while they have an unread email glaring at them can effectively reduce their IQ by around ten points. That's a substantial drop in performance, but it's just so addictive that we continue being distracted regardless. Let's use an email as an example; your phone pings and you see an alert on the screen. Already you get a hit of dopamine for the novelty of having something new. You quickly respond to the email and press send and you receive another hit of dopamine for completing a task. Despite not knowing that task required your action just a few seconds earlier, you have been rewarded twice for staying off course and getting distracted. It's an irony that a central part of what makes us human – the pleasure we have evolved to get from solving problems – now means that we've created devices that are so distracting in the short-term pleasure they bring, they stop us from being able to concentrate on actual problems.

Another reason you may feel a little flustered and confused when you have too much on your plate is actually because you need more on your plate. More food, that is. Continually switching from task to task uses up more energy, which we ultimately get from food. Considering our brains only make up about 2 per cent of our body weight, they burn about 20 per cent of the calories we intake. And that's on a quiet day. When you start taxing your noggin, this can shoot up and you will need to eat more to keep thinking straight. Performing too many jobs and not giving your brain enough juice can lead to difficulty focusing and a feeling of exhaustion. I know that I am a semi-professional procrastinator and get distracted easily, my brain is nearly always too busy and I am often left with a hazy focus. I need to eat more and think less. Do you know what? That's going to be my new life moto: 'eat more, think less'.

Thing 12:
Having said all that, if it's not going to kill you in the next few seconds, don't sweat it

It's also worth keeping in mind that this stuff isn't just about concentration and mood. In fact, our relationships with our various screens might be contributing to the general increases in anxiety being reported.

Humans weren't made to live in the concrete jungle and, as much as we avoid the thought, we are just a few million years removed from chimpanzees. If it wasn't for our huge brains we'd still be living in caves – hunting, gathering and dying at the age of twenty-two because we stubbed our toe on a dirty rock and it got infected, or a wolf tore out our jugular.

The shape of our lives has changed beyond recognition since our hunter-gatherer days, but our bodies haven't. We aren't built for the long-term, modern-day stresses of being overworked or not having enough money to pay the mortgage. The world has changed so much recently that it actually seems that those whom you'd assume would be carefree are suffering the most. Rates of depression and anxiety have risen by 70 per cent among young people in the past twenty-five years, with as many as 19 per cent of millennials reporting issues of this sort. Recent surveys have shown that a third of women and one in ten men suffer from panic attacks. When I asked my followers to tell me how often they felt anxious, 39 per cent said 'some of the time', 41 per cent said 'often' and 18 per cent said 'all of the time'. Only 3 per cent said 'none of the time'. For my mum's generation, it was the norm for teenagers to leave school, enter an apprenticeship and work their way up the ranks, staying with the same company until they retired. Many also went to university, but the majority of them still knew what job they would enter on graduation. With so many options open to people around my age and younger, it's easy to assume that they are spoiled, but the truth is, with all this choice comes uncertainty and uncertainty is very stressful. These people spend longer in education than ever before, the careers they wish for are more competitive and harder to come by, exams define success and this results in dragging out a stage in life they have little control over. Because of this, people are settling down, getting married and entering the property market later and later. It's getting more expensive to get the education they need to end up with the job they want, and all the while they are bombarded with advertising and social-media posts of the perfect life they feel pressured to be living.

Our bodies are geared up for short, sharp, adrenaline-induced stress, the type that's caused by suddenly being chased by a sabre-toothed cat. But seeing as they're less of an issue now, we don't get this very often and our stresses are much more drawn out and incessant. The trouble with this is that we only have one stress system and when it's overworked, it does bad things.

There are two parts to our autonomic nervous system: the 'sympathetic' and the 'parasympathetic'. Everybody's heard of *fight or flight*, but I don't think a lot of people realize that a huge number of us have grown accustomed to living with this as our default state.

The parasympathetic nervous system is the state in which we should spend most of our time. It's when the coast is clear and our bodies are balanced. It's an opportunity to rest and digest. It's basically the opposite of the sympathetic state.

The sympathetic nervous system is all about action; it's there to make sure you get out of stressful situations alive. To help you remember the difference between the two, think of it this way: the sympathetic nervous system is *sympathetic* to your body. When it sees a snake it tells you to either fight the serpent and bathe in its blood, or to run like the wind. The para-sympathetic system on the other hand is not so sympathetic, it completely ignores you and keeps your body running smoothly and efficiently at times when there is no perceived threat.

The sympathetic nervous system responds to a threat in less than a blink of an eye. Ever walked into a dark room and thought you saw a murderer waiting to stab you to death, only to realize that it was actually the towel you left hanging over the door? You get a sudden rush! Your adrenal gland sends a bunch of hormones into your bloodstream to make sure your pupils dilate, your heart rate increases, your muscles contract, your saliva production and digestive functions are reduced, your lungs let in more air and your immune system shuts down. You will recognize this feeling as the sudden alertness you feel when you step out onto the road without seeing the car which swerves just in time to miss you, or when you unexpectedly bump into the person you seriously have the hots for, or just before you have to go on stage to perform in front of lots of people. Your stomach drops and you get butterflies. Your mouth goes dry and you feel like you can't get enough air in your lungs. Your heart is pounding and you can't stop shaking.

All of this happens to prepare your body for action. Having larger pupils means that more light enters your eyes so you can assess your surroundings more efficiently. Your body channels the energy used to power your immune system to more immediately valuable places. Digesting food takes a back seat, so blood rushes out of your stomach (hence the butterflies) and into your muscles, giving you more of a chance of outrunning or outfighting said murderer. The term 'being shit scared' or 'shitting oneself' when terrified didn't come about because of how easily it rolls off the tongue. Next time you watch a wildlife show, keep an eye on the zebra's bottom when the lion starts chasing it; if you're lucky, you might just see a little poop escape. With all of the body's resources being pumped into keeping it alive, holding on to your stool is of very little consequence. So if the zebra – or indeed the human – was storing any waste, it might be involuntarily evacuated.

This system evolved in an environment where stress was, in

the main, more short-lived and often induced by a life-or-death situation. Today's stressors, such as the general anxiety an increasingly large number of people are suffering from, or more specific examples like studying for exams, making sure the bills get paid or worrying about what the future of your career looks like, are a lot less life threatening but tend to be much more drawn out. This leads to constant activation of the sympathetic nervous system. But rather than making us super alert and mega strong, it can actually have detrimental effects on our health. This is because we're remaining switched on for extended periods of time, which takes its toll on our bodies and can lead to high blood pressure, stomach ulcers, constipation and being more susceptible to illnesses.

It's kind of ironic, isn't it? A system that evolved to keep us alive in a time when life was very different is in fact making us ill in the world we live in today. But whatever the issue you're stressing about, I would wager that it's not worth having a heart attack over.

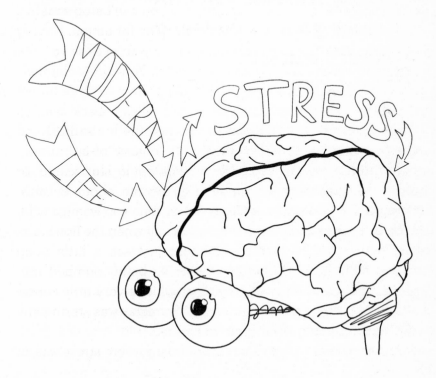

49

The world we have created for ourselves today is still terrifying, but in a very different way to the things that scared us thousands of years ago – our environment has changed faster than our biology can keep up with. It's much easier said than done, but try not to sweat the small stuff. The longer you are stressed for, the shorter your life could end up being. So, if what you're worrying about isn't a hungry, sabre-toothed cat, or a man-eating wolf ready to gobble up your face, don't sweat it.

The bottom line is that feeling anxious isn't a weakness and doesn't mean your brain is broken; it just means that you are one of the many people whose brain is finding it hard to deal with a very unfamiliar environment.

Thing 13:
Also, exercise will probably make your brain feel great, so it's win-win

Getting a good sweat on is one of the most tried and tested of cathartic activities. Whether it's lifting weights, sprinting, jogging, swimming, tennis or cheese rolling (that's an actual thing, and it's very dangerous), regular exercise benefits the body and mind. It's also super addictive, but unlike other addictive pastimes, such as a heroin habit, this one is going to make life better.

After falling off the bandwagon, eating pizza and not working out for a while, it's really tough to get back in the swing of it, but motivating yourself to turn up, committing to work hard and, if you're taking it fairly seriously, altering your diet (that means less pizza) can be a real shock to the system. You discover that you won't look like Brad Pitt after two days, it's a complete change to your normal schedule and chicken and broccoli is much less tasty than pizza. That's the reason a lot of new year's resolutioners don't make it to February, but once you break through that stage and it begins to become habitual, it genuinely feels great! And that's science.

My twin brother is a very qualified personal trainer and semi-genius, and knows a lot more than just what muscles do what and how to get buns of steel. We had a big old sciencey chat and this is what I took from it about why working out is good for you: serotonin is a neurotransmitter found in your brain and stomach that has a huge impact on your mood. Higher levels are associated with a chirpier disposition, while lower amounts can mean that you are more likely to feel grouchy or down – it's even linked to clinical depression. And guess what? Regular exercise and motor activity can give serotonin production a little bump. There is a lot of truth in people saying that exercise can make you feel good, and that's before you start to consider that, typically, the more you do it the better your body looks, which can have a huge impact on your confidence, sense of worth and self-esteem.

I'm certainly not The Rock, but when possible I try to get to the gym on most days. When that's not possible because I'm travelling, I'll take fifteen minutes in the morning to jump around my hotel room like a lunatic, doing burpies and press-ups and more burpies. I do it because I like to see the results aesthetically, but much more importantly I do it because it sets me up for the day. If I have a lot going on and a busy brain (which I suffer from quite a lot and can often lead to me feeling somewhat anxious), a good workout helps me to focus, to feel better about life and see things more clearly.

I wasn't gifted with hand–eye coordination and I'm not com-petitive enough to play most sports, so my workout method of choice is weight training with a sprinkling of cardio, because the movements are usually fairly simple and I'm only compet-ing against myself. It's one of the most important parts of my day and I can't emphasize enough the change it's made to the way I feel and my outlook on life. Looking better is a bonus too. Sometimes, when I have to drag my lifeless body to the gym super early in the morning, I question why I bother, but it soon makes sense as I get to work and focus on getting sweaty instead of the trials and tribulations that come with being a person (plus, nothing wakes you up like holding a heavy weight above your head).

Thing 14:
You wouldn't like me when
I'm hangry

Before people squashed together hungry and angry into one word, we had to waste time saying 'I'm angry' and then waste time thinking if it was because we were hungry. Now we can just say 'I'm hangry' and everyone understands what we mean. Because it's a new word, it comes along with a sense that it's silly and somehow not real, but there have been numerous studies that show that our blood glucose levels have a massive impact on our moods.

Personally, I've come to realize I need to eat regularly and, if I don't, the world becomes a very dark place for myself and anyone unfortunate enough to be around me.

Stage 1

This is usually at around the T +3 hours mark ('T' being the last meal you ate). It can vary depending on how much you consumed at your last sitting and the amount of physical activity you engaged in between feeding sessions. You start to feel a little hungry and may or may not realize it – I rarely notice when I'm at Stage 1 – but social interaction becomes less appealing and you find yourself going a little quiet and/or feeling distant. Others around you may think that you're tired or just have little to say, when in actual fact the clock is ticking to Stage 2. This stage is the first warning that your relationships with those around you are going to begin to suffer.

Stage 2

At T +4 hours your mental clarity begins to waiver. Not in a hallucinatory way, but more of a jet-lag type of feeling. If your job, like mine, is to talk to a camera all day, you may find that the number of bad takes begins to increase fairly rapidly. Control over your tongue becomes arduous and basic conversation is challenging. You'll be slow to respond when someone says your name and feel generally dazed. At this point it's almost too late. You can feel it coming on. You want everyone to leave you alone but you haven't reached the point where you feel so hangry that you're comfortable with being blatantly rude to people. Now your relationships with those around you are being put to the test and you've probably started to make a few snide comments or bitchy remarks. If you haven't, others are certainly making them about you.

Stage 3

You've reached T +5 or beyond. Everyone around you should be at code red. As far as I'm concerned, if they're in your proximity it's their own fault and they deserve to be hanger fodder. You are completely beyond reason and anybody foolish enough to engage in an argument with you (that you undoubtedly started) will be demolished, regardless of the integrity of their input, social standing or moral high ground. The real you is still in there, somewhere, but he/she is unreachable and has given up all hope of ever being seen again. You have well and truly thrown your toys out of the pram. Oddly, you're so full of anger by this point that you almost don't think of food until someone puts some in front of you.

There doesn't really need to be scientific evidence for all this because, let's face it, we all know it's a thing, but nevertheless, scientists in Israel discovered that judges are much more likely to be lenient with criminals in the session after lunch, compared to just before. Interesting as it is, it leaves me wondering what some people have been sentenced to or got away with based on the contents of the judge's stomach.

The main energy source our brains function on is glucose, which is made when our bodies break down carbohydrates into sugars. Without it your grey matter starts to perform suboptimally and you'll find yourself a little slower and, most likely, significantly more grouchy than usual while your body adapts to use alternative methods of fuel. So, if you have a job interview, an exam or you just want to be a pleasant human being, remember that your blood sugar level will have a massive impact.*

Of course, post-hanger, one always realizes what an utter knob they've been and begins to apologize profusely. My wife has actually learned to see the signs even before I'm aware of where I sit on the hanger scale and will source food for me. It's very sweet of her and it keeps my embarrassing mood swings to a minimum, but it's completely in her own self-interest. I don't blame her. On the rare occasion when she falls off the wagon and her hangry rage is directed at me, I see my life flash before my eyes.

---

* And drink more water too. It may seem the same as when Mum asks you when the last time you did a poo was, when you have a stomach ache, or tells you that going outside with wet hair will give you a cold. But research has shown that even a drop in hydration as small as 2 per cent can have a massive impact on your ability to concentrate.

Thing 15:
For something we spend a third of our life doing, we're not really very good at sleeping

Sometimes, sleep is hard. If you find it difficult, you are very much not alone. The Clinical Sleep Research Unit at Loughborough University reckons that almost one in three of us suffers from what they call 'significant sleep difficulties'. There are thought to be a bunch of reasons for this – from our 'always on' lives, to the blue light that our screens produce and the ways it messes with our bodies' natural rhythms. Whatever is doing it, we also know that the cycles our bodies go through when we sleep are incredibly important to us physically and psychologically. Ever seen new parents? They often seem to be operating in slow motion and look generally awful. Sleep deprivation is even used as an effective interrogation technique. In short, getting less than seven hours a night is just not a good idea.

Professor Richard Wiseman, a scientist and author who literally wrote the book on sleep, called *Night School*, reckons that a healthy night's sleep boils down to a few simple steps. These include: not looking at a screen for ninety minutes before you want to go to sleep; taking a bath or shower just before bed; avoiding booze; and making a list of things that are worrying you. If you can't sleep after twenty minutes, don't lie there getting more and more stressed, get up and do a jigsaw or do some colouring in. Weirdly, trying to stay awake is really tiring, so counting backwards in threes from a hundred or distracting yourself by naming a fruit with every letter of the alphabet will soon have you all tuckered out.[*]

---

[*] Or perhaps you could read a good book. If only I could think of one to recommend.

On the subject of sleep, let's discuss the conversations I have with my wife while she is in the land of nod.

Thing 16:
My wife is brilliant to chat to when she's asleep

Tan often has vivid and unusual dreams and she feels the need to tell me all about them when she wakes up (which drives me crazy because I can rarely recall my own). Sometimes, when I go to bed an hour or so after her, and with all the lumping and bumping required to remove my clothes and lie down, I stir her just enough that she ends up somewhere on the thin line between consciousness and the dream world. On these occasions, she talks absolute nonsense and it's brilliant. I even started writing these sessions down so that I remember them when the morning comes. Here is an actual conversation I've had with her in the past:

> *Me: Honey, can you stop grinding your teeth, please? [She's a grinder and the noise that comes from her face when she clenches her jaw makes me cringe in a way little else can.]*
>
> *Tan: You'd be grinding your teeth too if you were watching the same film as me.*
>
> *Me: What film are you watching?*
>
> *Tan: PRUNES!*
>
> *Me: Prunes? [To my knowledge 'Prunes' is not a movie, but when having a conversation with a sleep talker, you are very much a secondary member of the chat and it's best just to go with the flow.] But you know what prunes do to*

you, right? [Prunes give her wind. We joke about it
whenever she eats them.]
Tan: *Mmmmm, yummy, I'm hungry.*

Then she fell well and truly back into her sleep and that was the end of that enticing repartee. One of the things with sleep conversations is that there is very rarely a beginning, middle or end, and if you are one of those people that enjoys structure or needs a resolution from any dialogue, you will most probably be disappointed. Sometimes these chats end abruptly, sometimes they are disjointed, sometimes you can wait for an agonizingly long time for a response, and just when you think it's time to give up and hit the hay, you get something exquisite.

Tan: *Are you the doctor?*
Me: *Yes, I'm the doctor; what can I do for you? [I'm*
obviously not the doctor, but I've learned that it's
usually best to humour her on occasions such as this.]
[Very long pause]
Tan: *I want the cuddles to be warm like the broccoli.*
Me: *Broccoli cuddles?*
Tan: *Yes, warm like the broccoli. *Snore**

To give this one some context, Tan had made broccoli to accompany our dinner that night and had accidentally overcooked it to within an inch of its life. It was soggy, only held together by the fibrous outer skin. Inside was basically little individual servings of broccoli soup. It's fair to say the broccoli was warm.

Here's a creepy one from a few years back that resulted in me sleeping for all of about thirty-eight seconds for the rest of that night.

Tan: *[In a monotone, child-from-a-horror-film type voice]*
Who's watching you?
[It was pitch black in the room, I had my back to the door,
I was completely naked and, at that very moment, I felt
a stomach-dropping chill run down my spine. I felt like

Lucifer himself was somewhere in the room, enjoying
the show.]

Me: What do you mean? No one's watching me, I'm getting
into bed.

Tan: Someone's watching you.

Me: Nobody is watching me. [A little angry now and not
sure if she's doing this just to creep me out.] Are you
awake?

Tan: I'm at the party; who's watching you?

Me: No one is watching me. What party are you at?

[Then, obviously made uncomfortable by what was
happening in her head, she sits up, startled, scared
and panicked.]

Tan: Jim, is that you? What are you doing there?

Me: *What do you mean, 'Is that you?' Of course it's me.*
   Stop it. You're really freaking me out.
Tan: *Oh, phew, I thought that you were already in bed and*
   a stranger was standing over us.
Me: *Are you awake now or are you still asleep?*
Tan: . . . *[Asleep then, apparently.]*

It has been known, when she's asleep and my mental acuity isn't up to its usual standard (often when I'm jet-lagged), for her gobbledygook to make sense to me.

Me: *Tan, I need the scissors, where are they?*
Tan: *They're downstairs in the august drawer.*
Me: *OK, I'll go get them.*

It wasn't until I got downstairs to the drawers that it dawned on me that there was no such thing as an 'august drawer'. Also, it was June. So, I went back upstairs to find Tan again.

Me: *Tan, what on earth is the august drawer?*

She had woken up by the time I asked her that question and didn't have a clue what I was prattling on about. I had to explain what had just happened and, in the end, we christened the drawer that is full of junk and things that don't really have a home (including scissors) the august drawer. Now, whenever I ask for the scissors and Tan tells me that's where they are, I know exactly where she means. As a side note, if I was only semi-conscious and confused enough to mistakenly under-stand that the scissors were kept in a place that didn't exist, I should not have been playing with sharp things that could chop my fingers off.

Thing 17:
Technology sometimes gives us new ways to explore old problems

A constant refrain from anyone that spends time online is, 'Why do some people feel the need to be so mean to one another?' Whether it's trolling, name-calling, or cyber-bullying, you can't ignore the fact that, as well as all of the positive qualities of human connection the internet and social media enables, we also get some of the worst behaviour along with them. Technology offers us a layer of distance, too.* If someone in the street overheard something I said, even if they disagreed with it, they'd be unlikely to shout in my face that I was a waste of skin. But online, when it's anonymous, when everyone seems to do it, you'd be amazed at the things people feel OK saying. Certain behaviours are magnified. It's what the scientist Mary Aitken refers to as 'the cyber effect'. Basically, it means that all sorts of behaviours, good and bad, are accelerated when we're online. It's anonymous, easy and quick, and because it's hard to be held accountable, the consequences seem minimal. When you couple this with the ease with which groups of people can connect and communicate online, it's easy to see how this can lead to a pack mentality that can be really upsetting for anyone unfortunate enough to fall victim to it. This isn't a new thing. One of the fundamental ways that we have always defined ourselves is by what we are not. The easiest way to create a coherent group is to find a common enemy.

And it's especially difficult when you're a teenager, when fitting in, wanting to feel normal and special, wanting approval from your peers and feeling like you're competing for attention

---

* It's not just the internet either. You only have to look at what having a car between one person and another does during road rage to see that it happens to anyone at any age.

are all such a big deal. It's one reason why commenting on the way someone looks or something they've done is so prevalent; it creates an 'us' and a 'them'.

The bottom line is that there are always going to be people for whom being nasty about someone else, whether online or in person, is a way to make themselves feel better for a moment. Those people, just like the rest of us, have their issues – they just chose to be total plebs as a way to try to control those issues. They are the reason the 'delete' and 'block' functions exist.

At the risk of getting all 'self-helpy' and preachy, indulge me for a moment while I share with you a key piece of advice I was given by a very good friend when I first started making videos: 'Don't roll around with the pigs in the mud, because you'll both get dirty but the pigs will love it.' There will always be haters, it's human nature for some people, and many of them would like nothing more than a reply from you so they can engage in confrontation and feel some reward for their negativity. I can tell you from experience, though, that you have nothing to gain from encouraging that confrontation. If it makes you feel any better (it makes me feel much better), write out a brilliant response, including everything you would love to say to that person based on the hate they have sent you – it's a cathartic exercise – but don't send it. Instead, delete the text you have just written, along with their negativity, and move on. You win.

Thing 18:
You and 'you' are totally different things

So far, we've covered a few ways our brains aren't brilliant at dealing with certain things, and that's fine; I think it's important to know your limitations. Not to be a downer, but when Walt Disney said, 'If you can dream it, you can do it', he was wrong. I have dreams I can fly.

However, before we move to some of the amazing stuff we *can* do with our brains, I did want to add another to the list of 'stuff we're not so good at'. Specifically, the way we see ourselves.

I know that body image is a massive part of many people's lives. And I also know that, as a man, even though I feel it every time I catch my reflection or see myself somewhere, I only understand a tiny proportion of the pressures that are out there. But I'm a husband and a brother and I also have eyes. You just have to watch TV, read a magazine, see a billboard or check Instagram to see the sheer volume of stuff we are all exposed to. When I asked my followers how they felt about their body out of 10, the average score was 5.3. This is consistent with loads of other studies, which show that women and girls and, at a growing rate, men and boys, feel under significant pressure to look a certain way. This isn't a new issue: there has been an ongoing conversation around the impact that the media has on our attitudes towards our bodies. The idea is that the constant bombardment of shiny, glamorous images of physical perfection we can never match up to causes a constant sense of unworthiness. And you can totally see why: a brand that wants people to aspire to purchase their product wants to sell the whole package – 'Drink this beer and you'll have a six pack and be happy and the sun will always be shining'. What is new is the role that social media might now have to play. These issues are heightened online, where so much of what we see appears to be completely spontaneous and immediate. You don't get that illusion with a magazine or advert because you know that the model had hair and make-up and great lighting and possibly even airbrushing.

We all do it on our social feeds to some extent – we retake a photo if we don't like the angle. We put a filter on, we choose flattering lighting. I'm the first to admit that I do it. I have a lot of followers on my social platforms and whenever I post something, I open myself up to scrutiny and have set myself a standard to maintain; I don't want to upload a photo if I don't look as good as I could, so I will take it again from a different position or I'll change the light in some way. The danger occurs when we, as viewers, forget this process and start comparing the way our lives feel to the way other people's lives look. Trust me, if you could see behind the scenes on some of the shoots I've been on, you would know that they are nowhere near as glamourous as the end picture reveals, and believing they are is a shortcut to terrible self-esteem. Granted, some humans are blessed with great genetics, they may eat well and work out hard and they may be stunning to behold, but still not as stunning as they would have you think based on what they choose to show you. If you're under the impression that they're all effortlessly sun-glazed gods or goddesses while you're feeling particularly pudgy and pale, or that they're eating quinoa salads while you're gorging on peanut butter straight out of the jar, you're wrong – they just don't show anyone those photos.

It's not helped by the fact that studies have shown we tend to look more at other people's online feeds to give us a little 'pick-me-up' when we're feeling a bit down, so that gap between us and them is even more heightened. I look at guys with great abs on beaches and tell myself it's 'inspiration', but when I look away from my phone, I don't feel very inspired at all.

There's no easy solution and I'm certainly not qualified to fix it.* But, for now, trust me when I say that even though you might not feel like it based on my Instagram feed, I get it. I know a lot of models and they get it. I bet Brad Pitt gets it too. I can guarantee you that your body is utterly and entirely wonderful, because how can it not be?

Your body has been fashioned to carry the miracle that is

---

* As I've said previously, if you feel as if you'd like more specialist advice on anything the book covers, please do turn to the back, where there's a list of contacts as a good place to begin.

human consciousness – the important bit that makes you who you are. Your brain is the most complex structure in the universe, comprised of 100 billion neurons. The most powerful computer we are yet to invent is about 0.0002 per cent as powerful as that.

Your body is made up of 37 trillion cells, which in turn consist of 7 octillion atoms (7,000,000,000,000,000,000,000,000,000,000) and you produce 25 million new cells a second.

Your heart pumps 100,000 times a day, sending blood around your 60,000 miles of blood vessels. You have bones as strong as granite and muscles capable of extraordinary feats of strength. Your nerves carry signals down them faster than a Formula One race car.

Billions of years of adjustments and tweaks have led to the evolution of the perfect vessel whose only purpose is to pass on genes and keep the fragile bit that is really you safe. I've already explained how rare you are and the chances are that we don't get a second shot at all of this, so the best reason to keep fit is to allow the unprecedented wonder that is you to live for as long and in as healthy and happy a state as possible.

Bottom line, anyone who says there's not a big aesthetic aspect to looking after their body is probably lying, but just make sure you keep everything else in mind too.

Having said in previous pages that our genes have a big say in the way we behave, it's clear that they don't have total control. The following passage is an example of why this is the case.

Thing 19:
Some people aren't bad,
they just do bad things

I refuse to believe that my father was a bad man – I just don't think he was very well equipped to deal with life's problems and so he tended to do bad things. Unfortunately, life dealt him a pretty rough hand and the bad things he did in order to vent, or to regain control, or because he was angry, or for whatever reason he felt he needed to do them, were pretty unforgivable and resulted in his absence from my life.

While you're reading this, I first want to make it clear that this is not a tell-all, nor is it a glorified story told to garner sympathy or talk about how terrible my childhood was, because, in honesty, I believe I had a positive upbringing, overall. I'm not a special case and people have endured much worse than my experiences and I will not let the negative incidents of my formative years define me. One reason I am writing about this is because I frequently talk about my mum but have never mentioned my dad before and people often want to know why that is. But mainly I'm writing about this because, although my father has left his legacy in me in a fair few detrimental ways, he also taught me more than most people who have entered my life. I just don't think he intended to teach me what I learned from him.

When she was young, my brilliant mother met an attractive, charismatic man by the name of John Philip Chapman and fell in love. They got married and, when Mum was twenty-two years old, they had their first child: my big sister, Sam. Three years later, my other sister, Nic, entered the scene and another seven years after that myself and my twin brother, John, came to play. At some point between Sam and us twins, Dad found out that he suffered from multiple sclerosis. MS is a neurological condition that affects the nerves, brain and spinal cord, and as you can imagine, it isn't a walk in the park. It affects different people in different ways, but common symptoms include fatigue, diminished movement and less-able thinking as the nerves scar over. I recall regular massages, exercises and stretches that he had to do to stay mobile. One specific occasion springs to mind, when he took us to the cinema to see James Bond in *GoldenEye* (we were much too young but he got us in anyway). He gave us a child-friendly rundown of what MS is while stretching his calf on a ledge before buying the tickets. Setting aside the occasional moment like this, I feel like he thought that the world owed him a favour because this illness had been inflicted upon him and he was angry about it.

When I knew him, I was his child, and I idolized him. I was a daddy's boy and was far too young to know anything was wrong. Looking back, I feel like it should have been obvious, but as a kid, without experiencing someone else's childhood for comparison, how are you supposed to know that home shouldn't be that tense? That it maybe isn't all that normal for everyone in the house to be walking on eggshells in case he got upset.

This tension led to me developing a pretty successful 'out of sight, out of mind' strategy, around my father at least, but never my mother. I would keep my head down with my sketchbook and pencils and I would draw. I did it so much that I got pretty good for a boy of that age. For me, the thing with my dad was that I never knew what I would get. I was desperate for his approval but could ask him the same question in the same way on two separate occasions and I would get anywhere from undivided attention to complete dismissal, with plenty of anger thrown in somewhere along the scale. It was worse for my sisters; maybe because they were older and he expected them to be more autonomous and give him his space, or maybe it was simply because they were girls and he preferred his sons, but I remember that he was often very cruel to them.

It was much worse for my poor mum, though. When I was five or six, my brother and I were woken up by crashes and bangs. Understandably scared, we went to our parents' room to find him on top of her, beating her. This was the first instance I had witnessed, but it was far from the first time it had ever happened. As I grew up, I found that this had been going on for years. It's very easy to say, 'Why didn't she just leave him after the first time?', but it's not that easy when there are children to protect and a man that is willing to do a lot of bad things to make sure that they remain where they are. Mum remains the bravest person I have known and I can't imagine meeting anyone braver.

I was frozen on the spot when I saw what was happening. What on earth is a young boy supposed to do when one of the people who makes the rules is attacking the other one? My brother, thinking himself as invincible as always, dived on my dad in an attempt to stop him, but Dad just shrugged him off and sent him flying. I don't remember how it happened, but eventually the police turned up and took him away. I think that was it for my mum – once the veil had been lifted and everything she had tried to protect us from was unleashed before our eyes, she decided she had to act.

Cue a long and drawn-out process with lots of court dates and grown-up things that a six-year-old doesn't understand. Throughout this time, I would see my dad every other weekend (or whenever he would turn up, sometimes out of the blue, sometimes not for a long time) and despite it all I would still get really excited about it because I was still a daddy's boy. My mum somehow remained patient and would listen to me gush about how happy I was to see him and would console me when he didn't turn up. She respected six-year-old Jim enough to let him make his own decisions based on his own experiences: decisions that can take quite some time when you're young and confused.

There was no single turning point for me, more just a realization that I was not his priority and one too many scary experiences that left me with an uneasy feeling. Whether it be sitting, bored, in a pub all day waiting for him to drive us home too fast and too drunk. Or when he appeared at the house un-announced and took me from the window without consent, put me in his car and drove off until the police caught him. Or simply taking all of the furniture from the house when we were out, just so we knew that he was in control. At some point in the process, when I was about seven years old, I lost faith in him, chose to stop seeing him and I haven't seen him since.

For a short period, I hated him. I couldn't understand the situation and I saw the world in black and white, which resulted in the conclusion that he must just be a bad man. It didn't take me all that long to realize, though, that although he did some despicable things, we all have our issues that we struggle with and we all deal with them in different ways. I recently found out that he is still alive, although his MS is very serious and he is not at all well, which is terrible. Of course I was sad when I heard that, but if I'm being totally honest, no more sad than if I had heard the same news about someone who lives on my street, who I recognize but have never spoken to. It never really hit home for me because I don't have that many memories of him and he has become a stranger. He has not been a father to me for twenty-two years of my life and is about as estranged as it is possible to be. I'm not mad, I don't hate him, I just don't wish to know him. I have lived the majority of my life without him and in his absence I have been surrounded by people who I know love me without question, without hesitation and with-out limit, and that's plenty.

All of this has obviously left its mark in less than positive ways; I've never said this before, but I feel anxious much more often that I'd like, tension makes me uncomfortable in the extreme and I worry a lot. But I can work on all of this and, over the past few years, I have found it very useful to talk to someone about these things to help make sense of it all. As I get older, I realize that, in a reverse way, my father actually taught me a great deal. He has become something of an anti-role model – a cautionary tale of how your actions can leave you locked out of a loving family – and I have discovered that I often act in the opposite manner to the way I think he would behave in many situations. Without flattering myself, I can confidently say that I am kind, patient, caring, thoughtful and respectful. I am also stubborn, overly particular, pernickety and can be very hard work at times. But I am loving and gentle and I have my entire family to thank, including my dad, for helping me make the decisions that have led to this.

Thing 20:
Make memories

For all the wonders our world has to offer, cancer, we can all agree, is a detestable shit that we will not be inviting to family gatherings anytime soon. The trouble is, whether it RSVPs or not, sometimes it decides to show up unannounced and refuses to leave until it takes someone with it. Such was the case with Brian.

As you read this, I want you to appreciate that I simply don't possess the writing ability to do him justice; Shakespeare wouldn't even come close. Whatever opinion you form of him while reading this passage, know that he was better. Recognizing that it will not be enough, I want to write something about him anyway because he was special and deserves to be immortalized in writing somewhere.

In the early 2000s, my mother was out with my sister and a few friends. My mum is hot stuff, if I do say so myself, and it appears that Brian thought so too; with a little Dutch courage and a ton of Scottish charm, he went over to say hello. As it happened, I was in the car that picked the girls up from the bar they were at and I remember Mum telling us all about this guy that had chatted to her. She said that she couldn't really recall what he looked like, but she knew that he had a lovely voice and really bad hair. The main indicators of his 'really bad hair' were the bleach-blond tips and the fact that he used far too much gel. In his defence, it was the early 2000s and hair like this was not uncommon. In defence of hair across time and space, it was awful and should never have happened on top of anyone's head. Brian's was no exception to this. (This hair didn't last long, my mum made sure of that. When things got a little more serious between them, she insisted that it be banished for a more classic cut.)

Jude (that's what I call my mum sometimes, even though her name is actually Judy and you're supposed to call your mum Mum) said that they had swapped numbers but she wasn't going to call him because she couldn't even remember his face and surely that was a sign. But Brian called Mum the next day, ignoring the whole 'don't call for two days' rule, and he was so lovely and easy to talk to, and his voice was so pleasant and Scottish, that she decided to give him a chance and go on a date.

I'm not sure Brian bargained on inheriting twin fourteen-year-old boys, one troublesome twenty-one-year-old girl and a too-mature-for-her-twenty-four-years daughter, but he loved us like his own and took to fatherhood like a duck to water. On the first occasion my brother and I met him, we were in the back of his Vauxhall Vectra, arguing as all fourteen-year-olds do, and somehow we managed to spill an entire bottle of Dr Pepper on his leather seats. Rather than having a meltdown and cursing fate for meeting the woman of his dreams only to discover that she had managed to birth the most irritating brood of humans, capable of destroying his possessions in a matter of moments, he simply wasn't bothered. He just wiped the seats down and got back in the car. Jude knew then that he was a good egg.

I'm writing this on 23 February 2017. We lost him last night to a horrific and undignified battle with cancer and my heart is broken, along with the hearts of my family and all of the other people he touched. I'm twenty-nine years old now and I met him when I was fourteen. He was around for half of my life and twice as long as my biological father. He was infinitely better at being a dad to us and a partner to my mum and I'm only just starting to appreciate how much he will be missed.

We knew it was coming for a few months, as he started to deteriorate rapidly, and I had started grieving then, but something I have experienced with grief is that it comes in waves and it can knock you off your feet. We were all lucky; it's as much of a privilege to give love as it is to receive it and Brian was loved by us all. He knew that, and we knew that he loved us in return. We found a new member of our family and he stumbled into an entire horde of Chapmans.

The last thing I said to him (when he was able to listen and reply) was that I loved him, I was proud of him for fighting so hard and that I would see him next weekend. I knew he wouldn't last much longer but I wasn't sure if I would get the chance to be there when he went and I didn't want to scare him with a final goodbye. I went back to London with a very heavy heart, only for my brother to call the next day to say, 'If you want to be here when Brian goes, you might want to head back home.' So I cancelled what I was doing and got in the car.

Brian loved life and, despite the fact that when he was diagnosed his cancer was already at stage four and terminal, he wasn't going to let a little thing like that stop him without a fight. He ploughed through his initial chemotherapy like an absolute champ; he was exhausted, his hair started to thin, his immune system was so low that he would get all manner of sores and infections, he was in excruciating pain and towards the end he could barely breathe, but his resolve didn't waiver. He bounced back from most of his visits to the hospital with gusto, but the final one, which came a week or so after Christmas, was tough. We all knew that the treatment wouldn't destroy cancer, only shrink it and buy him some time, if he was lucky. He was part lucky, part devastatingly unfortunate. The unfortunate part was much, much bigger, as the initial cancer in his pancreas had shrunk, but had also spread to his lungs, his back, his stomach and everywhere else important.

In the end, he simply couldn't win against those odds, try as he might (and he certainly tried), and despite the emptiness I feel in my chest, despite the rage I feel at the waste of his life, I have fifteen years' worth of memories.

Brian was a bit of a dipstick; he could never get a saying right and would come out with corkers like 'I feel like a beached cow', to which we all replied, 'Beached whale, Brian', or 'Uh oh, I'm in the dog bed now' when he had done something to irritate my mum. 'Close, Brian, but it's dog house, not bed.' We called his little quirks like this 'Brianisms'. Another Brianism was that he was prone to sharing a story for everything; he always knew a guy who had done or experienced whatever the current conversation was about, and had a cautionary tale for every possible circumstance. Two of my favourites were a fable about a man who got eaten by a bear, all but the shoes, and the one he told when I was going snowboarding: how trees are the biggest killers of people on the slopes (apparently, people go too fast and hit them). As it happens, most of his little tales had an element of truth to them, but it was the way he delivered them that made them gold.

I could write an entire book just about the way I think his head worked, but in the end, the world continues to turn, the show goes on and life proceeds. The memories I have of Brian and lessons I have learned from him will make it all that bit easier. So, here's to my Brian and all the other Brians and Hillarys and Williams that live on in our memories. We will miss them, but we will remember them and we will live the best, most exciting, most extraordinary lives we can, with them in our hearts and minds because they were taken too soon and they deserved so much more.

The fact that death is the great certainty doesn't make it any easier to bear and, for anyone reading this who has grieved or is grieving, it's also little comfort to know that every one of us will go through it at some point. It really sucks and there is no way to sugar-coat it, but you should know that you needn't deal with it in isolation. Everyone experiences grief differently and there is no right way or wrong way of getting through it. The reason everything you say around death sounds so clichéd is because these clichés are true. It actually is better to have loved and lost than never to have loved at all, and although you are excused for feeling sad that it's over, you should also be happy it happened. It's not possible for me to explain what a huge part of my life Brian was and, despite the agony, I would never trade the pain I feel now for the opportunity to never have known him and to be blissfully unaware of his existence and his farewell.

I wanted to be honest and put the biggest things in among the smaller, sillier ones, because that's what life is made up of. I know that, as time goes by, life will keep going; small things will keep piling up because that's what life does. I have to remind myself that it's all too easy to get bogged down in the small things and neglect the big ones, when it's the big ones that really matter. Even if they don't seem that big at the time.

You are a product of your genetics and your upbringing, but they definitely don't define you. There is no ceiling. I certainly don't want this section of my book to make you feel hopeless or despondent, or like your future is set out in front of you. You are in charge and you can kick life in the arse! Here, as an aside, is the best antidote to feeling down that I have . . .

Thing 21:
Dream big

By far the best piece of advice I have ever been given came in the form of a scruffy little note, written by my wife and torn out of a cheap notebook. It consists of fourteen words and I'm not exaggerating when I say that it changed my life. She wrote it for me in 2014 and I still have it, face up in the drawer that I use most often in my office, so that whenever I go to get a pen or a charging cable, it's there, looking me in the face, reminding me to kick ass. This is what it says, verbatim:

DREAM

BIG

Make it happen.

Believe in yourself.

Think positive.

Don't ask 'what if?!'

For your reference, the 'dream' has bubble writing for the D and R, followed by regular capital EAM. I imagine Tan was worried she wouldn't manage to fit it all on the page if she continued with the size of the bubble letters, so abandoned ship after the first two. The 'big' is all in bubble writing, but seeing as it only consists of three letters, space was, I guess, less of an issue. In defence of shoddy penmanship, my excellent wife isn't known for her artistic prowess, nor her handwriting, but the point is not how it was written, it's how she knew to write exactly those words.

A big part of my job is to make videos for my YouTube channel and I pride myself on being a very hard worker, but, in honesty, I sometimes doubt that I'm cut out for it. It's not always just about applying yourself to making videos; people must find you and like you enough to watch and want to watch again. Of course, there are things I can do to help that process along a little: I can remind them how to subscribe or ask them to give me feedback on my stuff in the comments section so I can improve upon it, but really, there's only so much I can do. Those that discover me have to find me interesting enough, funny enough, helpful enough, insightful enough, attractive enough, intriguing enough, aspirational enough, or enough of whatever they are looking for to earn their time and that, for me, is very stressful.

Before this, I was used to jobs that rewarded you for your hard work. Granted, I detested them, but at least I knew how it went and could see a career progression laid out in front of me, if I were to continue down that avenue: newbie, middle management, management, regional management. Clearly, they were not the vocations for me, or I would still be working my way up the chain. I don't want to be misunderstood – I am very passionate about what I do now and I count myself as truly lucky to be doing something that I enjoy so much. But so much of it is open to interpretation and so much of it is out of my control that I worry it'll all come crashing down around me and I won't be able to do anything about it. Essentially, I worry about things that haven't happened yet and things that may never happen. It's a total waste of my time, I know, but that doesn't mean it's easy to stop.

I've been uploading videos for quite a long time now and have seen the industry grow around me, but being such an early adopter of the new medium is difficult because I have nobody to use as source material for getting an inkling on where it's all heading; myself, and others like me, have unwittingly become the blueprint for new content creators around the world. Often I feel like I'm feeling my way through, blindly, trying to make the right decisions and not cock it all up, and that can get on top of me; I'm something of a pessimist, I tend to worry and I nearly always overthink situations, and when the next step isn't always immediately obvious, it can be unnerving.

I really do believe that I have the best job in the world; I get to make content that I want to make for an audience of people who seem to really care, an audience of people that follow across platforms and media to support whatever it is I'm working on. I'm not subject to executives making decisions on whether I'm good enough to get the part because the people who watch are my casting board and have already deemed me worthy. I don't have to learn scripts (at least I rarely do for my YouTube content), I can broadcast whatever I want, whenever I want, to people all over the world and I have been lucky enough to experience things that just don't normally happen to people. But along with this can come the fear that, although I am putting my heart and soul into it and although I love it to pieces, it simply won't last in its current form and I must keep pushing forward so as not to be left behind.

That is where my wife comes in: she has been on the internet for a year or so longer than me and she just doesn't have concerns in the same way that I do. While I sometimes find myself terrified that it's all falling apart, she's aiming high and all but single-handedly kicking the world's arse. Things don't just happen for her. They don't just happen for anyone, but she won't stop working at them until they have well and truly happened and I love that about her. When it comes to her career, she is laser-focused, infinitely driven and is constantly onto the next thing. When it comes to my career, I tend to second guess everything, not know how to make the next step and hate to inconvenience people by asking for their help and time.

Tanya, however, believes that I'm a big deal and the letter that she wrote to me means that rather than asking 'what if?', I should be asking 'what if I don't?' That, if I have a dream, it doesn't matter if it seems too big to come true, I should believe in myself and make it happen regardless.

Since first reading her little note three years ago, I have done a lot of very cool, very exciting things that I can guarantee I would never have made happen if I hadn't ever laid eyes on it. There are lots of big dreams that I am currently working on and loads more that I haven't even dreamed up yet. I now realize that YouTube is just one platform among many others and I try to bridge the gap between mainstream media and the digital side of things, because I have interests in both. Since coming to this comprehension, I have branched out into lots of avenues that are not necessarily tied to my YouTube channel and I feel much more confident in the longevity of my career. Although I still have the more than occasional slight wobble (that's the beauty of having the letter though, I can pull it out and remind myself to keep my chin up), I will make things happen, I do believe in myself, I try to think positive, and 'what if?' is only a question I use in the context of 'what if an allosaurus went toe-to-toe with a giant squid?'

Try it:

DREAM

BIG

Make it happen.

Believe in yourself.

Think positive.

Don't ask 'what if?!'

DEATH
AND LIFE

Let's talk some more about life and death – beginning with death. Sounds a bit full on, but relax – I'm not going to get all morbid on you. In fact, I have a couple of personal stories to share with you, from which I have discovered things that I don't think you can learn any other way.

Not all creatures are the same, but the fact is that every one of us humans, if we're lucky, will get around 27,000 days to live. Minus around 9,000 spent sleeping. That leaves you 18,000 days. For the first 5–6,000 of those, you're basically just working out how all the equipment works – all the boring stuff like learning to control your bowels, or figuring out how to walk.

You're left with about 13,000 days into which you have to cram all of the people you'll ever know, all of the love, the joy, the pain, the laughter and internet memes. It suddenly doesn't seem very many days, does it? And that's if you're lucky. Obviously, I don't leap out of bed every day, greeting the dawn as a new opportunity for excellence. In fact, I'm not a morning person at all, and often get miserable when forced to leave the warmth of my bed. But I do genuinely believe that you're much more likely to do things you enjoy if you start to think of a day spent engaging in activities you hate as one of your 13,000 gone. Do what you love and 13,000 days will be plenty.

Thing 22:
Tempus fugit

My grandad had two sayings: 'There's another day tomorrow', which was a polite way of telling you 'you don't need second helpings of dessert, don't be greedy, nobody is starving to death here and there will still be food in the fridge when you wake up in the morning', and *Tempus fugit*', which is Latin for 'time flies'. He was a carpenter and had a particular penchant for clock making. My sister still has one of his *tempus fugit* grandfather clocks in her house. And do you know what? He was totally right, time really does fly and it's something you begin to appreciate (or at least grow more aware of; I do not appreciate it; I would like it if time didn't shoot by so fast) as you grow older.

From when you are born to your first birthday, that year accounts for 100 per cent of your life. When you hit two, each year is equivalent to 50 per cent and by the time you reach the age of fifty, the preceding year makes up a measly 2 per cent of the time you have existed on Earth. These percentages seem to be part of the reason your childhood feels like it lasts so long and why, as you get older, time goes so much faster; excluding the leap variety, every year is the same length of time, but later years simply account for an increasingly smaller proportion of your stint as a person.*

We're geared up to make the most of new things; we recall them more clearly because we must pay more attention to something when it's novel. That's how we learn things and why we are pretty good at not dying from eating raw chicken, or playing with sharp objects. We remember well and we pick things up fast. Think about when you first started driving a car (if you can drive a car; if not, riding a bike will do); to begin

---

* Actually, this isn't entirely true; technically the years are getting fractionally longer, but only by 1.4 milliseconds every century, so we'll ignore that.

with, you are acutely aware of absolutely everything. You have to really think about which pedal is the brake, which is the clutch and which is the accelerator, you need to remember the order in which to use these pedals to change gear, you must stay alert and remind yourself to check your mirrors, keep a look out for road signs, pedestrians, random animals and, if you're in Alaska, bears in the road. It takes a lot of brain power and it's not easy. But, after a little while on the roads, it all becomes second nature and you don't even need to think about it anymore. I sometimes do long journeys and could tell you nothing about the way I got there. I simply got in my car and did the driving thing. A similar comparison can be made for the years that make up a larger proportion of your life. Everything you've ever experienced has to happen for the first time once: first time you ate an apple, first time you got sand in your eye, first kiss, first time you fell out of a tree, first anything. As you get older, the number of novel encounters you have inevitably begins to dwindle. In a way, our brains are just too efficient at processing information and, as experiences become more habitual, or at least require much less mental capacity, time picks up speed and you coast through life.

Although my dear old grandad (Bilge, we called him, even though his name was actually Walter) was right – there is indeed another day tomorrow – unless we fill it with a brand new, brain-exciting adventure, we probably won't appreciate it and it will shoot past us. Trying new things as often as possible could effectively make time slow down, meaning you will feel like you've lived longer, and to the maximum, while also leaving you with some kick-ass stories to tell.

Leaving aside the people that freeze their heads in the hope that future science will find a way to turn them into Robocop, all of us know at some level that life is finite. However, the following creatures stick a middle finger up (not literally; none of them have fingers) to the grim reaper and keep living like the party will never end. Smug bastards. I can't wait for the Sun to swallow this planet up and teach them a lesson.

Thing 23:
It's possible for lobsters to live forever, but they don't

Have you ever looked at a lobster and asked yourself what possible circumstances could drive a living thing to look so alien?* Ever wondered what life would be like if they conquered the world? Want to know something weird? In theory, they are biologically immortal; if they don't get eaten, starve to death, suffer from disease or find themselves in some horrific lobster accident, they could potentially live forever. But they don't.

Most other living things grow throughout the first chunk of their life until they reach maturity, at which point they will cease getting any larger and start the long, depressing journey of dying. Not our troubling underwater crustacean friends though – they keep getting bigger and bigger throughout their entire life. In order to grow, our cells (and the DNA within them) need to replicate themselves, but the majority of those in the human body, for example, can only do so about forty to seventy times. After that, we have reached our physical peak and we begin to age.

Picture a shoelace; without the plastic bit on the end, the lace would unravel and tying your shoes would be a nightmare. Your DNA has similar plasticy-end-bits called telomeres that prevent all the information that makes you who you are from unspooling from the structure and creating a mess. Every time a cell copies itself, the telomeres get shorter, until they are so tiny that replication becomes impossible. At this point, you have to live with what you've got and run down the clock.

The magic with lobsters is that the telomeres in their DNA don't seem to get any shorter when their cells replicate, mean-

---

* Who was the first person to see a lobster and go, 'Yum, I'm eating that. In butter'?

84

ing that they can always do so and they stay forever young. So, if they don't die of old age, why are they not the dominant species? Why are they not so plentiful that they pour out of your tap when you run yourself a bath? Why have they not overthrown the human race and started boiling and eating us?

The answer is partly that they live in an ecosystem where bigger things with sharper teeth (or nets) want to eat them, there isn't always enough food to eat and the world is a grubby place full of bacteria, germs and viruses. The answer is also partly that they keep growing throughout their entire lives.

'Where's the problem in that?' you might be asking yourself. 'Surely if a lobster lives long enough to grow to the size of a bus, nothing is going to be brave enough to attempt to eat it.' Well, the problem is that they wear their skeletons on the outside of their bodies and, as their soft bits get larger, it can get a bit cramped, so they have to shed their shell and grow a new one or squash themselves to death. This is a risky business because the larger a lobster gets, the harder it is to get out of the old exterior. They can exhaust themselves to death if they can't squeeze out, or end up with an injury that leaves scar tissue, making it much more difficult to repeat the process next time, or contract a bacterial infection.

Let's assume they had no predators, lived in a sterile world, their habitat was an all-you-can-eat smorgasbord and they developed some sort of shell-removal machine. Then, in theory, they could be immortal. And bloody gigantic. And we'd all have to learn to speak lobster because they would rule the world.

Thing 24:
Immortal jellyfish are a little bit more immortal than lobsters, but not much

Do you ever have that fantasy of going back to a younger stage of your life but with the things you know now? There is a species of jellyfish that can actually do that.

The unorthodox aging of lobsters is yesterday's news when you consider *Turritopsis dohrnii*, aka the immortal jellyfish. For pretty much every other living thing, once you've reached sexual maturity, that's it, there's no going back. That's not the case for these little guys though, because when the going gets tough, they just revert back to a simpler time.

Once a jellyfish egg is fertilized, out pops a miniature larva that swims its way to the bottom of the ocean, attaches itself to the sea floor and transforms into a whole bunch of polyps. These polyps each become a fully-fledged, genetically identical, sexually mature, biologically immortal jellyfish. I suppose the equivalent with humans would be getting asked a difficult question on an exam or at a job interview and suddenly becoming a toddler. Obviously, this is entirely impossible, but I do like the idea of shrinking down and starting again in the hope that you will be more prepared next time.

If it falls on hard times or gets sick or old, it will simply go back a step and transform itself into a colony of polyp clones and start again. This may sound simple, but usually mature cells that are assigned a job will have the same job forever. A skin cell, for example, can never not be a skin cell – its job is to be skin. But *Turritopsis dohrnii* does a thing called 'trans-differentiation', which alters the purpose of mature cells and turns them into polyp cells again.

I guess, technically, when adult jellies arise from these

polyps they are not exactly the same creature, but they are genetically identical clones. We'd be arguing semantics and it actually makes no difference. It's believed that these little blobs could do this indefinitely too. 'Senescence' is a term used to describe the fact that, once organisms reach their physical peaks, they start to reproduce less and die more. It seems that whenever these jellyfish start to feel the aches and pains of age or their environment stresses them in another way, they just tell the cells that were making them a jellyfish to make them polyps again.[*]

---

[*] By the way, if, like me, you've ever wondered whether jellyfish sting themselves, the answer is no. They have special receptors in their tentacles that recognize their own species and put the safety catch on.

Of course, in reality, jellyfish are a form of plankton and just float along fairly inanely, so many of them get eaten regardless of what stage of development they are at. Also, seeing as any jellyfish that come from the same original larvae are clones of one another, if one of them is genetically at risk of getting a jelly disease, they all are. So, the immortal jellyfish is not all that immortal after all. I wouldn't say it's false advertising necessarily, because the potential to live forever is there. But it's definitely something of a wobbly definition.[*]

Thing 25:
Hydras are even more immortal than lobsters and immortal jellyfish

Another sea creature that has a bit of an ego and massive delusions of grandeur, the hydra is in fact not the serpent monster from Greek mythology, but a tiny little, centimetre-long, tentacled freshwater organism. A tiny little, centimetre-long, tentacled freshwater organism that never ages and has regenerative abilities, even if its head has been chopped off.

Just like Wolverine from the comic books, you might be thinking. Well, check this out: they also have claws that shoot out. Kind of. They're actually barbs, but they're coated in a neurotoxin that paralyzes their prey, which I think is much cooler. Their tentacles are covered with sensitive hairs that, when brushed by something tasty, trigger the dart to shoot forth and pierce whatever is in the way.

Seeing as they are fairly simple creatures, they don't really have a brain, so if their head (or any other part of them) is

---

[*] Forgive me.

removed, it's not the end of the world, they simply grow a new body around it. They do this by unleashing stem cells. You might have heard of stem cells before, but if you're unsure of what they are, essentially they are cells that don't yet have a function – they aren't a lung cell, or a cell for the lens of an eyeball, and because they are jobless, they are free to be anything they want to be. Think of them as cells that are on a gap year.

Long-term studies have shown that hydras don't even age. Every month or so their entire body is replaced by new stem cells that keep them young, forever. Or at least until they get eaten, which is all the time because they are a bit rubbish at protecting themselves. Still, if there's a ninja hydra out there somewhere, hiding in a nice little freshwater crevice where no predator will find it but plenty of food touches its tentacles, it could be older than super old (and probably really bored).

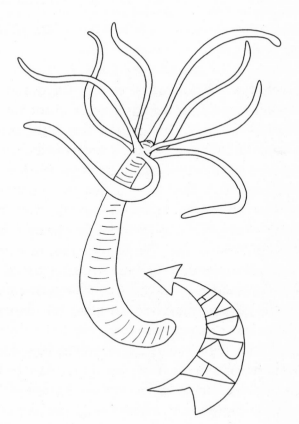

Thing 26:
Tardigrades aren't immortal, but they're so tough that they might be aliens

You know how some people speculate that the ancient Egyptians were actually aliens, due to the fact that we still don't know how they managed to build the pyramids with the limited technology they had available? Well, if this is ever going to be proven true, I'm pointing the finger at tardigrades as the extraterrestrials that crash-landed and birthed humanity.

For tiny micro-animals at 0.5mm long, they are actually pretty cute. Most creepy-crawlies are bloody disgusting, but tardigrades have earned the monikers 'water bears' and 'moss piglets' for their cuddly appearance. They are harmless little bugs that like to suck the water from foliage, and are about as near to impossible to kill as you're ever going to get.

When the faeces hit the fan, tardigrades shrivel up and die. For a little while. Then they just decide to resurrect themselves and carry on living their lives as if fresh from a power nap.

They can withstand pressure up to six times that of the deepest point in the ocean. There is literally nowhere on the surface of our planet that exerts that much pressure, which does beg the question, 'Why are they so well and truly over prepared?'

They laugh in the face of radiation and can shrug off loads more of it than would kill you or me or a horse or an elephant.

Despite the fact that their purpose is to suck the water from moss, they can live for at least ten years without a drop to drink. When dehydrated, their bodies can go from about 85 per cent water content down to 3 per cent.

Another reason their water level drops is because, if it froze (oh yeah, moss piglets can survive temperatures of -272°C, which is nearly as low as temperature can go), the expanding ice crystals would tear them apart.

Speaking of temperatures, you could boil a tardigrade in water and it would think you were running it a nice bath. They can tolerate 150°C heat.

Seeing as these things are so tough, obviously they've garnered the attention of scientists, who, in their infinite wisdom, decided to put them through their paces. The most hostile environment they could think to expose them to was, of course, the vacuum of outer space, where there is no air, no pressure and massive amounts of radiation. And guess what? They gave zero shits and carried on being tiny and adorable when they touched down on home turf again.

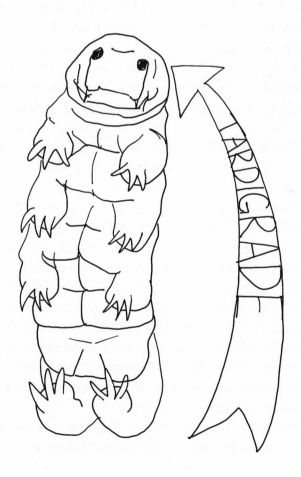

Considering they can live through ridiculous amounts of pressure, temperature, radiation and don't mind being more than a little parched, it's not entirely unreasonable to believe that a small colony of tardigrades could be smuggled inside a meteorite, enjoy an elongated journey from one world to another and begin a civilization in an entirely new part of the solar system, galaxy or universe. All hail the moss piglet.

You might think it was only moss piglets that get sent into space as experiments, but it's happened to the cells from a human, too.

Thing 27:
Since her death, enough of Henrietta Lack's cells have been produced to fit around the Earth three times

Most human cells divide around forty or so times before they begin to die away. It's the main reason we age. But a poor, African-American tobacco farmer by the name of Henrietta Lacks had something different about her. In 1951, she went to hospital with an aggressive form of cervical cancer where the doctor took a tissue sample. Back in the 1950s, 'informed consent' was not a thing, particularly for a poor African-American woman (in fact, the hospital she visited was one of the only ones in the area that would treat black people), so nobody asked her, but her sample was handed over to a specialist for study nonetheless. It was discovered that the cells of her tumour kept dividing, seemingly without limit. In fact, sixty-six years later, under lab conditions, they are still going strong, long after Henrietta herself succumbed to her illness.

Granted, the cells are cancerous, but they still hold a lot of similarities to those of a healthy human and, as such, have been invaluable to medical endeavours; the vaccination for polio, for example, being just one. These HeLa cells (so called by taking the first two letters of Henrietta's first and last name) have been mass-produced on such a scale that one estimate states that, if all of them that had ever existed where piled together, they'd weigh over 50 million tonnes and would be able to fit around our planet more than three times. Considering one cell weighs pretty much nothing, that's a lot of one person's matter to be floating around.

Thing 28:
If you spent your life in a basement, you'd bend time and might live longer than everyone at street level

Albert Einstein is a total legend and theorized that time is affected by gravity; the more powerful gravity becomes, the slower time moves. It's simple maths (it's not; it's like rocket science in Latin).

A black hole is a point in space with so much gravity that not even light can escape its grasp (hence why it is black; there's no light reaching your eyes) and so it stands to reason that time moves very, very, very, very, very, very slowly there. There are two types of black hole – supermassive and stellar mass – and the way you die in each varies.

As the name would suggest, a supermassive black hole is quite large. They hang out in the centre of galaxies while everything orbits around them. The one in our galaxy is called 'Sagittarius A*' and it has the equivalent mass of about 4 million of our suns.* A stellar mass black hole is much smaller, by comparison (usually between three and ten times the mass of our sun), and is made when a single massive star collapses at the end of its life.

Let's just say that you were on your morning space stroll and were unfortunate enough to fall into the reach of one of these singularities; unless you could move faster than the speed of light, which you couldn't because it's the speed limit of the universe, escape would be impossible and you'd be in for a very weird, time-bending experience, culminating in the coolest death space has to offer.

As you were pulled closer to the centre, gravity would increase so rapidly that a big difference would actually be felt, even across the relatively tiny length of a human body. Let's assume you were heading towards our black hole head first; your noggin would start to stretch; as the rest of you caught up, it would too, and you would get longer and thinner until you were nothing more than a stream of atoms hurtling towards oblivion. Believe it or not, the technical term for this is 'spaghettification', and I imagine it would hurt.

If you were heading for a supermassive black hole, people watching from a safe distance would miss you turning into pasta. To them, you'd simply appear to move more and more slowly as time warped, until eventually you just stopped. Then you'd get dimmer and fade to red as light waves were stretched under the huge force of gravity and, finally, you'd turn black when the waves extended so much that your mates could no longer perceive them.

For a stellar mass black hole, things are a little different, as

---

* I love it when science gets like this. 'What's the mass of this in suns?' 'About 4 million, mate.'

the point of no return (or 'event horizon') is slightly more forgiving and, although you would be totally screwed, a little light would still make it back to the onlookers' eyes. For you, it would all happen in real time; you'd be spaghettified and stretched out of humanity, while the people watching would witness you slowly, very slowly, elongating. So slowly that it could take years or even lifetimes. If you were to look back at them (this would have to be before the spaghettification ripped your eyes and brain apart), you'd see them age super-fast as time slowed for you, kind of like when the guy drinks out of the wrong cup in *Indiana Jones and the Last Crusade*.

Obviously, black holes are an extreme example, but even on planet Earth, gravity becomes more intense the closer you are to the Earth's core. In fact, living the entirety of a seventy-nine-year life in a basement would buy 90 billionths of a second of additional time. It's not a huge amount, to be honest, is it? I would also wager that the health issues you'd face from spending all that time in the cold, dark, damp isolation of a basement would far outweigh the 0.00000000009 of a second's worth of extra life gained, but it's your call.

But what about life after death . . .

Thing 29:
Even if the other sort does exist, I choose to concentrate on life before death

Life after death is a very complicated thing to think about but it is fascinating and there have been some really interesting studies into the 'life at death' stage – after that it all gets a bit supernatural – which suggest some aspects of brain function continue after the heart stops beating, at least for a few minutes (there is even evidence that unfortunate souls remain conscious for a little while, even after a sudden and very thorough beheading).

In honesty, I have no idea what to believe. The logical part of me is convinced that we are biological matter and nothing more. That when our brains stop working, we are reduced to a husk that used to harbour life, but will soon be worm food. However, there is a big part of me that simply refuses logic; having had an experience or two (you'll read about them a little later), I totally believe in ghosts. How can we just be a biological machine if, once our synapses cease to fire and our bodies are gone, we can still be seen and felt? There are just too many coincidences for it to be ruled out. Unfortunately, *Ghostbusters* is fantasy and we will likely never have the scientific capabilities to know for sure what happens after our bodies have had their time on this Earth. Maybe, either way, simple belief is enough.

BIRTH, CHILDHOOD, ADOLESCENCE

As fascinating as the subject of death is, let's move on to life for a bit, and as everyone knows, life begins with the miracle of birth.

Actually, wait. Before birth, you should know about the pee and the frog thing.

Thing 30:
Before pregnancy tests, we injected lady pee into frogs and it worked

Going to the local pharmacy to pick up a pregnancy test is actually a fairly recent privilege; before that, to know for sure, women would have to wait for the obvious signs, such as missing a period, growing a huge tummy or giving birth. But it's not like the tests we have today suddenly appeared out of nowhere. Believe it or not, less than a century ago, if someone wanted to find out if they had a bun in the oven, they'd have to get some of their urine injected into the hind legs of an African clawed frog. If the woman was indeed pregnant, the addition of the pregnancy hormone – 'human chorionic gonadotropin' (hCG) – to the frog's system would stimulate ovulation in the little amphibian and by morning she would have laid eggs.

By this point, if you're anything like me, you've probably asked yourself the following questions: 'Who injected a woman's pee into a frog?' 'How did they know this would happen?' 'What possible circumstances could have led to someone holding a syringe full of urine in one hand and a frog in the other?' Good questions. The answers to which mean that this story gets worse before it gets better. Shortly after hCG was discovered, scientists (who, let's face it, historically and as a whole, aren't exactly known for being the guardians of all creatures great and small) wondered what would happen if they started injecting it into wildlife. They did this pretty willy-nilly, mainly using the usual suspects in animal experiments: mice and rabbits. After a day or so, they would cut out the fluff-ball's ovaries to see if it had had any effect and, as it turns out, they proved to be pretty reliable indicators of pregnancy in humans. But, of course, the animals had to die and get dissected in order to yield the results, and destroying one life to possibly confirm another didn't seem like a fair trade-off (plus, for the scientist who didn't care about the cost of life, it was also inconvenient and fiddly).

What they needed was an animal that ovulated outside its body. That way no creature needed to be dissected and they could be reused again and again. Cue Mr Lancelot Hogben (great name), who discovered that African clawed frogs would do nicely. They proved to be so talented at predicting pregnancies that they were shipped all over the world to various labs and quickly became the international standard. They were used up until the 1950s, when more modern, more immediate, less weeing-on-live-frog-based tests were created.

Thing 31:
Human babies are super-cute and utterly pathetic but it's entirely necessary

One of the biggest mistakes of my life was watching an elephant give birth on YouTube. I'll spare you the gory details, but rest assured it was a grim affair. What I find truly amazing though is that, throughout most of the animal kingdom, babies are born ready to go. In the case of the elephant, its mother squeezed it out from a height, it fell to the floor, Mum then proceeded to kick it in the head (I assume to wake it up and welcome it to the world), it got to its feet and started living its elephant life.

Clearly, this makes a ton of sense; unless you are the top of your respective food chain, the chances are that you share your habitat with lots of things that want to eat you. This is a big problem if you're small and weak, because you can't run or fight. As a result, evolution has favoured those that can be as mobile as possible as quickly as possible. So why do humans give birth to infants that are entirely useless for such a long time?

Personally, I can't wait to start popping out little ones (I say 'popping out', but I'm fully aware that children don't just 'pop' out; there's a considerable amount of pain, discomfort and pushing involved), but I know that adding an infant to my life is not conducive to the way I am currently living. Sleepless nights, early mornings, being covered in poo and vomit and a crust of various foodstuffs, carrying a tiny human everywhere you go and teaching it how not to kill itself by accident with the infinite possible ways available for it to kill itself by accident is a responsibility that I am not quite ready for. I want to be secure and totally available for my child when he or she comes, so this part of my life is about setting the scene for that to take place.

Chimpanzees are our closest living relatives and they too give birth to fairly dependent children. A mother chimp has a baby with a brain roughly 40 per cent the size of an adult's, while a human newborn's is only 30 per cent that of its parents'. A difference of 10 per cent doesn't seem all that huge, but when you consider the fact that our brains are so jam-packed they weigh about three and half times more than a chimpanzee's, it brings into perspective just how little our offspring can actually do.

To birth children at the same level of development as a chimpanzee baby, our gestation period would go from the usual nine months to somewhere between eighteen and twenty-one. Clearly these children would be gargantuan and it would be impossible for any woman to pass something so huge through her birth canal. If all the females died because growing such monstrous offspring broke them, we would lose the ability to reproduce and it wouldn't take long at all for the rest of humanity to go the way of their mothers.

So why didn't women just evolve wider hips to allow babies the size of toddlers to slip out? I hear you ask. Well, the theory goes that our hips developed to make bipedal locomotion more efficient. It's important for humans to walk on two legs because it requires less energy over long distances, frees up our hands and, as our viewpoint is higher, allows us to see things from further away. The wider our hips, the more our posture is compromised, and so a trade-off between hip width and gestation period had to be reached.

Your poor mother's burden doesn't end with the size of her pelvis either; pregnant women need to consume a lot of calories to keep both themselves and their baby healthy. In fact, by the six-month mark, they will typically be burning through energy at twice their normal rate. As the foetus grows, so does this figure, but there is a limit to how much energy the human body can cycle through before it gets dangerous. Once again, in this scenario, growing a massive baby kills the mother. Also, we take for granted that we can swing by the local supermarket with £10 and leave with enough food to last all day. Things weren't that easy thousands of years ago and simply getting that much food into your body would have posed a real challenge.

We are pretty bright as a species and we're really very good at learning. We pick up complex things quickly and the sooner you can take a baby out of the womb (assuming it is developed enough to survive the outside world) and introduce it to its environment, the sooner its mind can begin the process of making neural pathways. You know the saying 'you learn something new every day'? Well, you really do, particularly when your brain is new. It's what smart people call 'plasticity' and it basically means that, when you're young, your mind is like a sponge.

My mum actually told me the other day that my twin brother was a cuter baby than me. He was chubby, had mischievous little eyes and blond, curly locks like a cherub, but regardless of who was cuter, the first chunk of your life is spent under near constant supervision while you learn the basics of how to move, how to talk and how not to poo yourself. My brother wouldn't be so cute if he made it past toddlerhood and still struggled to control the passing of waste.*

We need our giant brains to create language and culture, which teach us how to communicate and not to bite the brightly coloured wiggly stick, because it might turn out to be a snake that will eat you whole. A lot of the world's creatures are born in miniature adult form and don't need anything explained to them; all they must do is eat, avoid getting eaten and fill one another up with babies. At the most basic level, our lives fill out the same functions, but we went about it in a slightly different way. If human foetuses were kept in the womb for longer than necessary, not only would there be a huge risk to both mother and child, but the baby would miss out on learning how the

---

* Not so cute now, are you, imaginary incontinent twin?

world works, and when the world has sabre-toothed cats and woolly mammoths, you really don't want to be skiving off in your mum's tummy, because there are some tests you can't resit.

So, the bottom line is that not being able to do things but being able to learn how to do them is an essential part of what makes us human and where some of our greatest achievements as a species come from. In fact, it's this 'flaw' that is our greatest chance of surviving as a species.

However weird human babies are though, they can't hold a candle to kangaroos. We have to talk about them for just a minute.

Thing 32:
Babies may be a weird miracle, however, little is more disturbing than the inside of a kangaroo's pouch (except its three vaginas and the newborn joey)

Unless you're from the land down under, most depictions of kangaroos we're exposed to are based on dirty lies to divert our attention away from just how weird the truth is. The majority of marsupials depicted in popular culture (I'm looking at you, Kanga and Roo from *Winnie-the-Pooh*) have big fluffy pockets on their tummies for joeys to snuggle into. It wasn't until I was curious if such a cosy spot could be suitable for human infants to nap in that I did some research. What I discovered shocked me to my core and ruined my entire childhood. Brace yourself.

Australia has been in isolation from the rest of the world for a long time and evolution there started to take a slightly weird turn. As a result, female kangaroos ended up with three vaginas: two for sperm and a very small one for giving birth. If you're interested, the structure looks a little like a pink, soggy tennis racket, with the handle being where the three tubes merge. At the base of the handle is the entrance/exit, while the outer rim of the racket is made up of the two vaginas that transport sperm to a uterus (each) at the crown. Connected to the uteruses is a third vagina that the joey travels down when the time is right. It runs down the middle of the racket and connects to the handle area.

The drawback, though, is that vagina number three is tiny. The narrow birth canal of female roos restricts the size of anything travelling through it, and as a result they will actually only gestate for a period of about a month before squeezing out a teeny tiny joey less than an inch long (about 40,000 times smaller than its mother). If you ask me, that's nowhere near enough time to create complex life and the baby enters the world resembling a blind, hairless, translucent red jelly bean that has spent considerable time on the floor, on a hot summer's day, next to a swamp. If you've seen the final Harry Potter film, picture a minuscule version of the wretched Voldemort-esque creature from under the bench in the King's Cross Station dream sequence, but much, much more wretched.

Somehow (most likely witchcraft), this joey has the instinct and forearm strength to drag its underdeveloped body from its mother's vagina, up her body and into her pouch, where it will find a choice of teats to suckle from. It picks the best one, latches on and doesn't let go for love nor money. There it will stay, nursing from its mother's milk, growing big and strong and about 7 billion times cuter than when it first entered.

Its temporary home is not a massive, fur-lined pocket, handy for keeping all the paraphernalia it takes to be a roo, it's actually a stretchy, nearly bald orifice that the mother will stick her own head into and lick any dirt out of (and seeing as it doesn't velcro shut and these things live in the outback, there will be plenty of dirt in there). Think of it as a hot, sticky, semi-external, spare womb with easy access. Once you've come to terms with that mental image, picture opening said hole to find our blind, bald, veiny, half-developed joey clinging on to one of a few elongated nipples.

As the joey grows and gets a bit more adventurous, it may pop its head out from time to time. Eventually it will venture its entire body out into the real world for short periods before hopping back in, head first, covered in all the grub, dust and detritus the Australian outback has to offer. Often by this time our little joey friend will have company, because the mother kangaroo can actually produce two different types of milk from her various nipples: one suited for a new, gross, jelly-bean joey and one for our little guy who can now come and go as he pleases. This means that, if the going is good, with two uteruses

and two types of milk, the adult female kangaroo can literally always have a pouch full. A mother kangaroo's milk changes as her baby grows, but only the milk coming from the nipple that that joey attaches to. All her 'spare' nipples are ready to give milk suitable for newborns as soon as another baby comes along. When a joey leaves the pouch for good, the milk from that joey's nipple returns to being suitable for a newborn again. It's like a kangaroo conveyor belt and the vast majority of the work seems to take place in the most abused orifice in the animal kingdom.

Meanwhile, all the males have to worry about is the fact that they are the only animal in the world to have testicles situated above their penis. Seems like a small price to pay.

Whenever you think about babies, but especially after thinking about kangaroos, it's important to clarify one thing. Nipples.

Thing 33:
Men have nipples because they weren't always men

I have nipples, you have nipples, we all have nipples. Obviously, females use theirs to feed children, but if you stick an infant on either of mine, as hard as they suck, nothing is going to come out. Maybe a little blood if they really go for it, but certainly no milk.

So why do males have a completely superfluous part of their anatomy? Most parts of the human body have (or had, in times gone by) a reason for existing; after all, developing, growing and maintaining them cost a lot of calories, so the juice has to be worth the squeeze. For example, eyeballs need a lot of nutrients to work, but they help you see food, predators and things that you would stub your toe on, so are totally worth it. My nipples are completely pointless (despite being actual points) and grew only to exist on my chest and get erect when it's cold. My chest would be fine without them and I can tell if it's cold or not without the help from my nipples, so what's the point?

The truth is that there is no point, but there is equally no point in not having them. They are a by-product of development in the womb and not worth disposing of. Having nipples doesn't really have much of a downside, other than me overthinking why I have them, and in the grand scheme of things, it doesn't cost the body all that much to grow them and it's because of this that evolution never selected against them.

During the first four weeks of development in the womb, male and female embryos are indistinguishable. There is no little willy, no tiny testicles, but there are wee nipples because we are all female. Sexual dimorphism takes effect when the male-specific Y chromosome does its thing (if one is present), turning the baby into a biological boy. Testosterone is released, which stops breast development, fuses the labia into testes and transforms the other lady bits into boy bits. But seeing as the nipples don't really do any harm and they are already there, they stick around as a reminder that we all started out as girls, and sometimes, if you run for a long time, they can chafe a little.

So, it turns out that us men weren't always as masculine as some of us appear. For me, it also explains at least some of the variations between us. Gender is fluid and nipples are a permanent representation of this. Wear them with pride.

While we're talking about embryos, we should probably talk about twins.

Thing 34:
Being a twin is brilliant, most of the time

Whenever I tell people I have a twin, the first question I'm always asked is: 'Are you identical?'* Nope. I think we look more like cousins than siblings, although we resemble each other most when I'm tired. He looks a bit like me, only puffier. Depending on how much he smiles, his eyes can all but disappear, sandwiched between squashy cheek and squishy eyebrow. His jaw is slightly softer than mine and his abs are much harder. He's a personal trainer and a very good-looking son of a gun, which can actually kind of ruin the dynamic between us. If ever we're in the gym together, he looks like He-Man while I give off something of a lanky Gollum-esque wretch vibe, lifting half as much weight, for half as many reps, with half as good

---

* The second is: 'Can you read his mind?'

form. I suppose that's what I get for being twelve minutes his junior. I put it down to getting less nutrients in the womb. Greedy bastard.

His name is John, John Philip Chapman (named directly after our father), and he's my best mate. We are, though, completely and utterly different. I can be a bit uptight, I'm prone to pessimism, and self-deprecation is my go-to sense of humour/defence mechanism. Meanwhile, he's a bit of a moonchild. He's a kind of 'nothing is a big deal' (even if it is in fact a massive deal), 'everything will be all right in the end' (even if it definitely won't be), 'get some perspective, man' man. Sometimes I find this more than a little infuriating; for example, when I just want to moan about the lack of 4G on my phone, I don't want to be told to 'get in the moment'. I don't want to get in the bloody moment, I want to share the bloody moment with my Instagram followers, all right, John? All right?

You know what they say about absence making the heart grow fonder? Well, it works with twins too. John and I had pretty much identical upbringings until we left school. We have always been very different and although we've always loved each other dearly and had each other's back, when we were younger we would argue. A lot. And fight. A lot. John was always stronger but when he pushed me too far and my temper would flare, he'd always be the one to start running. Apart from that one time when I had him pinned down and was threatening to dribble in his mouth until I accidentally pulled the trigger and the spit tumbled from my lips and slowly dripped into the inside of his cheek where it became indistinguishable from his own saliva before I could suck it back up. On that occasion, I was the one running. In fairness, he still owes me a major dead arm for that.

As I was saying, it wasn't until our lives began going off in different directions that we realized just how important we were to each other. I went on to further education, while he became a carpenter's apprentice. Spending less time under each other's feet, not cramping each other's style, being interested in new things without feeling an obligation to take the other one along for the ride and making separate friends who don't view you as 'the twins' made growing our own personalities much easier. John and I would struggle to be any more different, and although we were always BFFs deep down, it's the time apart that allowed us to hone these differences and that's what made it easier to tolerate each other without resorting to the name calling or violence that was so often the case when we were growing up.

THE TWIN VENN DIAGRAM

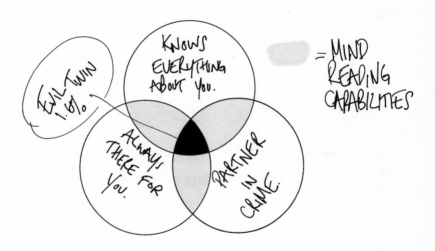

The reason why having a twin is brilliant 98.4 per cent of the time is because you know there is someone out there who's had the exact same upbringing as you. They know everything about you: they remember the time you fell off someone's shoulders and nearly broke your coccyx, they know that you don't like spiders and they have made mud pies and planned myriad mischiefs by your side. They know with just a look exactly what you're thinking, and they will always, always be there for you whenever you need them. No questions asked, no explanations needed and nothing wanted in return.

The reason why having a twin sucks the other 1.6 per cent of the time is because the person whose shoulders you fell from were his, and you didn't fall, you were pushed. They throw spiders at you because they know they are your weakness. They push you under the bus and blame you when you get caught for the mischief you both get up to (while you swear blindly that it was all him). And by knowing what's going on in your mind, they can out-think you and always call shotgun before you can – because, apparently, there's a stupid rule about being able to see the car before you can shout it and he's faster than you are. But despite the sore coccyx and that spider that laid eggs in your bed, knowing you've got someone who will always have your back when you need it makes it totally worth it. I'm very lucky to have a twin like John.

Thing 35:
Girls are born with all of the eggs they will ever have, already inside them

Which means that when your grandmother was pregnant with your mother, half of the genetic material *you* are made from was already inside your mum. It makes you think of those Russian dolls, doesn't it?

Families are pretty weird. I grew up with one sister a decade older than me who was off being a teenager and young adult, getting into all sorts of mischief, before I was even ten years old. I remember her (and this will sound awful, but it wasn't, I promise) tying a dressing-gown cord between my bedroom door and the banisters of the stairs opposite so my brother and I couldn't leave our room while she threw a party. My other sister, seven years older than me, left secondary school the same time I started – all the boys in the year below her (who were the oldest kids once she left) fancied her, which meant that nobody really messed with me during my first year because they thought word might get back to her and she would never date them. Not like she was going to anyway. Then I have a twin who, despite sharing basically every single experience I had up until fifteen years of age, turned out totally and utterly different from me in nearly every way. And a mum who was a total legend (and still is).

I don't think there's any way of 'solving' the amazing tangle that is family. But I do know that experiencing other people's allows you to take comfort in the fact that, although yours is undoubtedly odd, so is everyone else's, in their own strange little ways.

Thing 36:
On average, a four-year-old child asks 437 questions a day

Have you ever found yourself completely stumped by a toddler?

'What's that?'

'That's an oak tree.'

'Why?'

'Because it grew from an acorn.'

'Why?'

'Because it dropped in the soil and then the right amount of water and carbon dioxide and sunlight caused it to sprout.'

'Why?'

'Because that's how oak trees grow.'

'Why?'

'Because of evolution.'

'Why?'

'Because life wants to continue.'

'Why?'

'Because . . . Because . . . Because.' *Sobbing* 'I don't know.'

I feel as if spending time with someone and trying their brain out for size is an essential way of keeping things in perspective. Kids are brilliant because they haven't yet stopped asking the questions that we all should ask. They do the things that make them happy and that's enough. They dance without worrying how they look; they do (let's be honest) objectively rubbish paintings for the joy of doing them. They laugh at how delicious foods are, they spend whole days noticing things and asking questions and wanting to know more. It's totally fascinating and, although I can scarcely remember being that age, trying to get into their headspace, where everything is an adventure, fills me with wonder. It's a cliché to say that we can learn from children but you know who don't care about clichés? Children. So, I'm going to say it anyway – get more why in your life. Why? Well, I just explained it, didn't I?

Here are two bonus things that kids ask and their answers.

Why is the sky blue?

Light, which appears to be white, is actually made up of lots of different colours with lots of different lengths of wave. These travel in straight lines until they hit something, at which point they either reflect, bend or scatter. The colour with the shortest wavelength is blue, and because it wobbles up and down much more than the others in the same amount of space, it hits the most particles and scatters the most. Therefore, it is represented more in the sky. It's quite complicated to explain this to a young one though, so until they understand that light comes in waves, I would advise you to stick to 'Just, because' when they ask.

When lightning strikes the sea, how come all the fish don't die?

Any fish near where the lightning strikes probably do die. But water is such a good conductor and the sea is so full of it that anything further than a few metres away from the bolt will most likely feel nothing more than a light tingle as the bolt dissipates quickly through the water.

I feel as if you only just get used to childhood, and then you're a teenager. Basically, one minute someone's going 'Ooh, it's a big birthday – double figures' and the next you're dealing with the ridiculousness of adolescence – being absolutely adamant that everyone else in the entire history of the universe is and always has been wrong, nobody has possibly gone through what you are currently enduring and all people in the surrounding area should just shut up because you are right and that is that.

Thing 37:
No matter how big you are, you are never big enough to stand up to your mother

Dear Mum,

I'm really sorry that I shouted at you and told you to shut up when I was sixteen. I can't even remember what we were arguing about, but I was a total moron to think that I was ready to take you on like that.

It was the first and definitely the last time I will ever speak to you in that tone and I really regret it. Mostly because you did your scary-eyes-flarey-nostril thing to a level I had previously not encountered and it was the single most petrifying experience of my life. But also because, although I can't remember why I got so riled up, I can guarantee that you were in the right and I was being a dick.

I recall that, shortly before this incident, I had just had a bit of a growth spurt and found myself taller than you. I think it went to my head, and that, combined with the masses of puberty-related hormones knocking around my body, led to the delusion that I was tough enough to tell you where to shove it. I was an idiot and you will always wear the trousers.

I realized this as soon as I had said what I said and witnessed your reaction. The look you gave me (and the terrifying finger point, which only showed up on occasions when I had royally pissed you off) made me want to back-pedal, apologize profusely, do the washing-up for the rest of my time under your roof and have a cuddle, but I had gone too far and was compelled to commit to the course of action I had initiated.

That was when I slammed the door for dramatic effect. Unfortunately, the effect was much more dramatic than I had anticipated and the glass panel shattered. That was when I ran.

While I was out of the house, avoiding your wrath, I thought about living the rest of my life on the road, just coasting from town to town, but then I got cold and hungry and had to return with my tail between my legs.

I guess the good news is that, after this event, I was no longer labouring under the illusion that just because I was bigger than you it meant that I didn't have to listen to you anymore. Once that notion was shattered, you didn't have to endure any more pathetic outbursts from me. I've always been a quick learner and it certainly didn't take me long to grasp that particular lesson.

Even when you're old and frail, you will always be right and I will never attempt to usurp you ever again.

Love you big time,

Jim

Thing 38:
Puberty is a mess, it just is

Puberty is no fun and being a teen is tough for everyone. Your hormones are all over the place – one day you hate everyone and everything and the idea of kissing is gross because, as far as you're aware, all girls definitely have cooties. The next thing you know, all you can think about is sex with anyone unlucky enough to brush past you in the corridor and physical contact with the object of your desire becomes the most important and stressful experience of your life (as I became acutely aware when I was fourteen, and developed a strangely powerful crush on the new girl, Jenny McDonald. She was Scottish and had bright-red hair that I thought was exotic).

As a teenager, your prefrontal cortex (the part of your brain that is rational, reasonable and thinky) is among the last areas to get really honed to adult standards, which means that you are much more likely to be governed by your amygdala. This little blob is in charge of emotional impulses and instinctual behaviour and can account for a lot of a teenager's 'act first, think later' actions. Until the prefrontal cortex catches up, adolescents genuinely have diminished control over themselves, because the bit of their noggin that will convince them that maybe downing a bottle of tequila before hurling themselves from the neighbours' roof might not be the best idea isn't fully functional yet.* You start to get unusual urges that you've never experienced. You have next to zero control over your bodily functions and, if you're a guy, you end up with unwanted erections in geography class (that, no matter how hard you pray or think of your nan, refuse to deflate before everyone gets up for the next lesson).

Everyone is different, but for the most part people go through these changes at roughly the same time, in roughly the same order. My family were the exception to that rule. I should have taken the hint from my two big sisters, who were the last kids in school to start their periods and grow boobies. But I ignored the signs and started secondary school with the expectation of growing a beard by the end of the first week. A decade later and I was counting the sparse hairs on my chin as my twin

---

* What this means is that, in the same way we don't mock old people for being a bit forgetful because their brains are no longer able to find memories, we shouldn't mock teenagers for having brains that aren't yet set up optimally to make certain sorts of decisions.

brother and I were back for another onslaught of 'Chapman vs Puberty: This time it's sticky'.

I shaved once in that entire five-year spell and that was only because I was curious to see if I could work it out in the absence of a father figure to teach me. My adult teeth didn't even come through until I was fifteen, and even then some of them never emerged at all. My voice didn't break until the final term of my final year at school, and I didn't grow taller or more muscular until well after that.

The crux of the problem was internal. I had the body of a prepubescent child, but the mind of a young adult. I liked girls and wanted them to like me back. They rarely did, but on the odd occasion when I was surprised by requited affection, I was woefully under-equipped and far too nervous to do anything about it. I yearned for more responsibility, but when you look like an eleven-year-old, that's hard to come by, and, as with most adolescents at this time, I was painfully self-aware.

During puberty my body just started to go . . . a little wrong. My hands and feet grew large and I became very clumsy. My limbs finally extended to accommodate them years later, but only in length. I went from being one of the shortest kids around to one of the tallest in a matter of months. You'd think that was good news, but my mass was just spread over a bigger distance and, despite having a lot more body, my weight didn't alter at all.

Being gangly was one thing, but the fact that it happened so suddenly meant that my tendons struggled to grow as fast as my bones and muscles. As a result, I developed a slightly lopsided, *T. Rex*-type stance before everything stretched to accommodate a more human-like posture. Flexibility went out the window, and after growing so rapidly I couldn't even touch my toes.

I had braces, because the Chapman teeth seemed to get worse with each subsequent sibling. Sam has great teeth, Nic has great teeth minus one adult one that never came through, John had three adult gnashers missing and I had five. My teeth

PUBERTY

have always been straight and quite white; I just don't have as many as I should. Five baby teeth came out and there was nothing to grow in their place so a brace had to be fitted to close the gaps left in their milky wake.

I then developed something affectionately known as 'pubic breast', which, according to my doctor (who by this point was sick of feeling every part of my body for various pubescent problems), is caused by an imbalance in those raging teenage hormones. It got worse before it got better and there was a noticeable bulge around the breast area until it began to dissipate and make its way to wherever it needed to be.

And then (this is a fun one), I had to be circumcised at the age of fifteen. In my opinion, fifteen is far too old for a circumcision; still, needs must. I'd been to the doctors and hospital a number of times to undergo uncomfortable and invasive pokes, prods and slices in an effort to steer clear of the snip, but in the end it had to happen. I like to joke that it was just too big to fit, like an overcooked sausage that threatens to burst the skin. But in truth, it was the equivalent of being tongue-tied – just further south – and, rather than the inability to pronounce your 'L's, it leaves you with slight issues and some discomfort when performing *other* activities the way the body intended.

It all got a little much, and I have to say I didn't handle the news that the doctor wanted to remove part of my penis as well as I could have. My British stiff upper lip failed me and I may have shown a little weakness. My mum had to step in and give me some perspective. I distinctly remember her saying, 'Listen, Jim, in a few years you'll look back at all of this and laugh. You'll have great teeth, you'll be walking upright, your nipples will be fine and your willy will be unstoppable.' It took a little more than a few years - my body hadn't quite finished embarrassing me - but, on the bright side, all of that drama remains a constant source of amusement which is still much appreciated at family gatherings.

If I could write a letter and give some advice to my teenage self, it would go like this:

> Dear young, weird-looking Jim,
>
> When you're going through it, puberty is all-consuming and a constant source of stress, embarrassment and bodily leakage, but it does get better and it leaves you with a new and improved adult body.
>
> You'll find that, if you are willing to laugh at yourself, you'll gain a wicked sense of humour that will see you through.
>
> Get some perspective and realize that, even if you do need braces, or you can't walk properly for a while, or your nipples are a little inflated, or you require a surprise circumcision, it's all temporary (apart from the circumcision, which is definitely permanent, but totally

worth it) and you will survive. You'll realize that these problems are all superficial and that there are people out there who have real, enduring issues and that you have nothing to stress over.

So rub some dirt on it (probably best to avoid your penis in this instance), stop whining and get on with your life.

Yours sincerely (and actually),

Future Jim

PS: Learn to swim, learn to play piano and learn French – you'd be much cooler if you could, you know, do stuff.

The headline is this: PUBERTY IS *INSANE*. It's OK to be getting over the trauma of it well into your eighties. However, for some reason, this is exactly the moment, while the hurricane of nonsense that is adolescence is taking place, that we ask our teenagers to decide what they want to do with their entire lives. Genius.

Thing 39:
Higher education is not
100 per cent essential (but being
interested in something is)

When I was at school, it was ingrained in me that if you didn't go to university you were just counting down the days until you ended up on the streets and died a slow and painful death.

I'm the only one of four siblings who went to uni, and arguably the one that took the longest to find his career path. My career path, incidentally, has less than nothing to do with my chosen degree. I'm not saying that you shouldn't go into higher education, only that nobody should feel forced to. In my view, having a curious mind, passion and hunger for something, no matter what it may be, is what's important. If your passion lies in English Literature or Medicine (or countless other areas), then you're going to need to get yourself a degree to pursue it. If your interests lie somewhere a little more off the beaten track of academia, there are a million other options open to you. You know what they say, 'Find a job you love and you'll never work a day in your life.'

I have a BSc in 'Psychosocial Sciences' (basically, psychology) from the University of East Anglia and half a masters degree in psychology from the University of East London. It's important to point out that there is actually no such award as 'half a masters'. What I mean to say is that I was doing my MA, part-time over two years instead of one (while working at the Levi's store in Chaplefield shopping centre, Norwich, to pay for it), when this YouTube thing I was doing on the weekends started to show real promise. I enjoyed that much more than psychology so I just never went back to studying.

I've always been very arty and when I was younger I wanted to be a comic-book illustrator. After a chat with the careers advisor at school, I realized that I had no idea how to get into it and, although I was good at drawing, I almost certainly wasn't good enough. I truly love what I do now but one of my biggest regrets is that I decided to be boring and shelve the idea rather than working to get better and chase that particular dream. I regret it, not because I wish I was doing that instead of my current calling (I wouldn't trade my career for anything), I lament it mostly because, like with any skill, the less you practise it, the more it slips away from you. I rarely draw anymore and my ability is a fraction of what it was, and that fact makes me very sad.

When I took psychology as one of my A Levels, I discovered that I was really good at it (I actually got 100 per cent in some of my exams). I found it interesting and figured that there would be a viable route into a credible career. What I didn't realize is that opting to get into a ton of debt and making huge decisions about your entire future, based on a couple of years of low-level study at the age of eighteen, is a ridiculous notion. How anyone is expected to know what they want to do with their life at that age, when all they have experienced up to that point is studying a select few subjects, is something of a mystery to me.

Fairly quickly, the realization hit me that my interest in the subject had peaked during my A Levels. I found the next three years a little bit dull, if I'm completely honest. The subject just didn't grab my attention the way it had previously. Nonetheless, one of the things I pride myself on most is that I always commit myself 100 per cent to everything I do. So I got on with it, studied hard and did well.

After graduating, I expected to magically find the best job on the planet, but the reality is that, in order to start a career in the nitty-gritty of psychology, you need to take your degree further. I waited a year, so I could travel and work and save money, and went on to study for the masters that I half completed (I guess I don't *always* commit myself 100 per cent, after all).

The moral of this story is that, although I had a good time at university and I wouldn't want to tempt fate by changing anything (who knows? Maybe I wouldn't have found myself where I am today), I do feel like I could have done more with those four years of my life. I could have been gaining real life experience in a different area. I could have been drawing more and getting better. I could have discovered YouTube earlier. Coulda woulda shoulda. There's this sense, at various points in your life, that once you go down one path you're stuck. That's it. You can't do a different course because you haven't already done another one. You can't do that job because you're on the wrong career path. Now, I'm not saying that I'm going to win a gold medal in gymnastics any time soon, but I think that's massively overplayed. You should never feel like you can't change. Of course, some career paths require a degree and, for people that want to go into those jobs, you need one or it won't happen.

A career like the one I have been fortunate enough to pursue is testament to the idea that higher education may not be essential. Not everyone can do my job – it's the nature of it. If suddenly everybody was doing what I do, it wouldn't be special anymore and no one would climb to the levels that I aspire to reach. But remember that, when I first started making videos on my YouTube channel, it barely existed as a credible career path. I had no idea where it would take me and what brilliant things I would get to experience along the way. Mine was an accident, but you don't have to wait around for the universe to hand you your calling; all you need is curiosity, passion and a little bit of gumption.

Speaking from personal experience, the chances of knowing what you want to do with your career at eighteen and making decisions that will dictate the rest of your life when you've only been allowed to drive for a year, you can just about drink alcohol legally and you probably haven't even cast a vote in your first general election, is totally ludicrous. If this is you right now, it's OK if you feel like you're fumbling in the dark. In fact, I would go as far as to say that it's more than OK; it's totally normal and entirely to be expected.

When I was studying, the internet was slow. Now it's everything. I'm definitely not saying that you should burn all the books and expect to be the next Mark Zuckerberg in a fortnight, I'm just saying that learning a single subject for years and ending up with specific knowledge in one area shouldn't be the default that young people are expected to adhere to. New industries and opportunities are opening up quicker than an education regime can be written around them. With hard work, creativity and resourcefulness, there are limitless options and the world, as they say, is your oyster.*

---

* I've never understood that saying; why would the world be an oyster? OK, so once you've opened them, you can get the edible bit inside, but loads of people don't like oysters, loads of people do get sick from them and either way they're over really quickly – you have to have, like, a dozen at a time. Personally, I think they taste like the sea with the consistency of cold phlegm. If there's a worse

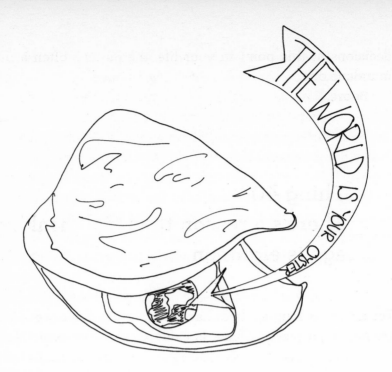

Combining the idea of a fixed path through life with a volatile, fast-changing world is a recipe for disaster. There are entire industries that didn't exist five years ago, so to ask one eighteen-year-old to effectively predict the future is only going to make them feel anxious and trapped.

I think it's useful here to think back to the beginning of everything. The fact that there are humans at all is because we're pretty good at rolling with the punches and adapting. Once you see education as you acquiring the resources you'll need to be able to adapt in the future, rather than it giving you a finite list of things you need to know, it will all appear less stressful. The most clever people I know are the ones who keep trying to find new ways of explaining things to themselves. Sometimes that involves university, sometimes it doesn't.

I should also say that, as well as the more complex, psychological and developmental reasons it's hard to make good

---

metaphor for life, I don't know what it is. I like mussels, though, the world can be my mussel.

decisions at this point in your life, there's also often a more mundane one.

Booze.

Thing 40:
There's a reason the legal drinking age is eighteen

For nearly as long as there have been civilizations, we've been trying to get pissed. There is evidence that we were brewing booze from as early as 10,000 BCE. Fast forward 12,000 years and I remember the first time I got drunk. Actually, I was too drunk to remember it, but my brother was more than happy to fill me in on the evening's escapades the next morning. I was fourteen or fifteen years old and was celebrating New Year's Eve at my friend's house. His parents were throwing a party and told Dan (my friend) that he could have a few people over too, and seeing as it was a special occasion and we were all under adult supervision, we were allowed to have a few drinks.

Other than having the odd sip of my mum's wine, a drop had never passed my lips before that night. Because of this, and because booze has a slightly delayed effect, and because I had no idea how much a fourteen- or fifteen-year-old should be able to tolerate, I got wrecked. Absolutely smashed. Completely and utterly trolleyed. Undisputedly wasted.

I was always the boy that friend's parents would like to have around for dinner or sleepovers; I was a polite young man, would always say please and thank you, could handle small talk and would help tidy the kitchen after everyone had eaten. Apparently, this was less the case on that evening. I wasn't rude or obnoxious and I still respected the adults, it seems I was just a little overfamiliar; I started calling them all by their first names because, after all, now that I was drinking, I was officially a man. I would confidently join their conversations, as if I was the oracle about things that I was totally under-equipped to understand and I was well out of my depth. At one point, I spilt a beer, clumsily wiped it up with the nearest towel and threw it at Dan's dad. I guess I thought he was paying attention. He wasn't; he was actually having a civilized, grown-up conversation until the tea towel, sodden with an entire pint, sloppily thwacked him on the side of the head. Bearing in mind my level of inebriation at this point in the evening, I'm surprised it hit him. Then again, I was probably aiming for the sink.

Soon after, midnight struck and Dan's mum said (very firmly, with thin patience) that we had seen in the new year and that we should all go to bed before anyone else threw anything else at anyone else's head (she used a lot of 'else' words, but was referring only to me). The room was well and truly spinning by this time and I was starting to feel a little claustrophobic and nauseous, so I didn't need to be told twice. I headed up the stairs to Ben's room, where I would be sleeping on the floor, very shortly before the shit hit the fan. I was suddenly aware that I was going to vomit in the next few seconds. I pushed my way into the bathroom to find someone sitting on the toilet; I told them to move but they were midway through their pre-bed poo and wouldn't be shifted for hell, high water or a hammered teenager. So, I took the only other logical option left open to me and was horrendously sick in the sink.

It went downhill from there; Dan's mum had to clear out the sink while I immediately fell asleep on the bathroom floor. I couldn't stay there because there were only two bathrooms and lots of people in that house, so she woke me up and put me in my makeshift bed. That was a mistake on her part; a few people holding their bladders a little longer would have been nothing compared to the carnage I was about to unleash. I was sick many more times that night and the vast majority of my up-chucks were not in the toilet. They weren't even in the bathroom.

They were in my bed, on my brother's bed, on Dan's bedroom carpet, even on his bedroom door (in my defence, I tried to make it to the toilet for that one but couldn't get the door open. In defence of Dan's door, my earlier vomiting meant that, to get out of the room, you had to pull said door over the vomit, which just mushed it into the carpet).

Needless to say, that wasn't the way I had intended to see in the new year. The next morning, I snuck off without saying thank you or sorry to Ben's parents and I never went there again (Dan said it was probably a good idea when I suggested never going back). In fact, I haven't seen them since. To be honest, I haven't seen Dan since I was sixteen either, but they're definitely on my list of 'people to avoid for the rest of my life' (other entries include a student from my sixth form named Eddie Moon whose sister I kissed after telling him I wouldn't, and Tracy Emin, but how she got on that list is a story for another time).

Being underage, alcohol was hard to come by, but even if it had been readily available, I was scared off it for a few years after that experience. It wasn't until I was seventeen or so that I started accompanying my sister on a few nights out, and I think she loved it; she had loads of friends and enjoyed having her little brother along with her to show the ropes to. She looked after me well too, just like a big sister should, perhaps too well. She has seven years on me and I think she had used most of that time building up an impressive tolerance to booze, a tolerance that I was very far from earning, yet whenever a new round was bought, I would find myself with fresh beverage in hand. Going at the pace she and her friends set was my undoing on many a night. I was sick very often and hungover more often still.

When you consume alcohol, ethanol (the stuff that makes you drunk) is absorbed into you bloodstream via your stomach lining and small intestine. It then heads to your liver, which decides that ethanol is toxic and releases various enzymes to do their bit in breaking it down before disposing of it. Your liver transforms the ethanol into another toxic substance called acetaldehyde, which is easier to break down, once more, into acetate. Acetate won't do you any harm, so your liver sets it free to be passed out of your body via urine, and assuming you haven't drunk more than it can handle, you won't be drunk. However, if you continue to drink, your liver can't process the booze fast enough and the ethanol it hasn't got around to dealing with yet is free to swim around in your blood, where it reaches your brain. Here, it gets up to all sorts of mischief, inhibiting some neurotransmitters that usually cause lots of signals to be sent and exciting others that are usually quieter. It affects the cerebellum, which leads to lazy motor-function control. The prefrontal cortex is slowed, so reasoning and information processing is reduced. This also means that the limbic system, which oversees emotions, has more of a say and can make you more outgoing or prone to crying, laughter, aggression or to making risky decisions. Now you're pissed. If your liver can't cope, your body will attempt to purge itself of the toxins, and vomit. Given enough time though, your liver will do its thing and process the ethanol into acetate and you'll sober up with a headache and a dry mouth.

By the time I got to nineteen, I still hadn't learned when enough was enough and decided to stop drinking altogether. I didn't touch a drop for the following seven years. Then, when I was twenty-six, at Vidcon in Anaheim, just outside LA, after an extremely long day of meeting thousands of viewers (you'd be surprised how exhausting that can be), I suddenly felt the urge for a beer. I only had two, but after my stint of being teetotal, that was ample. I discovered two things that night: I'm a lightweight; and I had finally found where my limit lies. From that night on, I became a much more sensible drinker.*

---

* I remember a huge amount of pressure to drink when I was younger. It often ended badly. In fact, when I made the decision to abstain from alcohol I got ridiculed on multiple occasions. I never understood why people tried to make me feel like choosing not to drink was uncool – it's just something

If you were deciding on a recipe for chaos, an adolescent's brain plus booze would probably be a good start. But adolescent brain, plus booze, plus sex? Now that can often be a perfect storm.

But before we get into the specifics of that sexy storm, it's time to consider love, in all of its glorious forms.

---

you drink. I wouldn't judge you if you decided not to eat a tuna sandwich. Besides, some of the stupidest, meanest, most dangerous things ever done have happened because someone has been drunk.

Thing 41:
Love is love

It's as simple as this: love, no matter who you feel it for (opposite sex, same sex, all sexes, everyone, yourself), is love. Equally as powerful, equally as triumphant, equally as heartbreaking, equally as all-consuming, equally as overwhelmingly, entirely and utterly wonderful, and all forms of love should be celebrated. Not merely tolerated, but celebrated. Unfortunately, that is not always the case.

At the very base level, before you even start to consider anybody else's feelings but your own, the only thing you have to ask yourself is this: 'If what that person is doing isn't harming themselves or anyone else, and I can continue living my life, unaffected, why should I object to it?' Another person's sexual preference does not change my life in any way, therefore, I have no right to interfere. That, I believe, should be every human being's bare minimum when it comes to tolerance. Clearly it isn't, because homophobia is still a huge issue and people from the LBGTQ+ community are judged and persecuted in every town and every city in every country in the world.

Of course, the bare minimum is just that: the very least you can do, and who wants to do the least of anything? Especially when there are too many people out there that don't even come close to that standard, it's more important than ever for everyone who celebrates love in all its forms to make it clear that anything less than 'the least you can do' is unacceptable.

The thing with sexuality is that it's a human trait, just like personality, or height, or skin tone and, as such, it's not just black or white, on or off, gay or straight. It's a continuum, and continuums are very difficult to measure. Seeing as we, as a species, find it more comfortable to give things names, we end up with strict categories that lump people together but that no single person fits into. Everybody falls somewhere along the spectrum, from those who are entirely heterosexual, to those that are curious, to those that are 100 per cent homosexual and every possible integer in between. Personally, I'm attracted to women, but I can definitely appreciate other men and have more female friends than male ones. I would say that I hold quite a number of characteristics that would typically be described as 'gay' (certainly in some of the playgrounds I grew up in), but here I am, heterosexual and married to a woman.

People differ in every possible minutia of every possible distinction and until we stop trying to categorize one another as one thing or another, prejudice will never disappear. We're a long way from that mark, but while we're waiting, imagine how boring the world would be if we were all exactly the same. There would be no point in finding love because there would be no difference between my wife and my next-door neighbour. We would all listen to the same music, if we had music at all, our days would be strict and regimented and identical, and we would all know exactly what we all required at exactly what time. It would be totally shit and completely boring. It's the same changes – whether they be minute or massive – along the infinite spectrums that make each of us completely unique, that also create a world that is worth living in. Our dissimilarities bring art, they bring music, they bring conversation, they bring connection and they are what pulls us towards certain individuals and allow us to fall in love, regardless of who we fall in love with.

I've been making my videos and talking with my audience on various social-media platforms for about seven years now and one thing that gives me hope is that, although homophobia is still very much a thing and there are still far too many people of the LBGTQ+ community being treated unfairly, there have been, and there continue to be, huge improvements in people's attitudes. I have real hope that, soon enough, everyone will be free to express their gender and sexuality in a way that suits them, without fear of repercussions for doing something as simple as living as they wish.

Thing 42:
Love begins in your brain, not your heart

We use the word 'love' to mean lots of different things. There's the sex drive, the evolutionary motivation to reproduce and then deep attachment. We're not sure exactly what's going on when someone feels attracted to someone else but scientists are pretty confident it has a lot to do with pheromones.

Dr Helen Fisher and her colleagues at Rutgers University put a whole bunch of people in love into a brain scanner. What they found is that, when they were shown the person they love, a bit of the brain called the caudate nucleus was activated via big hits of dopamine. This is a part of the brain associated with 'the rewards system'. Interestingly, other things that follow the same path are addictive substances, like nicotine and certain drugs (and it's the part of the brain connected to wanting chocolate, too). The dopamine then spreads throughout the brain, making you feel euphoric and joyful and, more importantly, making you want the person more too, like a chemical craving. It also means you can't stop thinking about them. It doesn't stop there either; there's another chemical released called norepinephrine, which gives you butterflies, a pounding heart and that shaky feeling.

Relationships go on and become many other things besides the physical, but those initial feelings we all associate with love begin in the chemical. This is not to devalue the greatest thing about being alive, but it might make you feel a bit less intimidated by it.

Thing 43:
First times can be overrated

My first kiss came much too early, was much too sloppy and left me much too traumatized to try it again for a long time. It was forced upon me, it all happened so fast and I can't even remember the name of the girl who inflicted it upon me. I do remember that I was primary-school age and that it took place at New Buckenham village hall at the birthday party of Florence Hall. Her friend, who went to a different school, must have decided that it'd be a fun challenge to kiss as many boys as she could in as little time as possible. Now, bear in mind that I was very young – everyone (bar the adults) at that party was young – so young, in fact, that I hadn't even started to show any interest in girls yet. I could think of nothing worse than a big, wet, open-mouthed snog.

I turned up to this party a little later than most, so by the time I arrived it was already in full swing and I remember seeing this girl move around the place, kissing boys seemingly at random, and I thought 'gross', but figured it was all part of a game that I wasn't playing. I was wrong, because as soon as I had taken off my coat, stepped into the hall and prepared to cut some serious shapes on the dance floor, I felt a tap on my shoulder. I turned to see who was trying to gain my attention and was met by a grotesque, damp orifice hurtling towards my face. I was a polite little boy and have a vivid memory of thinking to myself, *Oh no, I don't want to kiss this girl, she's kissed everyone and she has germs, but I don't want to hurt her feelings. How can I get out of this?* Of course, this thought process took longer to navigate than the time required for her mouth to engage with my own, and there I found myself, having my first kiss, forced on me by way of guerrilla tactics, with a mouth that I had just witnessed slosh around twelve other boys.

It was not a pleasant experience, I had my eyes wide open

in shock and I couldn't fathom how the inside of someone else's mouth could feel so vastly different to my own. And then it was done and the mystery girl from a different school went off to find her next victim. While she did that, I went to the bathroom and literally washed my mouth out, because I was paranoid that I might catch the lurgy or something.

Fast forward a few years, and secondary-school Jim is still so traumatized by his first foray into the world of passion that he tries very hard to avoid kissing girls at all costs, while the other boys his age are snogging left, right and centre at the school disco. I was pretty successful at keeping my face away from other people's, until Laura from the year above me came over while Weezer was playing and actually said the words, 'I'll make it all better,' in what I imagine was her sexiest voice that she had been practising for just this occasion. As she leaned in, all that was on my mind was *Make what better? What's wrong with me? That line is completely out of context unless someone has something wrong with them for you to make better.* That, and avoiding her mouth. History has a way of repeating itself, but I had learned from previous experience and managed to pretend that I didn't realize she wanted a kiss and thought she was going for a hug instead. As I wrapped my arms around her and turned my face out of the line of fire, I could feel her lingering for too long and trying to regain control of the smooch (probably thinking that I really was oblivious to her obvious attempt and that surely I would love to be kissed by her) until, eventually, after an agonizingly long and excruciatingly awkward cuddle,* she got the message and moved on. After my first experience, I wanted to be sure that any future canoodling was mutual and not forced on me or out of the blue, accompanied by a cheesy line.

It seems odd, given that I had avoided frenchies for so long; you'd think, seeing as I was so protective over it, that it'd be quite a big deal when it happened, but I honestly can't remember who my first proper, reciprocal kiss was with. My brother

---

* I think I may have even made that 'ahhh' cuddle noise.

seems to think it was Tiffany Clarke, who was my 'girlfriend' from the end of primary school till the second year of high school. I use the inverted commas because we didn't even hold hands (we barely even talked to each other), so I'm confident that it wasn't her. Whoever it was with, I'm pretty sure it was at another school disco, because where better to put your tongue in someone else's mouth? There're plenty of dark corners (but also lots of your mates around to show off to afterwards), there's music and the teachers have had to stay at work late, so they would struggle to care any less about what you get up to.

I'm sure that the fact that I can't remember who it was with means that it wasn't exactly life-affirming. I've clearly carried on with my existence and, at some point, my brain has discarded this information as useless, which leads me to the conclusion that first kisses are overrated.

But why do we even kiss at all? Studies have found that half of human cultures enjoy smacking lips, while almost all animals tend to give it a wide birth. There are so many biological reasons not to mash your bacteria-ridden mouth-hole against someone else's and yet we do. Why?

It's a difficult thing to trace back particularly far, but we know from hieroglyphics that the Egyptians didn't tend to.[*] We know that our close relatives, chimpanzees, do kiss, but it's mainly a kind of make-up thing between male apes after a fight and not connected to mating. Bonobos do actual frenchies, the sexy things.

We know our lips our packed full of nerve endings, so it makes sense to put those bits of the body together. Interestingly, a study of oxytocin, the hormone connected to feelings of bonding, suggests that levels are increased around the act of kissing in men but not women. So, men are basically ready to be attached from the first kiss, whereas women need a lot more. I guess this explains why some men can come on a little strong in the early days of a relationship.

---

[*] They just seem to have stood awkwardly close together.

Our best guess is that kissing is almost certainly connected to smell, as this is such a big part of mating decisions. Close enough to kiss means you're close enough to smell.

Thing 44:
Love doesn't happen in a heartbeat

I'm not sure I believe in love at first sight. I definitely believe in lust at first sight, but I think you need to learn someone's intricacies to really love them, and that takes time. Not always a lot of time, but I don't believe it's instantaneous. You fall for the things that make someone different from everybody else (if you didn't, you'd love everyone) and people don't often show that straight away. When someone is falling for you, they'll be at their most comfortable and will relax into showing you what makes them different from every other person on the planet, often without even realizing they're doing it. When that happens, assuming you enjoy these little quirks, you might find yourself falling in love. At least that's how it went for me.

My wife and I didn't fall in love at first sight, we didn't even fall in lust. The truth is, she thought she'd found her new gay best friend in me. Here's the story:

I was in my first year at the University of East Anglia in Norwich (I stayed at home because my mum lived five minutes from campus, they did a good course in psychology and it was cheaper) while Tan was still studying at the sixth form I had just left the year previous. She was only in the year below me but I had never spoken to her at school before. Not because it was a particularly busy school; in fact, it was quite small, but I had my routine and she had hers. I've always been slow and careful when it comes to making friends, so I wasn't exactly Mr Popular. I had a small group of people I would spend most of my time with and we simply tended to hang out in the areas Tan and her friends didn't. Plus, I was terrified of girls and, most likely, wouldn't have spoken to her even if I had the opportunity. We had, however, crossed paths here and there. We recognized each other; not by name, but by face. I'm told that she and her best friend first laid eyes on me at a Bloc Party gig (that I went to on my own because nobody else wanted to accompany me. Rock 'n' roll).

The summer before I began uni, I started a new job in an independent clothes store and met my new best friend. His name was Ryan and he was in his second year of university and promised to show me the ropes. He lived with five other boys and they quickly took me under their wings and did indeed show me the ropes. I can honestly say that my fresher year would not have been anywhere near as fun without them. They lived off-campus and, even though my mum's house was much closer to work and university, I still all but moved in with them and we got up to all sorts of mischief.

Tan had met Ryan at a Babyshambles concert (held in the same location as the Bloc Party gig a year or so prior). He had a long-term-ish girlfriend and would never cheat, but he did enjoy a good flirt. He was very confident, very good-looking, and wore the skinniest jeans around, which, seeing as this was at the height of the 'indie scene' in 2006, may as well have been a pair of very tight babe-magnets. He had this troubled, mysterious, loner-in-a-group-of-friends vibe that girls seemed to be really into and he enjoyed the attention (while I mostly watched in awe).

During the gig where Tan and Ryan met, Ryan invited her and Kate (still Tan's best friend to this day) to a house party that he, myself and the other five boys were hosting a few days later at their grotty, damp-carpeted, 'why does the inside of your house smell like humid yeast?' house. Of course, when the night of the party arrived, Tan and Kate had to get a bus from the village they lived in and Tan was so keen to meet the boy she had been obsessing over that they were the first guests to arrive. Way to play it cool, Tan. I answered the door, and had been enjoying a little 'pre-drinking' to socially lubricate myself, so when I saw her, I said (I may have slurred it a little), 'I know you; where do I know you from?' We made the connection and the girls entered the house to find Ryan, in the kitchen, with his girlfriend.

I could see that Tan's little heart was broken and, seeing as Ryan had made a run for it up to his bedroom, the other boys hadn't even poked their heads out of theirs yet, and the girls were the only guests that had arrived, I felt an obligation, as a quasi-housemate, to entertain them. Plus, we had school as a shared experience and I was still fairly new on the university scene and was acquainted with the other soon-to-be-guests about as well as I was with Tan and Kate, so I figured I would keep them company for a while.

They told me that Tan had the hots for Ryan and that she thought he was single and interested in her, to which I told her, as sensitively as I could, and without betraying my friend, 'Join the queue, love' and got them both a drink. At some point in the evening, Tan and Kate's other best friend Emma (again, still best friends today), joined us and the whole time I just thought that Tan was the most stunning creature I had seen. We all got along swimmingly and I even made them all laugh on a few occasions. I remember thinking that Tan had very nice teeth (I have a thing for good teeth) and I loved the way her mouth moved when she smiled. She had (still very much has) a beautiful smile that touched her eyes and was truly heart-warming. She had a silly haircut, but then, looking back, so did I. I found myself pretty smitten with her, so decided to flirt my arse off.

As it turned out, I was undeniably diabolical at flirting and apparently did not make my intentions clear at all. We did manage to swap numbers (which I thought was mission accomplished), but only because she thought I was a good listener and that we could talk about boys together. It wasn't until after that party, when they were heading home, that Tan said something like (and I wasn't there for this bit, so I'm telling you what the girls have told me), 'Isn't Jim lovely? I have an opening for a gay best friend.' It was Kate who replied something along the lines of, 'Tan, I don't think he's gay, just really unthreatening and a nice guy. He's gorgeous. You should go on a date.' I have actually quizzed the two girls on this little exchange a number of times; after all, it's a conversation that completely changed the course of my life. They are not 100 per cent clear on exactly how the chat went, but that's the gist of it. One thing they are sure on though is that Kate used the word 'gorgeous'. I'm not telling you this so you think I'm a hunk, because she didn't mean it that way. I'm told (and I take great pride in this) that she just meant that I'm a gorgeous human being. A gorgeous soul.

The next day, Ryan and I had work. We were both feeling a little fragile but I would not shut up about the girl I had met the night before. I told him the story about how she had fancied him and how I had been her shoulder to cry on and, 'Wouldn't it be weird if I were to pursue it after that?' To which he laughed. On the way home from work, we were coming up to the Starbucks where Tan worked on the weekends. I was midway through talking myself out of going in and striking up a conversation with her, when Ryan simply pushed me through the door and continued his journey home. I saw her behind the counter and, when she spotted me, we exchanged sheepish, cheeky grins. She looked happy to see me. I hated coffee but didn't know what else to have, so ordered one and took it upstairs. Tan popped up to say hello on the pretence of wiping down tables and, when I asked her, she told me that her shift ended in two hours. So I waited, with a cold cup of coffee that I found disgusting. When she clocked off, we walked around the shops the long way to her bus stop and chatted. Not about anything specific, just chatting outside of the context of a house party with lots of alcohol and other people. At this point, I knew I liked her, but I had no idea I would love her.

We texted and called each other a lot, she would swing by to see me at work or meet me on campus and I would wait in Starbucks for her to finish on many occasions. I was very inexperienced with girls so I would text her things like, 'I like you, can we go on a date soon, please?' I had no idea that that wasn't the done thing. Apparently, you were supposed to play it really cool and leave it two days before getting in touch, then be really mysterious and unavailable when you did. Whatever was the norm, Tan said she liked my approach and we saw each other as much as we could.

I am a very hard man to please and my standards are extremely high. By now, if you've read much of this book, you might have realized that I'm interested in the scientific method; not that I'm qualified in science, just that I'm thoughtful, can be quite pensive and I'm methodical. I tend to analyse and think hard before making decisions. I always want to know how things work or why things do what they do, but Tan came charging through all of that like a bull in a china shop, clumsy and quirky and jam-packed full of charm, and I fell in love with her within a month or two, which I think is fast.

She fell in love with me first, though. She told me so via a text message when I was at work one day. Not the coolest way to let someone know, but she was seventeen, I was eighteen, and it was easier to tell someone like that than put your heart on the line. I wouldn't change it.

Thing 45:
If you've never experienced a broken heart, I suggest you hurry up. It's an educational experience

Dear Samantha,

You may not remember me, but I was obsessed with you during the summer of 2005. I thought we were going to be soulmates and live happily ever after in a townhouse, with three children. A lot of time has passed since then and it's possible that I may have come on a little strong; as such, I would like to extend an apology your way.

To refresh your memory, I worked in the independent clothes store, Elements, while you temped next door, in Asylum. I was seventeen and you were the first girl I liked outside of the school playground and it's fair to say I was a total rookie when it came to courtship. I remember buying strawberries to take to you at work because you said you liked them once. I would text you from the next building while we were both on shift and I would 'just happen to find myself' in your store on my days off. I texted you much too often, for any reason I could think of, and I wanted to be in your company so much that, if I discovered you would be going out with the girls, I would plan a night out with my friends at the same location.

In hindsight, this may have been a tad too much, but in my defence, you did tell me you liked me and that you were going to break up with your boyfriend. One night you even asked me to stay at your house, in your bedroom, while your parents were away. I like to think I can look back on this time with objectivity and I can see where I was a bit over the top, but to this day, I still believe that you invited me to sleep at yours as a test, to see if I was man enough to pluck up the courage and make a move. Of course, I was nowhere near man enough, was far too scared and chose to lie on your floor, where I didn't sleep a wink for arguing with myself about the pros and cons of just going for it.

I appreciate now that your boyfriend, who was also seventeen (but actually looked seventeen, while I looked fourteen), was a much better catch than me and that you strung me along because you liked the attention. That was totally normal on your part, but I had never had much attention before and I may have got carried away. I told my big sisters that you were my girlfriend (they both still hate you for breaking their little brother's heart, by the way) because I was delusional enough to feel that we were just days away from making it official. I imagined us having proper conversations where you would confess your undying love and, on more than one occasion, I pictured myself challenging your boyfriend to a duel.

Anyway, it was only a year or so later that I met Tanya, who is now my wife, and I realize that, no offence, I had no idea what love was before her. I would like to thank you, though, because I learned a lot from the utter mess I made of my attempt to woo you. I was a little braver with Tan and told her that I liked her early on. I still thought (and still think) about her every minute of every day, but was sensible enough to not let that turn into odd, semi-stalkerish behaviour. Apparently, I got the balance between being everywhere she was and playing it far too cool for her to know I was interested just right, too.

Who knows? Perhaps meeting her was fate and it would have worked out regardless, or perhaps I learned my lesson from making such a terrible job of courting you. Either way, I'm sorry for being such a needy weirdo and thank you for teaching me just a little bit about how to behave around women that aren't your siblings or your mother.

I hope you're well and very happy. If you happen to pick up a copy of this book and read this little letter to yourself, drop me a line.

Yours truly,

Jim

(who is much more normal and can definitely talk to you without risk of swallowing his own tongue now.)

Thing 46:
The science of heartbreak

It's all very well looking back on a distant break-up and being able to keep things in perspective, but I know that, when in the process of experiencing one, it can feel excruciating and unending. Scientists have actually looked at what happens in your brain when you're in love and then when you're heartbroken (it doesn't have much to do with the heart at all).

When studies have shown people undergoing difficult break-ups images of their ex, even though they rationally knew the relationship was over, the brain kept trying to follow the same reward circuits discussed earlier, but without the same reward. The part of the brain that deals with behaviour control and learning from emotions tries to take control. The brain is basically in a battle against itself, between the rational and the desire for pleasure. Interestingly, there is also activity in parts of the brain that fire when physical pain is experienced.

This is all a way of saying that feeling stuck in a vicious circle, trying to battle between logic and irrational behaviour and having a physical feeling of loss after a break-up doesn't make you weird, obsessed, too sensitive or broken. It's a completely natural, physical response to a broken heart. The good news is that our brains are astonishing things, capable of building new connections at phenomenal speed. As useless as it may seem to those people who miss their ex, the old advice of getting back out there and making new memories can be really helpful. If you give your brain enough time to make new connections, you can break free of the old circuits.

Thing 46.1: While we're on the subject of heartbreak

One of the least helpful ideas ever created about love is that there is the 'one' out there. Your heart's counterpart. The yin to your yang. The only person that will ever truly understand you. I totally get it; when you're in love, you feel as if no other person could ever be as special in your life. It really does feel as if they are the only one you could possibly love. And it's true that no one else could ever be in your life in exactly the same way. But the maths just doesn't hold up. Think about it for a minute – if there is a 'one' for everyone on the planet, what are the chances that so many of them come from the same school, the same office, or the same town? If there was a 'one' for everyone on the planet, surely they'd be dispersed randomly, separated by thousands of miles, never to meet. With 7 billion individuals spread across the face of the Earth, if every person had only one soulmate, the world would be full to the brim of lonely humans.

But you should definitely not drunk text. That is never a good idea.

Thing 47:
Whatever you have to say, it should probably wait until you're sober

'YOU ROCK MY WORLD' was a drunk text I once sent to a girl that I had a crush on. To make matters worse, my phone was a little dodgy and would often send texts twice. Needless to say, I didn't get a reply. Also needless to say, when I bumped into the recipient a few days (and a horrific hangover) later, it was extremely awkward.

The thing is, I had been playing what I liked to call 'the long game' with this particular girl, and by 'the long game', what I really mean is 'never saying or doing anything'. This poor person had absolutely no idea how utterly obsessed with her I was because I had given her a total of zero signs to that effect. So, when she received two identically desperate messages at 2.30 a.m., demonstrating the depth of my emotions, I can see now, with hindsight, that she may have been a tad surprised and how it could make things a tiny bit awkward. My bad.

Still, a valuable lesson was learned. Never drunk text.

An Interlude, but not a Thing

Let's be honest, people can talk about love all they want, but the nitty-gritty of the sex bit is really strange. It's such a deep-seated drive in all of us that we rarely stop to think about it, but trust me, it's mental. Just for a minute. 'Well, she was wearing a top cut so I could see the shape of the glandular and fatty tissue of her chest, which is generally thought to be very attractive and which caused my external intromittent organ, which by the way also serves as a urinal duct, to fill with blood.' We all know what happens next. And yes, I know that's definitely not how every-one has sex but that's the bog standard 'when a mummy and a daddy love each other very much' description that still gets pre-sented as the norm. And no one's saying, 'That's mental,' because of course it's one of the most deep-seated drives we have. Even the forty-year-old virgin got laid eventually and the truth is, whether you wait until midlife or not, the chances are you put a ridiculous amount of pressure on yourself before you realize how simple an affair it is. We've been doing it for a very long time and it's not rocket science, so if you are one of my more inexperienced readers, fear not, there isn't much that can go wrong, despite what your friends might say. Just be safe, hey?

Intercourse is just one more odd thing in the long line of odd things that go along with being a human. I want to cover a load more things about being a human that are peculiar. But first, if you think *we* have it weird, be grateful you're not a honey bee.

Thing 48:
Honey bees' testicles explode after they use them

Unlike wasps, which will go out of their way to sting you on the eyeball just because they believe that everyone has jam somewhere on their person, honey bees are gentle creatures that will only resort to violence to defend themselves or their hive.

They make quite the sacrifice too, for their stingers are barbed, so when they enter the skin of their target, they're not easy to get back out. In fact, when the bee pulls away, the stinger and venom sack are usually left behind, ripped from the insect's body, leaving a mortally wounded bumble, not long for this world.

Only female worker bees have stingers, but it would seem that male drone bees have a problem with penetration too. When they mate, their testicles explode and guess what? They die.

Drones don't have a stinger, they don't collect nectar or pollen, they tend to be bigger and stouter than workers and have huge eyes. This is because they don't live long but, during their short life, they have one mission: to inseminate a queen (usually from a different hive), and to do that, they need to be able to fly and see well.

Queen bees only mate once in their lives, so when they do

it, they go big and they go hard. What ensues is a huge gang bang in mid-air. All of the lucky lads that latch on will ejaculate into her before dying, content in the knowledge that they have completed their life's work. Presumably exhausted after the massive orgy, their little bee balls go boom. The force of the drone emptying his testicles is so violent that it can make an audible 'popping' sound and the bee is actually blasted backwards, exiting the queen but leaving his penis behind to plug the space and prevent any sperm from escaping.*

---

* So, you know, in this context, not messaging someone enough seems pretty minor.

The queen then heads back home, where she will stay, full to the brim with various drone bees' sperm, drip feeding it to her ovaries in order to lay up to 2,000 eggs a day, every day, for the rest of her life.

As an interesting side note, the queen of any honey-bee colony was not particularly special until the hive decided that a few specific larvae were potentially the chosen one. Worker bees feed all youngling workers a secretion known as 'royal jelly' from a gland in their heads, but the possible future queens are fed this nutrient-rich substance exclusively for the rest of their lives.* Because of this diet, the queens receive upgrades that the rest of the hive does not, such as ovaries and a smooth stinger (allowing for multiple attacks without leaving it in her provoker). Once a queen emerges, she will seek out the rest of the budding royals and fight them to the death, leaving only one new ruler.

---

* The rest of the bees just chow down on pollen and honey.

THE
HUMAN
BODY

One of the easiest ways to stop taking things too seriously is to step back and look at the human body objectively. We get so caught up in aesthetics, we don't think enough about how strange our bodies are. Here are some of my favourite ways to remember that.

Thing 49:
There's a good chance we're from space

Before we get going, do you know what really blows my mind, perhaps more than anything else? The idea that this planet came from nothing but water, rocks, dust and random chemicals, yet, somehow, life emerged. The first ever living organism, the thing that sparked every variety of life that has been, is and is yet to come (on our planet, at least), the common ancestor of every bacterium, fish, mammal, amoeba, marsupial, insect, arachnid, plant, fungus and slime mould, ever, wasn't born, because there was nothing to birth it. Life just happened and that makes my brain feel floppy and overwhelmed.

Of course, this happened billions of years ago, so all we have is theories, but I love a good theory and this is one that accounts for us, badgers, bacteria, *Velociraptors*, octopuses and everything in between. It's a big one. It seems pretty obvious, to those with scientific sympathies at least, that life emerged from chemistry. We know that atoms interact to form molecules; for example, two hydrogen atoms and one oxygen atom form one molecule of water. These molecules, in turn, interact with other molecules and form larger structures and compounds.

Everything is made of molecules, from the air we breathe to the nose and lungs we breathe it with. Absolutely everything. Interestingly, some special molecules, that we once thought could not exist outside of a living thing, have been discovered on the inside of meteorites that have landed on Earth from outer space. This doesn't necessarily mean that we are all aliens, but it does suggest that these molecules are not as rare as we once thought. It seems that they quite like existing and, if the conditions are right, may form on their own.

The ancient seas of our planet are sometimes referred to as the *primordial soup*, which basically means that all the bits and bobs required to build life were hanging out, apparently just waiting to get to work. Nobody is entirely sure how these atoms, molecules and structures started collaborating to form the genetic code found in DNA, but a theory suggests that one hollow, sphere-like structure formed around a column-like structure, and the first ever semblance of a cell was formed, with the sphere acting as a wall to protect the important bit inside.

Of course, this is a very fleeting visit to a massive concept and if you do decide to do a little digging yourself, you'll likely discover the wonders of RNA, amino acids, chemical evolution and metabolic pathways. It's all a lot to take in, so I shall leave you with this thought: if indeed life was not a random chance and molecules do self-organize and self-assemble, regardless of how tiny the probability, with the sheer number of Earth-like planets out there in the universe, maybe the chances of life existing elsewhere aren't all that low.

Thing 50:
Your brain is in your head because your anus is at the other end

Most people's brains are located in their heads. In fact, the think boxes of a lot of living things are found in their noggins. But why? It seems to me that, seeing as our brains control everything we do, they should find their home right, smack bang in the centre of us. As someone who continuously falls over his own feet, surely I would be more coordinated if my brain was in my stomach. I could control exactly where my feet were with much less of a delay than having to wait for a signal to travel all the way to my head, compute that I'm about to trip and send a corrective response back to my size elevens. Often, by the time that process takes place, I'm already face down.

Our brains are the most sophisticated piece of kit we have; they are very heavy, unnervingly delicate and require a huge portion of our daily calorie intake just to keep us functioning and in a tolerable mood. So why is mine balanced atop a scrawny neck at the dizzying height of six foot three inches?

The real answer lies with your anus. Kind of. Way back in the early days of living things, lots of the world's creatures were simple and radially symmetrical. Think jellyfish, coral or starfish. Radial symmetry refers to organisms that are symmetrical along many axes. Let's use a jellyfish as an example: they have no discernible front or back, so if you had an aerial view (which, in my opinion, is the only way jellyfish should be viewed because the tentacles are weird and will definitely sting you to death), you could cut it like a pizza. Along any of those slices, each half of the jellyfish would be near enough identical to the other opposite half.

Over time, this started to change. Maybe an ancestor of the jellyfish went rogue and decided to only face one way when it swam; maybe it's sensory organs where more heavily focused on one side, so it began to favour swimming with that part first (this is the much more likely scenario, as jellyfish can't 'decide to go rogue', because they're too stupid). However it happened, it was a very successful trait that had major meaning for the future of nearly all complex life.

With directional movement came a need for a change of anatomy, because if you're moving forward, it makes sense for your mouth to be at the front of your body. If your mouth is at the front of your body and your digestive tract starts from your mouth, your butt is going to be at the other end. All of a sudden – it actually took millions of years – you have a front and a back and you have reached bilateral symmetry. Animals that are bilaterally symmetrical are mirrored down only one plane. For example, if you sliced me lengthways down the middle, both halves would have one eye, one nostril, one ear, half a mouth, one nipple, one arm, one leg, one testicle and, assuming it's not too cold and I'm wearing the right underwear, half a penis. Similarly, if you sliced a spider down the middle from mouth to anus,* you'd have a complete mess, far too many legs and a mouthful of vomit because spiders are gross, but you'd also have two symmetrical halves.

Hopefully you don't need to go on slicing things in two to recognize if it has bilateral symmetry or not, because most things do. If it has a face at one end and a rectum down the other, the chances are it fits the category. Dogs, lobsters, birds, butterflies, horses, sharks – most things. A lot of these living things have brains in their heads.

Going back to our early bilateral friends, as the environment forced organisms to become more competitive to find food and all the cool kids started being bilaterally symmetrical, over time simply swimming in the same direction that your mouth was pointing wasn't enough. Sometimes it's nice to

---

* For the avoidance of doubt, this should all be done in your imagination. No spiders, jellyfish or me should be harmed during this process.

YOU ARE NOT A JELLYFISH!

know where your food is, so it makes a lot of sense for you to get some eyes and/or ears and/or a nose. It also makes sense for these things to be located in a similar vicinity to your mouth, so you 'sense' your food into it.

These sensory organs, though, are metabolically expensive and require a fair bit of computational power, so nerves began to cluster to deal with all of the information they were picking up. The closer these nerves are to their respective organs, the quicker they can process this information, and as these organs tended to find themselves around the mouth, lots of nerves clustered in the head. Over time these nerves would become more abundant and more powerful as the animals grew increasingly complex. Give it plenty more time and it would lead to the evolution of the central nervous system and the brain. Millions and millions and millions of years later, you get to humans who started walking upright. Standing tall allowed us to conserve energy by walking on two legs and gave us a higher vantage point from which to see predators and prey. As a result, our butts ended up down one end and our precious, delicate brain matter up the other, suspended, haphazardly, many feet above the ground. Fast forward a bit more and you reach one individual human freaking out about why evolution took this path, why his brain is so far from the ground, and seriously considering wearing a helmet around the house to keep it protected.

Thing 51:
Having two nostrils is not purely aesthetic

We have two ears so we can detect which direction a sound comes from, we have two eyes so we can focus on objects and where they are in relation to other things, and we have one mouth because we can't taste direction like a snake with a forked tongue. We have a notoriously naff sense of smell though (mine is particularly bad) – it's certainly not good enough to gauge the specifics of location with a huge amount of success before our other senses do the rest of the work for it, so why do we need two nostrils?

The answer is not 'just because we look better with two nostrils'. We certainly do look better with two nostrils, but I'm sure if we all had just the one hole in our noses, we'd soon get used to the way it looks. The answer is that, at any given time, one nostril will be inhaling air at a more efficient rate than the other. It has nothing to do with breathing, but more with the particles that enter our noses as we breathe. Impulses are sent to the olfactory receptor in our brains, which analyses what those particles may be and that is how we smell things.

The microscopic bits and bobs that end up in our nostrils are absorbed at different rates. Some need to be sent straight to the brain for scrutiny, others require some time to be soaked up and others still need a moment to ruminate before we can process them. If both nostrils breathed at the same rate, some things would be rushed straight to the lungs before they could be sensed and others would be absorbed by our skin, or destroyed before they reached the receptors. Having one nostril that is sucking things up more quickly and one that is a little lazy allows us to make the most of whatever information is heading into our faces.

Thing 52:
We have bad teeth because we have excellent heads

The majority of humans have far from perfect teeth. In fact, many of us look like we could chew an apple through a fence, and for those who do own a good set of chompers, the chances are that they look that way via artificial intervention. The reason for this is that a few million years ago our diets consisted of a whole lot of fibre. Our ancestors were pretty much exclusively vegetarian, and roots, seeds, leaves, twigs and tubers require a lot of grinding before they can be swallowed and digested efficiently.

The thing is, even when they are digested, they tend to be a little low on the calorie scale, which doesn't leave a great deal of nutrients for the brain once the body has had its share. Then, about 2.3 million years ago, some bright spark discovered that eating meat provides more calories chew for chew, and if it's cooked, there is less chance of dying from food poisoning. As a result, and because meat is softer anyway, we needed to chew less but got more bang for our prehistoric buck and were left with enough spare juice to grow some mighty impressive brains.

But every silver lining has a cloud, and as we became more and more adapted to a diet that included a lot of meat, although we got super intelligent, our jaws began to get smaller and weaker because we didn't need all that extra crunch. That doesn't sound so bad – I mean, nobody wants a chin like Mr Incredible. But when you consider that we still have the same number of teeth, only crammed into a smaller area, things can get ugly and uncomfortable.

As mentioned earlier, I am actually a few teeth short. Because I was left with a little extra room in my mouth, when my wisdom teeth came through I barely felt a thing. For a lot of people, this is not the case. With a mouth that is already crammed to capacity, inviting some hefty strangers to the party can cause all sorts of mischief. I have a friend who got an awful mouth infection, lost a stone in weight because he couldn't eat anything, had to go on a long course of antibiotics and then have his jaw broken so his wisdom teeth could be removed, because the dentist couldn't gain access any other way. He couldn't talk and had to eat through a straw until the wires were removed. Obviously, that's worst-case scenario, but his tiny jaw and the fact that he has too many teeth would have been the death of him before antibiotics were invented. The moral of this story is that sometimes we can be too smart for our own good; the same thing that led to our big brains also led to our mouths shrinking, which, in turn, could have resulted in my friend's death. But in the end, it doesn't really matter, because having such big brains means we are smart enough to solve the problems that arise from our tiny jaw, so I guess there isn't really a moral to this story at all. Sorry to waste your time.

Thing 53:
Thank God we can talk, otherwise we'd choke to death for no reason

We can all sit up in our ivory towers, talking about how great we are compared to the other animals, but we'd better be careful not to talk too much while eating. If we do, we may choke to death while the rest of the animal kingdom makes weird laughy-noises (they can't actually laugh as their voice boxes aren't in the right place) and grunt, or bark, or meow about how the mighty have fallen.

During evolution, as we and the chimpanzees went our separate ways, we made a trade-off that led to better communication skills for a risk of choking on a bacon sandwich. Humans are the only mammal that can asphyxiate on their own food and it's all because our larynx (air and speaky tube) separated from our oesophagus (food tube) lower down our throat.

Next time you see a human, hold their mouth open and look in; you will see one throat hole, exactly the same as if you were to do this with your dog. The reason your dog can only make variations on a bark noise is that, shortly after the point you can see when looking down its throat, the oesophagus and the larynx become distinct. In fact, because most mammals' windpipes and foodpipes are set up in a similar way, they can actually breathe while swallowing. We cannot. Don't try it. You will choke.

Our vocal chords are located further down our throat, more towards the lungs than other animals, because this location allows us to make the plethora of noises we are accustomed to when saying words. That's all very well and good, but from the point you've chewed and swallowed your bratwurst, it has a little way to travel down the throat where the two tubes are one before being shoved down the oesophagus. Having the pipe you breathe through and the pipe you eat through fused together for such a distance can lead to difficulties; you can't block it up with food and still expect to breathe. Our epiglottis (a kind of valvey-type bit over the larynx) is in charge of making sure we can eat and inhale independently, by opening when we breathe and closing when we swallow.

The epiglottis isn't known for its intellect though, and if you decided to speak, laugh or inhale at the same time as chewing on a pickled egg, there's a chance you'd suck it down your windpipe and choke to death. Still, I quite like talking and listening to other people sing, so I think we traded up. And what's life without a little risk, anyway?

Thing 54:
We all like big butts and we cannot lie

Butts are brilliant. Have you noticed how the human rump is larger and more bulbous than that of most other animals? Each cheek is made up of two fairly large muscles (the gluteus maximus and gluteus medius), as well as a generous helping of fat that makes them super comfy to sit on. These muscles and fat are what gives our buxom bottoms their shape, but the anatomy alone doesn't explain why we need such voluptuous rear ends. Surely we could have those fat deposits on our feet to make sitting less necessary, or spread over our entire bodies for better insulation, or we could have altogether smaller gluteus muscles to save on the energy it costs to run them? The reason our bodies are so bootylicious is because we walk upright, and it's our derrière that helps make this so.

Did you know a well-conditioned human can outrun a horse? Not for speed, but over distance. Being bipedal is a more efficient way of covering ground than walking on all fours, but it does require a rather large behind to keep us upright and balanced. It's totally worth it though, because it provided us with the means to hunt for our food before we learned to use traps and projectiles. When an animal is scared (in this instance, it's the horse we are going to eat), it will likely bolt off, full tilt, to escape the danger. Running like this can't be sustained for long and, before you know it, our horsey meal is exhausted and will either slow to a canter or stop altogether. That's a great strategy if you're running from a lion, because they too can only sprint in short bursts and, as long as the horse gets far enough away before they are both pooped, the prey animal lives to run another day. However, humans are not your typical predator and, while the horse is having a lie-down to gather its energy, good old Blorph-the-padfoot (that's the name of our big-butted

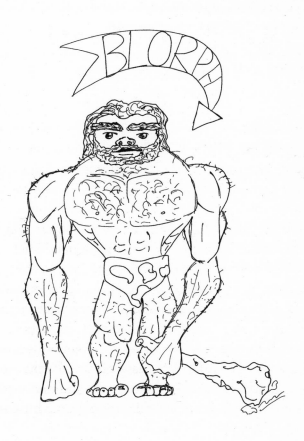

hero; he's really good at tracking, by the way) has been following its trail at a steady jog. Once he catches up to the exhausted and defenceless animal, he quickly dispatches it, dismembers it and carries it home for the tribe to eat. The horse gets eaten and Blorph is a champion (in reality, Blorph would most likely have had accomplices, but I couldn't think of anymore prehistoric names, so I kept to just Blorph, the lone wolf).

Although we are not that fast over short distances compared to most creatures, over long stretches there is little that can match our speed, and we owe a lot of gratitude to our buns for making this possible. But not all of the gratitude. Our butts are brilliant, but they don't deserve all the credit. In fact, a lot of our body has adapted to prolonged running:

- We have less hair over our bodies and can sweat more efficiently than most animals, which allows us to rid ourselves of unwanted body heat

- Despite having a high centre of gravity, our inner ears are particularly good at assessing our balance, allowing us to continually correct it

- Narrow hips prevent waddling and rotation that would waste energy and slow us down

- Short ligaments in our necks keep our heads stable while on the move

- The arches of our feet, our Achilles tendons and ligaments in our legs act as springs, storing and releasing energy at the correct moment of each step

- Shorter toes provide more torque while the big toe on the inside of the foot prevents the knee from rotating inwards

We even find a good butt more physically attractive (well, I know I do), which makes total sense when you consider how important it was to our survival. Someone with lots of muscle is much more likely to enjoy a decent running speed for a decent amount of time and someone with a healthy helping of fat will have plenty of energy reserves for when food is more scarce or, specifically in women, for when pregnant or breast feeding.

In the immortal words of Sir Mix-A-Lot, 'I like big butts and I cannot lie'. In the much less immortal words of Jim Chapman, 'I like big butts . . . because they help us to walk upright and cover long distances more efficiently, which was very important when hunting and so a very important part of our development as a species.'

While we're talking about butts . . .

Thing 55:
There's more to sphincters than butts

A boy (Gavin Day, I believe his name was) once called me a sphincter in the playground by way of insult. I had no idea what a sphincter was, so I asked around and all the kids told me that it was another name for a butthole. *Good insult, Gavin*, I remember thinking. *I'll adopt it as my own and use it when the time is right*. When that time came, I unleashed this brilliant zinger, certain that it would stop anyone in their tracks. I delivered it like a pro: 'Shut it, you sphincter.'

My mistake was not doing enough research; the kids I had asked for clarity on the offending word had also all fallen victim to Gavin's mirth and had used only one source of information (Gavin himself) to explain. It worked on a bunch of newbies like us, but it did not wash on my big sister, who had a much more extensive knowledge of anatomy than me.

There is little more embarrassing than delivering a killer one-liner like that, only to be factually incorrect, or at least completely overstep the boundaries of your knowledge. I knew I was out of my depth when my sister replied, 'That's a weird comeback; do you even know what a sphincter is?' I panicked and quickly realized that, if this show-stopper of a retort didn't have the desired effect immediately, then maybe there was more to the word than I thought. So, I did what any eleven-year-old would do and responded with the classic, 'Yeah, I know what one is, it's you,' losing all credibility and supplying my sister with enough ammunition to end the confrontation with, 'Don't use words you don't understand in an argument; you'll make yourself look stupid.'

In my defence, I was kind of right, and if I had not bottled it and followed through with the confirmation that I did, in fact, know what a sphincter was, things could have been different. Although I doubt it. Your anus is a sphincter but sphincters are not anuses: a sphincter is characterized as a ring-like muscle. They can contract or relax to open, close, restrict or enable bodily passages. Unless you've been in some sort of accident, you'll have fifty of them inside you. There's one in each eyeball that contracts the iris in the presence of bright light. One that prevents stomach acid from making its way up your oesophagus. One that controls the excretion of urine when you gotta go. Two in your anus (one we can control voluntarily and one that does its own thing) and forty-four others dotted around, keeping you alive and/or making sure your body works.

It is a bit of a weird insult, if you think about it. Bloody Gavin Day.

Thing 56:
Eating mould can save your life, but it could also kill you

Mould is a variety of fungus and there is a whole bunch of fungi that you definitely shouldn't eat. Some lead to hallucinations, while others will straight-up murder you in a disgusting, gurgly, anus-leaky fashion. There's even a type that grows inside the brains of ants and turns them into zombies – more on them later. However, certain types of fungus are so brilliant that they have saved more lives than we can even begin to imagine.

Up until the late 1920s, if you were particularly unlucky, something as simple as a splinter could get infected and kill you. Any wound could get riddled with bacteria and end up being fatal. That was until a bacteriologist by the name of Alexander Fleming accidentally got some mould in one of his petri dishes. As it turns out, this was one of those fortunate accidents, because the mould in question, which was called *Penicillium notatum*, had destroyed all of the bacteria that came into contact with it.

Fleming realized he was onto something and set to work; he discovered that the mould was producing a chemical that prevented the enzymes that build bacteria cell walls from forming. Without a cell wall, the bacterium has nothing to keep its insides inside it and so it dies. Fleming called this chemical 'penicillin'. You might have heard of it – it's only one of humankind's greatest achievements.

With the help of two other exceptionally clever chaps, Howard Florey and Ernst Boris Chain, they achieved the very difficult task of cultivating penicillin and making it into the antibiotic we take for granted today.

Thing 57:
S'not there for no reason

Every opening on your body is guarded by mucus, the sticky liquid that lubricates and protects its respective hole. Your eyes, nose, mouth and butt all produce it in some way or another and for good reason. The world is a wonderful place, but there is a lot out there that wants to kill you, or use your body as a warm, wet place in which to multiply. Mucus is one of the first lines of defence that we have to prevent germs, bacteria, viruses, parasites and tiny bugs from doing any damage. For example, when you breathe in nasty bits and bobs from the air, much of the harmful stuff that was in that breath will be trapped by snot before it can reach your lungs and start getting up to no good. Once it's secure in your snot, it'll either get sneezed out or swallowed and destroyed by your stomach acid.

It's simple but effective, and you probably don't realize it, but you will produce about half a litre of nasal and sinus mucus on any given day. That is until you get a common cold, then all manner of sloppy stuff breaks loose. You don't usually notice your snot because it is produced slowly and evaporates quickly before it can exit your nostril. However, in response to infection, mucus secretion goes into overdrive to give your respiratory system extra protection. You will certainly become aware of how much snot you're producing then. Typically, you have a thin layer of mucus coating your sinuses, nasal cavity and throat, but when excess is produced, blockages form, you can feel bunged up and your face leaks. You will also notice that your snot won't be the harmless, transparent liquid you're used to; it'll be green and viscous. Don't worry about it; that's just the culmination of the various pusses and dead white blood cells that have been saving your bacon and that your body is trying to now rid itself of.

Any time you're feeling like you need reminding of the

sheer absurdity of life – just think about snot. Everyone's got it – kings, presidents, Brad Pitt, that seemingly perfect person over there making you feel like a troll. We're all just bags of liquid and some of it is leaking out of our holes.

Thing 58:
Paper cuts really do hurt more than most others

Your skin is amazing. It's your body's biggest organ, accounting for 15 per cent of your body weight. Every hour you shed 30,000 dead skin cells and there are 1,000 species of bacteria living on your skin. However, it's helpless against a piece of paper.

I like to think that I have a relatively high 'ouchy' threshold. I don't whinge or complain when I have an injury and I'm usually fairly successful at shutting the pain out. Paper cuts, though, are my weakness. And it is a weakness that is not mine alone, because by general consensus, they suck. Here's why:

Paper cuts tend to be on your hand, seeing as they usually occur when you handle paper. You use your hands more than pretty much any other part of your body and it makes sense that your awareness of a nuisance on an area of your body will be greater the more you use that area. It may sound obvious, but being more aware of a cut increases your focus on the pain.

What your hands are used for also plays a role; a good sense of touch is important for us to be able to manipulate objects efficiently, and we have achieved this by cramming a whole bunch of sensory receptors into fingers. These receptors respond to inputs like temperature and pressure. A paper cut will slice through these receptors, which will throw their toys out of the pram, completely overreact and send a mess of pain signals to your brain. Also, fingers are very dexterous, and seeing as cuts like these don't bleed much, they don't provide the layer of protection you would get from a scab, meaning that every time you bend the affected finger, it can open the cut again.

To rub salt into the wound (quite literally), because our hands are such busy parts of our bodies, if the slice keeps opening when we are cooking, eating, cleaning or doing pretty much anything, more nasty bits and bobs can work their way into it and royally piss it off. If you want to avoid the pain of paper cuts, either never touch paper again, turn pages with your elbows* or wear gloves.

Thing 59:
The composition of eye bogies

As we've just covered, the skin cells on your body are constantly dying, falling off and being replaced (a disgustingly large proportion of household dust is comprised of bits of you and the people you live with). As it turns out, your eyeballs are no different.

I'm going to assume that your peepers are of some importance to you. Your body also knows the value of sight and puts a lot of effort into making sure the surfaces of your eyes stay in tip-top condition. The cornea (the lensey bit of your eye that covers your iris) is coated in a 'tear film'. The tear film is a layer

---

* Although, be careful with your elbows. There's a really important nerve that runs behind them called the ulnar nerve, which is really easy to squash against a nobbly bit of your arm bone, which is why hitting your funny bone feels so weird.

of mucus consisting of water, salt and protein to keep your eye lubricated, and it has a thin layer of oil on top to prevent the mucus from evaporating and further focus light heading to your retina.

During the day, you blink a lot, so the leftover dead cells that were clinging to your eyeball, as well as any other crud, junk or detritus that happens to find its way in, are removed. Think of your eyelids as someone who washes your windscreen when you get to a red light, removing all the dead bugs after you've been driving on the motorway.

Unless you're the scariest person in the world and sleep with your eyes open, when you take forty winks your eyelids aren't doing a great deal of window wiping, so the eye gunk works its way to the corner of your eye where it collects and, hey presto, you've got yourself an eye bogie, patiently waiting for you to pick at in the morning.

Sometimes they're crusty, sometimes they're gooey, sometimes they're somewhere in between. The consistency of the bogie simply depends on how much mucus is in your eye and what the debris is made up of.

While we're talking about eyes, can I just say this?

Thing 60:
Non-criers have feelings too

As far as I recall, I have only cried twice in my adult life. Once through sadness and once on the happiest day of my life. The first time was when my grandad passed away, and even that emotional outburst had a delayed reaction and didn't last long when it emerged. I was at work when I found out, but he had been poorly for a while and we were all expecting it to happen, so when it did I took a deep breath, finished my shift, clocked off and headed home. It wasn't until I saw my mum after, walking through the front door, that I crumbled. I always thought my grandad was invincible and the realization suddenly hit me that he was no longer the strongest man I knew and he wouldn't be able to pin me down and shout 'ARROWS' as he prodded me in the abdomen (much harder than I think he intended) and he would never call me Jim-lad in a pirate's voice again and, for the first time since I was in school, I cried.

The second occasion was about eight years later, on my wedding day. The ceremony wasn't until 3 p.m. and, despite being full of nervous energy from the moment I woke up, I honestly didn't expect to cry. I had even made sure to tell my bride-to-be not to feel sad if my eyes remained dry; after all, she knows me better than anyone and would be aware that it doesn't mean that I don't love her, just that I don't weep. I walked down the aisle, smiling to all of my friends and family, even throwing the occasional cocky wink, really enjoying my moment. Then the double doors opened and Tan came through and I lost my shit. The walk from those double doors to my side was very long, but to me it happened in an instant and I was completely overwhelmed. As a result, my wedding video consists mostly of me sniffing.

Although there hasn't been a great deal of research carried out into the science of crying, some wise guys have found that what makes up emotional tears is different to that of other tears (from when something gets in your eye, for example): there are higher levels of hormones that diminish pain as well as those associated with stress, which you don't want lingering around your system. One theory states crying may be your body's way of disposing of waste and toxins and that this is why you often feel better after you've cried it all out.

It's not like I view tear shedding as a weakness or anything; in fact, I sometimes envy people that can have a good old cathartic cry, people who can get it all out and feel a little better. I think I just have a very high waterworks threshold, a particularly stiff upper lip. I've seen *The Notebook* many a time and, while everyone I've ever seen it with is in bits, my eyes don't even water. I can watch Leonardo DiCaprio die over and over again after an ill-fated ride on the *Titanic* and, while I'm sorry for Kate Winslet's loss and I think it's a real shame that Jack will never paint anyone like one of his French girls again, my eyes always remain dry (partly because that film makes me much more mad than it does sad. There was definitely room for him on that bit of wood).

I know my tear ducts are in perfect working order because, after one of my sneezing frenzies, my eyes will often stream. Plus, before I had laser eye surgery, the opthalmist did his due diligence and was very proud to report that my eyes are plenty moist (I also have rather thick corneas, which is a compliment indeed, so I am told).

What's really interesting is that scientists think there are at least three different sorts of tears. The first, called basal tears, are the ones that are on our eyes all the time, keeping them moist. The second type, called reflex tears, appear when the eye needs protecting from chopped onions or bonfire smoke or a strong wind. The third kind, emotional tears, which happen when we watch videos of dogs being reunited with their owners, have a different make-up to the other two, though generally speaking they're all made of salt, proteins and hormones. Speaking of which, scientists don't really know why we cry when we feel sad. However, we know that women cry more and for longer than men. Although, I'm fairly sure that would even out if men were expected to get any part of their body waxed regularly.

The good news is that it looks like this is a good thing, as crying actually makes you feel better, releasing endorphins and potentially even flushing stress hormones out of your body.

What is clear is that people fall somewhere on a spectrum between crybaby and watertight stoic badass. Although the boffins aren't entirely sure why this may be, it would appear that I fall more towards the stoic end of the continuum. That doesn't mean I am void of emotion, it just means that I don't tend to display my emotions via facial leakage. I, like every other person, am a complex human and I deal with my thoughts and feelings in a way that works for me. I think (I tend to overthink). If I'm sad or concerned, I can turn pensive. I can be hedonistic. I feel all sorts of ways based on everything from the weather to my mum running over our dog; I just require less tissues than most people when I feel sad.

Thing 61:
A sneeze is not, in fact,
⅛ of an orgasm

A good sneeze can be really satisfying: you have a build-up of tingly anticipation while screwing up your face and temporarily losing control over most of your motor skills, you take short sharp breaths until it ends in a damp crescendo. So, you can understand that, when somebody once told me that a sneeze is the equivalent of an eighth of an orgasm, I figured it seemed pretty legitimate.

That was up until the day I clocked fifteen sneezes in a row, and felt nothing. Not even a tingle. I've always been an odd sneezer; they sound more like coughs and I tend to do them in batches of four or five. Fifteen is still my record and I'm fairly certain I suffered minor whiplash from the experience.* You'd expect, if every sneeze were an eighth of an orgasm, for fifteen to send you into pleasure land almost twice over. All that actually happened was that my nose ran and my eyes streamed. There was absolutely no carnal pleasure to be had. It did require a similar amount of tissues though.

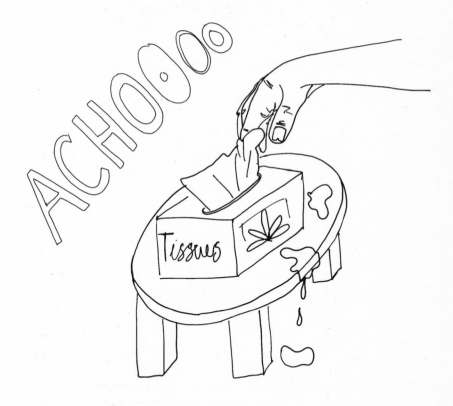

---

* Also, some people can sneeze with their eyes open, putting to bed the myth that your eyes would pop out if you didn't blink when you sneezed.

Thing 62:
We all have a blind spot
(no, not a metaphor, an actual
blind spot)

The retinas at the backs of our eyes are covered in photorecep-
tor cells. Quite simply, they take the data from the light that hits
them and pass it to the brain via the optic nerve, so you can
figure out what you're looking at. This is a constant process
and, because our eyes are always scanning the environment
and working as a pair to pick up each other's slack (and our
brains are very busy filling in what's missing), we don't even
realize that there is a little bit of blank space in our vision.

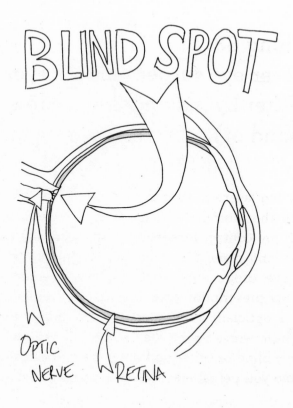

The retina coats the back of pretty much your entire eyeball, except for where the optic nerve connects, and that is where you'll find your blind spot.

If you're sceptical, you can test it: cover your left eye and focus on a point in the distance with your right. Hold out your right thumb at arm's length and, starting in the middle of your field of view, move it down slightly, then slowly manoeuver it to the right. Assuming you have held your gaze on the same spot and your eyes are in the right way round, at the point when your thumb ends up over the portion of your eye that is your optic nerve, you should realize that it has disappeared.

Once you've done your right eye, do the same thing with your left eye; cover your right eye, focus on a point, bring your left thumb up, move it slightly down and to the left and before you know it you'll be thumbless.

Thing 63:
Laser eye surgery makes eyes better by making them worse (kind of)

Before having laser eye surgery, my vision was shocking. Getting up in the morning and heading for the shower before putting in my contact lenses was a ritualistically risky affair. Travelling long distances or having late nights would mean carrying eye drops and spectacles for emergency contact removal. My prescription was -5.5 in both eyes, which, if you don't speak optician, is not good. It's not entirely awful either – people have worse vision than that – but assuming you are not actually blind or suffering from another medical condition, by the time you get where I was on the spectrum, it's all just varying degrees of blur, and moving down the scale doesn't make much difference in the real world because you're screwed if you don't do anything to correct your sight.

When light hits the front of your eyeball, it heads to a bunch of light-detecting cells at the back, called the retina. By the time it touches down there, it should have been focused by your lens and cornea, leaving a crystal-clear image for your brain to enjoy and prevent you from stubbing your toe on the bed, again. However, with *myopia* (short/near sight), the eyeball is actually stretched a little and the light information is focused before it hits the retina, leaving an image that is blurry and uncomfortable. The only way to get that image to make sense is to head closer and closer to it and force that focus point onto your retina.

Seeing as your eyeball is too long, laser eye surgery essentially flattens the lens, in effect distorting the point at which light focuses on your retina and giving you better vision. That's a very crude way of putting it; it's more scientific than that and there are lots of machines and a very talented, not very squeamish doctor who performs the procedure, but in layman's terms, that's what happens.

The way it happens sounds awful, but I've had it done and I have to tell you that it really isn't that bad. For me, and for most people, it takes around five minutes per eye, you don't feel a thing and the effects are instant. After you've had all of the checks and the ophthalmic surgeon clears you for the eye slice, you lie on the bed, have some numbing eye drops and the procedure begins. I was asked to look at a green light as the speculum (eye-opening clamp-thing) was inserted and an alien-looking eye-sucky-thing was put into place. This is the worst part and it's really not that bad. It takes about fifteen seconds and all you can feel is a little pressure as the machine puts a bit of weight on your eyeball to hold it in place. What the machine does is cut a circular incision, using a laser, on the lens to create a flap that can then be lifted. You can't feel the flap being made or lifted, but once it is moved out of the way, there is nothing to do any focusing and the green light you've been looking at becomes a total blur. Next comes the vision-correction part of the procedure, as another laser is used to destroy the cells on your lens, under the flap. This takes about five or six seconds and you may become aware of a slight burning odour. After that, the surface of your eye gets a quick sponge-down, the flap is replaced and you move on to eye number two.

Something my doctor told me that I found very interesting is that, technically, you could have this procedure done without having the initial incision from the alien-looking eye-sucky-thing and it would still work, temporarily. The surface of your eye is much like the rest of your skin, in that dead cells are constantly falling off and new ones are growing in their place. If you were to do it this way, within a week you'd be back at square one. The reason the incision is made is that having the correction carried out under the layer of lens that is continually being replaced will give permanent results.

Anyway, back to me, lying on the bed, having bits of my eyes blasted away by lasers; as soon as the flap on my second eye was placed back where it belonged, I was asked to sit up and enjoy my new peepers. I could see as well as with my glasses on, but without my glasses on. Everything was a little misty, like looking through a thin fog, for the first few hours, but it was sharp and focused.

Over the next couple of days, as the liquid that had made everything a bit cloudy dissipated and my eyes healed, my vision got better.

Last time I had a check-up, I had the vision of a kestrel. I can actually see as well as a bird of prey and it's all because I had the top lens of my eye flattened by a laser.

Thing 64:
If your finger gets cut off, don't panic – you can probably just sew it back on

My friend Claire has a sister four years her junior called Gemma. One day, Claire and Gemma's mum, Susan, chopped Gemma's finger off.

I'm told it was an accident and, in Susan's defence, I've known her for over a decade and she doesn't seem like the finger-amputating type. From what I understand, it was a simple case of 'Whoops, I slammed the door and didn't realize my two-year-old's finger was in the way, and now it's no longer part of her hand.'

We could play 'point the severed finger' all day to establish who was to blame (definitely Susan), but what happened next is what really blows my mind. I'd heard of people getting digits and toes sewn back on after various accidents, but never really thought about what that entailed before Claire told me the story of how Gemma was separated from her little finger.

As soon as something is no longer part of your body, it stops receiving oxygen from blood and its cells begin to die. Once these cells perish, they aren't very good at preventing bacteria from eating them and the process of decomposition begins. However, loose fingers can actually survive for longer than you might expect, so there's no immediate rush to stop whatever it is you're doing to reattach it (although I probably wouldn't want to hang around). If the finger is left in a warm environment, you've got somewhere around the twelve-hour mark, but if you're doing something particularly exciting and don't want to let a little thing like part of your body falling off ruin your fun, keep it refrigerated and you can buy yourself anywhere up to four days.

Fingers are very good candidates for reattachment, as they are mainly bone. Muscle has a much faster metabolic rate than bone or cartilage and because of this it will deteriorate more quickly. If you are unfortunate enough to find yourself with a severed limb, you'd better hope there isn't a big wait at A&E, because you've only got about six to twelve hours to get that thing back where it belongs before it's gone forever.

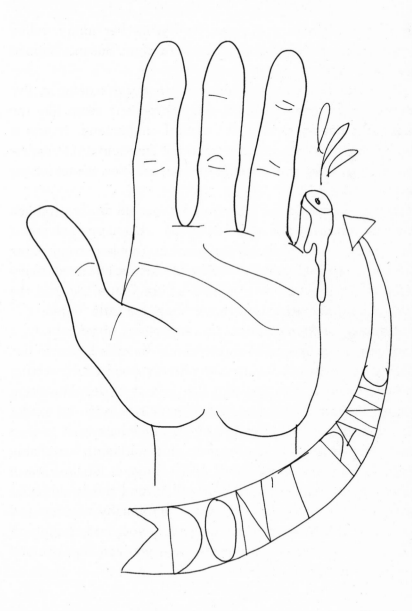

Anyway, Susan put Gemma's finger on ice and rushed her to the hospital, where the surgeons followed the usual protocol for such situations: they sterilized the rogue digit, removed any dead or damaged tissue and actually shortened the bone-end a little (partly so there was a cleaner end to the wound and partly to allow a little wiggle room for reconnecting the blood supply and nerves, which shouldn't be done under tension). Next, they drilled into the bone fragments in order to reattach them, then reunited the tendons, arteries, veins and nerves before adding a few stitches to secure the skin in place. Just like that, Gemma had her finger back on her hand, good as new, if slightly shorter.

If you think that's impressive, surgeons once had to reattach two left arms after a horrific tug-of-war incident involving over 800 people on each side and a snapping nylon rope. In 2009, Garrett Lafever lost his thumb in an accident but clearly had his priorities in order and decided to have his big toe removed and sewn on to his hand. Also in 2009 (a good year for severed body parts), a vet called Chang Po-yu was checking the inside of a crocodile's mouth when it tore off his forearm. His friend asked very nicely for the appendage to be returned to its owner, but the croc refused and a police officer shot it twice in the head. The rounds just bounced off but the animal did drop the arm and Chang underwent a six-hour operation that ended with a fully functioning arm and a kick-ass story to tell.

Gemma was two years old, so her finger healed quickly and worked perfectly, but if you're older than two and you're reading this and thinking about potential party tricks, I would strongly suggest you avoid chopping anything off that you might miss. The success rate of reattaching viable digits is about 90 per cent, which is brilliant, but among adults these off-again-on-again fingers often experience reduced motion, less sensation and generally don't work as well as they should. Besides, as far as party tricks go, it's pretty gross and requires zero skill (unless you count pain tolerance and a strong gag reflex). Everybody likes that person that can burp the alphabet or chug a litre of beer while doing a handstand, because both of these things are tolerably gross in an entertaining kind of way, but at nearly all of the parties I've been to, self-mutilation is not going to help you make friends – it's frowned upon at the very least and can really alter the party vibe.

Thing 65:
Body odour is much worse than you think but also kind of amazing

Microbes are everywhere: on the floor, in your fridge, up your nose and under your armpits. In fact, a very clever guy called Ed Yong has written an entire book called *I Contain Multitudes* about the sheer variety of life living on us and in us, and how important it is to our moods, digestion and immune system – basically our entire lives. It's estimated that there are 40 trillion of these microbes and every time we breathe, 37 billion of them are released into the air around us.*

A few of a specific sort of the little blighters that live on your skin enjoy breaking down the stuff found in your sweat and transforming it into the energy they need to divide and function. The by-product of this transformation is a variety of acids that have a nasty stench. Basically, these particular microbes poop on you and you breathe it in when you catch a whiff. Lovely. Let's move on . . .

Over the last few Things, I hope I've shown you how amazing, absurd, odd and surprising the human body is. But one of the things I think we need to keep in mind is that humans, though an especially impressive, intelligent and accomplished

---

* In fact, there's an argument to be made that collectively they are cleverer than the human they're on. If that doesn't put things in perspective, nothing will.

sort, are just animals. And often we're not even the most interesting.

It's time to explore some of the ways other animals leave us trailing in their dust.

ANIMALS

Thing 66:
Groups of animals have weird names

A group of crows is called a 'murder', a group of cobras is a 'quiver' and a group of owls is known as a 'parliament'. I have no idea why, when a bunch of the same species get together, we don't have one word that will do, but we don't. There are plenty to choose from: a herd, a troop, a shoal, a drove or an army, to name some of the less creative.

If it were up to me, I'd just pick the coolest collective noun and call everything by that. But it's not up to me and maybe that makes the world more interesting. Here's a list of some of my favourite names for when animals gather:

- A congregation of alligators
- A flange of baboons (ha, flange!)
- A company of badgers
- A battery of barracudas
- A cloud of bats
- A family of beavers
- A flutter of butterflies
- A destruction of wild cats
- A coalition of cheetahs
- An intrusion of cockroaches
- A kine of cows

- A pod of dolphins
- A mob of emus
- A flamboyance of flamingos
- A tower of giraffes
- A confusion of guinea fowl

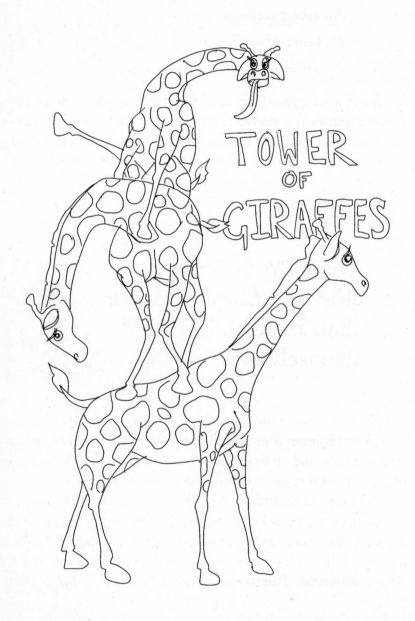

- A bloat of hippopotamuses
- A mischief of mice
- An embarrassment of pandas
- A rhumba of rattlesnakes
- A stubbornness of rhinoceros
- An escargatoire of snails
- A cluster of spiders
- A dazzle of zebras

Don't worry, you don't need to remember all of these. To be honest, if someone said to me, 'Run, there's a bloat of hippos on the rampage,' I'd have too many questions and would probably get trampled to death by the bloat before they were answered.

Thing 67:
Any land mammals much larger than an elephant would cook themselves alive

I'm six foot three, which is tall enough that people mention it. The tallest human ever recorded was Robert Pershing Waldow, who not only had an exceptional name but also measured in at eight foot eleven. But why aren't we ten feet tall?

Most dinosaurs lived their lives as titchy little blighters, no larger than a peacock, but some of them were bloody huge. *T. rex*, for example, could get to forty feet long, twenty feet high and weigh in at nine tonnes, and *T. rex* was a baby compared to *Argentinosaurus*. This beast could have been around seventy tonnes and, although the fossil records are patchy, there are bones that suggest other dinos could have been bigger still.

So what happened? When the dinosaurs went kaput, it seems our planet said goodbye to truly massive wildlife along with them. Unless there's a gigantic Bigfoot up a very strong tree somewhere, the largest land mammal we are left with today is the African elephant, which comes in at six tonnes. I've seen a herd of elephants on safari and I thought they were pretty huge, but it turns out they're actually over eleven times less massive than *Argentinosaurus*. Pathetic.

Animals have had over 65 million years to recover from the last mass extinction and, with the last dominant species out of the picture, mammals had the opportunity to diversify and grow into all shapes and sizes. Up until then, they hadn't really done a great deal. They were mostly very small and were all pretty samey, but with less competition for resources and less chance of getting eaten by *Velociraptors* at every turn, they had the chance to become the big dogs (literally, in some cases) of the planet and were able to adapt to nearly every environment mother nature could throw at them. They evolved into all sorts of weird and wonderful creatures and kept getting bigger (and smaller, and taller, shorter and hairier, and balder and smarter and dumber) until around 42 million years ago, when their size appears to have maxed out.

We know that prehistoric animals could grow to gigantic proportions, so what changed? Why is an elephant the biggest we can muster now? Why am I not taller than a giraffe? Why does my dog barely have any legs at all? What's life without a little fear that a rodent the size of a commercial jet may step on your house and squish you and your loved ones into oblivion at any moment?

The first reason you shouldn't worry about a rat hulking out and crushing your car is that, when dinosaurs walked the Earth, the climate was very different; it was warmer and muggier because there was much more carbon dioxide in the air than there is today. Plants love carbon dioxide, so they could grow huge and lush and plentiful, meaning that things that like to eat plants could gorge all day every day and use that energy to grow big and strong. In turn, carnivores could eat the herbivores that ate the plants and they too could start bulking. Having more calories consumed at the bottom of the food chain gives everything in that chain a chance to get some of those calories and use them to gain mass.

Also, a lot of dinos were lighter than you'd expect based on their size. Even *Sauropods* (the really big ones that walked on all fours with the long necks and tails), much like birds today, had air sacs in their skeletal structures to reduce their weight. It's thought that a mammal of equivalent size to one of these behemoths would weigh nearly twice as much. When you're that hefty, being a little solid-footed is the least of your worries – your frame might be simply too heavy for your bones to take, making it impossible to actually get anywhere. It makes sense that the largest animal to have ever inhabited the Earth is a mammal only when you consider that it's the blue whale; it's whole body is suspended in water, making it weigh two thirds less than it would on land.

But my favourite theory as to why mammals can't get supersized is that they would cook themselves alive from the inside. It's generally believed that dinosaurs were cold-blooded like lizards and used their environment to heat their bodies to the desired temperature. This makes you a little sluggish when it's chilly, but nice and toasty and full of beans when the sun is out. Also, seeing as you've absorbed heat from your surroundings and not generated it yourself, it doesn't cost you any calories. Us mammals, on the other hand, are warm-blooded and we use between 50 per cent and 80 per cent of our daily calorie intake just to regulate the temperature of our bodies. This means, for one thing (I'm getting to the bit where we'd cook ourselves), that a mammal needs to eat much more food, much more often than a reptile just to function, and any mammal that wanted to be bigger than an elephant would have to continuously consume calories, leaving little time for anything else.

Now we get to the cool bit. Not only do mammals have all of the scale-related conundrums I've just listed off, but in order to grow as large as some of the big dinosaurs, we'd probably produce so much heat that we'd roast our internal organs. It all comes down to the issue of surface area versus mass: the former grows additively while the latter grows exponentially.

To avoid you all getting your calculators and maths revision notes out, this basically means that mass will continue to grow at a much faster rate than surface area, which is a problem when you are a warm-blooded mammal of a certain stature. Body temperature is maintained within the mass of the animal and lost via the surface area (the skin), and the theory goes that, when this capacious beast reaches critical bulk, the temperature lost from its skin will not be sufficient to provide equilibrium with all of the heat that is being produced inside, and the animal cooks its own tissue and dies.

So that's why big things only get so big, but why are small things small?

Thing 68:
Sometimes a little less oxygen is a good thing

Have you ever questioned why a swarm of wasps the size of huskies has never overthrown a jam factory? Or why a mosquito as large as a Shetland pony hasn't sucked you completely dry, leaving your withered husk, along with the rest of the human population, all dried out like a bunch of raisins? A world where insects could reach such exaggerated proportions is a world that I would not want to live in. Lucky there isn't enough oxygen in our atmosphere for that to happen.

The largest insect around at the moment is the giant weta, which can grow to about 10 cm and weighs a hefty 35 g (about as much as a sparrow). It's found only in New Zealand, which makes sense because everything comes big there; even us humans. Kiwi men have an average height of five foot ten, compared to the global average of five foot seven. But the giant weta is tiny in comparison to a species of prehistoric *Meganisoptera* (also known as a griffinfly), which looked a lot like a dragonfly but was nearer the size of an actual dragon. Whereas the weta can grow to about 10 cm, this beast had a body of about 43 cm and a wingspan of 71 cm. *Arthropleura* was a millipede-like arthropod that could grow around two feet longer than I am tall. For something without a spine, eight feet is just too long. I don't care how tough the Maori or the All Blacks are; they could haka all they like, but if an eight-foot insect-train showed up, they'd all shit themselves.

Thankfully, bugs of this magnitude no longer stalk the earth or terrorize the skies, and a lot of that has to do with maths and the way they breathe. The maths part has its roots in the same volume-to-surface-area conundrum that won't allow a mammal to get much larger than an elephant without cooking itself to death, but in this instance, overheating isn't the problem. Asphyxiation is.

Insects don't breathe like we do; they have little holes called *tracheoles* along the sides of their bodies that take air in. These tracheoles divide and divide again and they keep dividing to the microscopic level until they can deliver oxygen to each and every cell.

Here's the issue (I touched on this in the previous Thing but to briefly elaborate): as something grows, the surface area (exoskeleton with breathy holes) increases by the factor of square (the measurement, multiplied by itself), while volume expands by the factor of cube (the measurement, multiplied by itself, then multiplied by itself again). So, with this considered, it would be difficult to cram enough tracheoles onto the exoskeleton of any massive insect for the oxygen delivery system to give every cell in its body a chance to respire.

The reason the good old massive griffinfly was eating the prehistoric equivalent of my dog 300 million years ago was simply because there was a lot more oxygen (32 per cent vs today's 21 per cent) in the atmosphere back then. More oxygen density means that, for every tracheole full of air, there is a higher payload that can be spread around the body. As oxygen levels dropped over millennia, the really big bugs died off or evolved into the smaller, marginally less terrifying versions we have today. I like my bugs tiny.

Thing 69:
Penguins are my favourite animal for many reasons; this is not one of them

If penguins aren't your favourite animal, you need to have a good long think about what kind of person you are. I love them for the same reason I love my tiny, rubbish dog: they're pathetic and clumsy but possess a ton of gumption and still exist despite seals and orca whales and freezing cold seas all trying to murder them. They just don't give a shit and will continue being tenacious little penguins no matter what mother nature has to say on the matter.

We all know they can't fly, but they've developed some nifty little tricks that make them perfectly suited to the little penguin lives they lead. They can even drink seawater, which is deadly to most of the rest of the world's avian kind and to the majority of land mammals too. There's no way us humans can drink it. In fact, if we did, the more we drank it, the faster we would die of thirst, and here's why: our pee is saltier than the water we drink, but our kidneys don't have the capacity to make it as salty as the sea. Therefore, in order to flush out all of the salt you've taken on board from seawater, you would have to produce much more urine than the amount of water you consumed in the first place. The more you drink, the further out of balance your levels of water and salt become and you will soon become fatally dehydrated.

Right, so we've established that we can't drink seawater, but what makes penguins so bloody special? What do they have that we don't? What they have is a supraorbital gland and I want one (not that I'd use it much, I don't swim in the sea that often, but it just sounds brilliant: 'Hey, wanna see my supraorbital gland?'). Some penguins don't even drink, per se; their food is fish, so when they swallow prey they also get a mouthful of the sea. The supraorbital gland sits just above the eyes and acts like a set of kidneys – that does the work of seven sets of kidneys. The penguin's blood travels through it, where excess salt is removed before it continues its journey around the rest of the body. Clearly it's very effective, as you can tell from the liquid that dribbles out of the little nose holes on their beaks. That stuff is not snot, rather it's the excess salt in a briny solution that is about five times more saturated than the rest of the liquids in the penguin's body.

I went swimming in the sea once and swallowed a mouthful of water that shot up my nose. I remember it burning and feeling very uncomfortable for hours. If I were a penguin, I can't say I'd love the idea of having a concentrated salty brine continuously trickling from my schnoz. I know I said I wanted a supraorbital gland, but I've changed my mind. I'll stick to freshwater, thank you.

Thing 70:
Horses can't vomit

The ability to spew, although not pleasant, is very important; if there is something nasty in your stomach, it's best to expel it as quickly as possible before it can cause too much damage. Keeping something toxic in your body for longer than necessary only gives it more time to get into your bloodstream and do terrible things to you. That's why most mammals can vomit. Most animals, but not horses. Their anatomy just won't allow it.

The muscles at their lower oesophageal sphincter are so strong that it makes it nearly impossible to open via pressure coming from the stomach. A stomach, by the way, that is located behind their ribcage, not in the belly, like in most other things. Digesting food here adds protection from external squeezes and bumps, thus reducing the need to evacuate what has just been consumed after getting a hoof in the gut. It even seems that a horse's gag reflex is very weak, if it exists at all.*

It does seem strange though. What if a horse gets food poisoning? What is it supposed to do then? The truth is that, although we know how a horse can't blow chunks, we're not entirely sure why they can't. One theory suggests that they need this super strong oesophagus sphincter because the motion of their gallop moves their stomach back and forth and, under a weaker system, would result in involuntary sick, all over the place. That's fair enough. I would hate to throw up every time I moved faster than a walk.

---

* The real irony of course is that a horse's mane would be the perfect kind of hair for you to lovingly hold back while they were being sick. But that act of kindness will be forever denied to them.

Thing 71:
The plural of octopus is not octopi

It's octopuses; so says the *Oxford English Dictionary*, the final arbiter of such things. Octopodes is also acceptable, but I've never heard it used in real life. Therefore, next time I say octopuses, don't be a smart-arse and tell me that 'actually it's octopi' in a smug tone of voice, because you'll be making a mockery of the English language and a complete tit out of yourself.

Thing 72:
Bats have reverse feet

I work out quite a lot and my grip strength is still rubbish. I often have to resort to using wraps to aid my hands in supporting the load, but if I were a bat, things would be different. It makes perfect sense for bats to hang upside down; they can't take off from the ground because their wings don't create enough lift and their tiny little itty-bitty back legs are too pathetic to jump from, so instead they must hang there, ready to drop and fly at a moment's notice. Have you ever tried to hang from a branch all day? I bet you can't do it for more than a few minutes before your hands give out. I couldn't. It's tough, but not for a bat.

For humans to grip things, our brains send messages to the muscles in our forearms that are connected to tendons in our hands and fingers. A bat's set-up is similar but with a key difference; their tendons are connected only to their upper body, not to any muscle. The muscle comes in when they want to open their claws, not close them. Essentially, this means that their feet work in reverse to hands. When they are relaxed, they grip, whereas they must contract muscles to open them. Our bat will fly into position, open its claws, put them where they want to be and then just relax – its body weight does the rest and it can stay there for as long as it pleases. Even if it's dead.

Thing 73:
Zombies actually do exist, they're just really tiny

Not created in a lab, nor contracted from the bite of an infected ape, there are a whole bunch of zombie insects on the loose, right this moment. And fungus is all to blame.

There are many varieties of the parasitic fungus, *Cordyceps*, and each one is specialized to attack a specific genus of bug. It all starts when a single spore from the *Cordyceps* lands on an insect, for example, an ant. The spore is so tiny that it can penetrate the exoskeleton of the creepy-crawly via the breathing tubes along its body. Once inside, it starts to grow by sending out thin, filament-like structures that fill any space within the ant. The ant doesn't know it yet, but the fungus is digesting it from the inside out to fuel its development. By the time the brain is infected, most of the insect is dead, with only the most vital bits left untouched to keep it alive.

Then it gets really weird (if it wasn't already weird enough before). The *Cordyceps* hijacks the motor functions of the ant's brain and alters its behaviour. The ant will wander away from the nest and climb upwards in search of a spot that is high enough and has just the right temperature and humidity for optimal fungus growth. Next, the ant is forced to walk onto the underside of a leaf (so that the top of its body is facing the ground) and bite down so that it will not fall off when it dies. Which it does, after an agonizingly long time. Do you know how it dies? The bloody fungus erupts from its bloody head, that's how!

Using up what juice is left in the ant, the fungus puts all of its effort into growing an impressive spire from the ant's cranium, from where it will release microscopic spores and infect more unsuspecting victims. It's so efficient at its job that, if the conditions are right, a single spore could infect one ant which could infect thousands more which could infect millions. Entire colonies are known to have been wiped out.

Yes, these zombie ants don't crave the flesh of their nearest and dearest, but it's the closest thing to a zombie that I can think of. They are infected, they rot (well, they're digested from the inside out, but same difference), they have no control over their actions and they can pass on the condition to many, many more victims.

Different kinds of *Cordyceps* affect different kinds of insects but, as far as science is aware, they are yet to make the leap to mammals. That said, if you happen to see your neighbour, upside down, clinging on to the underside of a lamppost with her teeth, grab your zombie survival kit (we should all have one by now) and hit the road.

Thing 74:
If there's one thing sharks are good at, it's making teeth; their skin is even made of them

Sharks aren't that much like other fish. Well, they are; they live and breathe in water and they look very similar, but they don't have bones. Bony fish are more closely related to us than they are to sharks. What is thought to be the common ancestor of both mammals and bony fish can be traced back about 300 million years, while the common ancestor of bony fish and sharks is theorized to have existed somewhere in the region of 400 million years ago.* The fact that they look and act similar is due to *convergent evolution*; they live in the same environment, thus many similar features proved to be adaptive for those living conditions. For example, fins help marine life to swim more efficiently, so when they started popping up, the individuals with fins would have lived longer or been more efficient at mating, therefore passing the fin trait down the generations.

Instead of bones, sharks have cartilage, which is lighter and more flexible. I know what you're thinking; you're thinking, *No fair, I want a skeleton made of cartilage; I hate my stupid bones. They're too heavy and they're not flexible enough.* Don't be silly; we need our bones. For one thing, inside them is where our red blood cells are made (sharks' are made in their spleen and a few other spots). We also don't live in water, so don't need so much aid with buoyancy, but we do need anchor points for our muscles. If you had cartilage instead of bones, you'd

---

* Just let that sink in for a moment. Sharks are as old to dinosaurs as dinosaurs are to us. I feel confident that the sharks are just biding their time, waiting for us to cock up so they can exit the oceans, eat our world leaders and rule on land with an iron fist (fin).

basically be a blob, unable to hold yourself up. You'd also be dead because red blood cells carry oxygen around your body. For sharks, though, never developing bones was a good move. They are lighter than bony fish of equal size, and much more manoeuvrable. 'But what do their muscles connect to?' I hear you ask. 'Muscle connects to bone and, without bone, why are they not just a vaguely shark-shaped hunk, drifting through the ocean?' Good question. To answer it, you must consider things with an exoskeleton (crabs, insects, spiders and the like); their muscles connect directly to their outer shell and, oddly enough, sharks have a similar set-up. Just under their skin is a layer of collagen to which the muscles attach.

Scales are handy things to have if you live in water – they provide protection while also allowing for freedom of movement. Many fish have scales and so do sharks, only they came about in different ways. Sharks don't have the necessary mechanisms to produce scales the way that most fish do, but there is one thing that sharks certainly have no problem producing: teeth. As such, their scales (otherwise known as *dermal denticles*) are covered in dentin, the same stuff that makes teeth. Seeing as they've had nearly half a billion years to work on them, the structure of these scales (kind of like tiny diamonds) is not only a natural repellent to the bacteria and plankton that bothers other fish, but it allows them to swim faster and more quietly by pulling water onto their bodies and over their surface.

Sharks did have a significant head start on us, but still, given 400 million years and assuming we haven't blown ourselves up, a meteorite hasn't smeared us off the plane of existence or aliens haven't made us their bitches, I would hope that we too could develop some badass features like tooth-skin or mind control or invisibility. Fingers crossed for invisibility.

Thing 75:
Horseshoe crabs are the original unsung heroes[*]

Horseshoe crabs existed millions of years before horses, eons before shoes and even well before crabs. They've been on Earth, virtually unchanged, for at least 450 million years, making them one of the oldest species of anything that is still around today. They're more closely related to spiders than they are to crabs and, if you've ever had an injection, they just might be the reason you're not dead.

The blood of most things we're familiar with is red; that's because it's iron-based and when iron reacts to the oxygen that is carried around within blood, it rusts. Horseshoe-crab blood, though, is copper-based and, if you've ever seen the Statue of Liberty, you'll know that when copper reacts with oxygen it turns blue. The fact that they have blue blood is cool and all, but that's not the reason it's so valuable to us. When we get a cut, our white blood cells run to the rescue and fight any bacteria that will inevitably be trying to kill us. When a horseshoe crab sustains a wound and bacteria tries to enter through it, their blood simply coagulates around the trauma, forming a viscous gel that the nasty little things can't penetrate. It's primitive but very effective.

The friendly little helpers in their blood are called 'amoebocytes' and some bright sparks (beginning with Fred Bang, who is credited for discovering this phenomenon) worked out that, if you draw some blood from a crab, separate the amoebocytes from the plasma, freeze-dry them and then add them to liquids

---

* So let's write them a song. 'Horseshoe crabs, horseshoe crabs. The best crustaceans in the lab. They're really old, their blood is blue. Their amoebocytes save me and you.'

that may later be injected into humans (in the form of vaccines, for example), you will quickly be able to tell if your juice has been contaminated. With the addition of a little crab mojo, anything that you want to put into a person would have coagulated lumps in it, as the amoebocytes go to work around the bacteria in there. It's best the doctor knows about it if there's some E. coli in the syringe of liquid that is moments away from being pumped into your left shoulder, and blue hunks seem like as good a way as any of drawing this to their attention.

Weirdly, this whole process is quite clandestine and people don't tend to know about it. I guess the powers that be made the assessment that members of the public wouldn't like the idea of bits of ancient crab-but-not-crab-more-like-a-distant-cousin-of-the-spider being needled into them. I, for one, can't get enough of the stuff. If it's good enough for a species of weird-looking arthropods that have been around for nearly half a billion years, it's certainly good enough for little old me.

A three-Thing aside about dinosaurs. * *I realize that I glossed over dinosaurs at the beginning of the book. This was because I worried that if I put them right at the beginning you'd think this was basically a book of 147 Things about dinosaurs. They are, it goes without saying, awesome, so I will now be spending six pages talking about them. If you don't like dinosaurs, you can skip to page 210. However, be warned that we probably can't be friends anymore.*

---

* And one Thing about avocados and giant sloths.

Thing 76:
Jurassic Park is full of lies

When asked what your favourite dinosaur is, if your answer is anything other than *Velociraptor*, you're dead to me. If you ask me – and this is my book, so I'm going to tell you even if you don't want to ask me – *Velociraptors* and all of their cousins were the coolest creatures ever to have walked the Earth. However, it's worth noting that they were not the same animal that featured in *Jurassic Park*.

I was six years old in 1993, which was the year *Jurassic Park* was released. I was at the very height of my dinosaur infatuation and, being six, I took the film as gospel. It wasn't until I did a school project on dinosaurs and started reading about them that I realized Hollywood had taken the term 'artistic license' and used it as an excuse to tell a *Diplodocus*-sized lie. Don't get me wrong, I still love the film – but if you've been living your life, happy in the knowledge that *Velociraptors* were faithfully portrayed, I'm about to burst your bubble.

Velociraptors came and went roughly between 86 and 70 million years ago, at the end of the Cretaceous period. Nothing to do with the Jurassic period at all, but, to be honest, most of the dinosaurs in the movie didn't exist at the same time as one another. The premise of the film is that the scientists managed to find DNA of certain species and they were working with what they had, so I don't blame them for calling the movie *Jurassic Park*. It's much catchier than *Various Dinosaurs from Different Eras Park*.

Now let's address the facts about a *Velociraptor*. They were named after the Latin 'velox', meaning 'swift', and *Velociraptor* literally means 'swift seizer'. Cool name, right? But here's the rub: they were nowhere near as big as the movie portrays. In fact, they were about the size of a small turkey. Let that sink in. A small turkey. When I first heard this, I nearly cried.

My favourite ever living creature – a hunting machine, a bio-mechanical force of nature – was not in fact as big as the teenagers it was trying to eat in the kitchen scene, but rather the size of a delicious, fat, ugly bird with too much skin on its face. It doesn't quite instil the same terror, does it? If the kitchen scene was reshot using more accurate raptors, the two teens would probably end up making a raptor roast dinner.

That's not where the avian similarities end, either. By now we all know that dinosaurs were the precursors to modern birds, and *Velociraptors* are actually among some of the most bird-like species we have discovered so far. Quill knobs have been found in some fossils, suggesting that the little turkeysaurus almost certainly had feathers. It couldn't fly, but it seems its ancestors could. Keeping its plumage may have provided an evolutionary advantage when it came to attracting a mate or regulating body temperature. So it was less the smooth, stream-lined, bipedal hound from hell depicted in the movie, and more like a large robin with teeth.

One thing that *Jurassic Park* didn't make up was the kick-ass toe claw. It was held, coiled, away from the ground, like a switchblade ready to be released when the moment was right. That moment was when it jumped onto the back of its prey, digging it in to get a good grip. Unlike in the film though, it wouldn't have been jumping on the backs of people. There are two reasons for this: the first is that people didn't exist yet, the second is that we would have been way too big for them to mess with. *Velociraptors* would have dined on anything they could scavenge, as well as hunting for insects, reptiles and other small dinosaurs and mammals.

No doubt you wouldn't want a *Velociraptor* as a pet (I totally would) on account of it being a vicious little scallywag and almost certainly eating your cat. But other than it giving you a nasty bite, I don't think there'd be too much to fear if Richard Attenborough did decide to bring them back from extinction.

But that doesn't mean the writers of the iconic dinosaur flick invented their raptors entirely. They're actually based on a larger cousin of the *Velociraptor* that lived about 25 million years prior. Yes, they too were probably feathered, but palaeontologists think they did bear more than a few similarities to the beasts from the film.

These bad boys were known as *Deinonychus* (although, at the time, they were probably referred to as roar, or growl; it's hard to tell for sure), which translates to *terrible claw* from the Greek. Like most species from the raptor family, it too had a curved, hinged claw on the inside toe of each hind foot that would stay perpendicular to the floor until unleashed on its dino prey, either for getting a foothold to clamber up and rend flesh with its teeth, or to slash and gouge to cause maximum blood loss, or both. Whatever the specifics, it was bigger, scarier and more powerful than that of its pigmy-sized cousin. In truth, the proportions of the talon in the film are much more closely matched to this theropod than the *Velociraptor*, so when Dr Alan Grant scares that mouthy little pre-teen douchebag with one, early on in the movie, it's best to assume it comes from *Deinonychus*, not *Velociraptor*.

In the film, the *Velociraptors* were discovered in North America, when they actually resided in modern-day Asia and Russia. *Deinonychus*, however, was American, born and bred. It was also of a similar stature to the ones featured in the ill-fated theme park, weighing in at about 80 kg, with measurements of 3 m in length and 1.5 m in height. As well as this, they had the stiff tail to help with balance, long fore-limbs and were, more or less (less than more, but close enough), anatomically consistent with those in the film.

Of course, the filmmakers still took the piss and fabricated a lot of what they were capable of; they weren't intelligent enough to use door handles, they don't seem to have hunted in packs and were also around in the Cretaceous period (definitely not the Jurassic). They weren't even all that fast or agile. But they were, undoubtedly, still badass, and deserve to be given the credit that *Jurassic Park* brazenly handed out to the wrong dinosaur just because it's easier to pronounce (and sounds much cooler).

The lesson to take home here is that Hollywood gives us unrealistic ideas. I'll never look like Brad Pitt in *Fight Club*; in fact, I will never be as cool as Brad Pitt in any movie, and *Velociraptors* were small, feathered and birdish. Still, they remain my favourite dinosaur to this day and I won't hear a bad word said about them.

Thing 77:
The sharpest tool in the prehistoric box

Troodon was a relatively small bird-like dinosaur that measured in at about 3 feet tall, but it was a genius. I mean, it couldn't do long division or anything, but its brain capacity was fairly large compared to its body size. Consider this: *Diplodocus* was a 90-foot leviathan with a brain not much bigger than a walnut (semi-official measurement) controlling its entire being. Its brain weighed 0.0001 per cent of its total mass, whereas *Troodon's* thinker was around the 4 per cent mark, not too dissimilar to some modern-day birds.

Troodon's brain was proportionally larger than those found in modern reptiles, and palaeontologists believe that it displayed some characteristics of crocodilians (earlier relatives to the dinosaurs), and some characteristics of birds, which evolved much later. This puts *Troodon* in quite an important spot on the evolutionary tree as a link between the two.

I like to imagine this clever little thing as a big, reptilian-looking, probably feathered bird that couldn't fly. It nested in the ground with its mate, but it's believed that it sat on its eggs to incubate them (the reason that boffins think this is that a fossil of a nesting pair was found a few years back). It would have been very agile and quick on its feet, eating bugs and small mammals and lizards. It had big, forward-facing eyes that allowed for good binocular vision, even at night-time. Whereas prey animals tend to have eyes on the sides of their heads to get a wider field of view, many predators have both eyes front-facing so they can focus on the meal in front of them and measure distance accurately. *Troodon*, it seems, was an intelligent little badass.

Thing 78:
There's no such thing as
a *Brontosaurus*

One hundred and thirty years ago was the time of the 'Bone Wars', which sounds epic and scary and like the name of a film I would definitely watch. In reality, it was more of a 'bone race' to see who could very gently brush the loose earth from a fossil and name a new species of dinosaur the fastest. It's hard to imagine the painstakingly slow and delicate process of digging up bones that have been in the ground for millions of years as a particularly competitive environment, but two palaeontologists by the names of Othniel Charles Marsh and Edward Drinker Cope (Othniel wins in the weird-name wars, that's for sure) took their jobs way too seriously and were in a bitter rivalry to discover as many new dinosaurs as possible before the other one.

Marsh discovered the partial skeleton of an *Apatosaurus* (one of those ones with a long neck and tail, like a *Brontosaurus*, only nothing like a *Brontosaurus* because *Brontosauruses* never existed) in 1877, but it was missing a skull. 'No worries,' he said. 'I'll just pop the head of a *Camarasaurus* on its body; no one will be able to tell the difference.'

A few years later, his team discovered another, similar looking fossil that Marsh, in his haste to outdo Cope, dubbed *Brontosaurus*. Only it wasn't a *Brontosaurus*, because, as I've said a few times already, there was no such thing. What had really been discovered was another *Apatosaurus*, only this time complete with a skull (which, if you ask me, is the most important bone). It only took a few years for Marsh's contemporaries to go, 'Woah, hang on there a minute, Othniel; we're not entirely convinced this is a different dinosaur at all. We actually think it's the same as the other one with no head, but with a head,' which I'm sure Cope lapped up and would not drop. Of course, by then the world had gone dinosaur mad, the *Brontosaurus* had captured the public's imagination and there was no taking it back. Also, let's face it, *Brontosaurus*, which means 'thunder lizard', is a much better name.

Thing 79:
Avocados are lucky to exist

Fruits are made to be delicious so that an animal wants to eat them and their seeds can go for a little journey through its digestive tract while the animal itself goes for a little journey across the land. That way, when the beast poops, the seeds are dropped far from the original tree in their own little pile of fertilizer, the animal has had a nice meal, a new tree can grow and everyone is happy. But what happens when the animals that eat your fruit all die? Without anyone to disperse the seeds, surely the future of that tree is doomed. Well, usually, yes, but not in the case of the avocado.

Megatherium was a giant ground sloth that lived in South and Central America and went extinct about 10,000 years ago (coincidentally, humans popped up in this area shortly before they died out. Classic humans). When I say *Megatherium* was giant, I mean it was bloody huge. The Natural History Museum in London has one on display and, when I stood next to it, I came up to its ribcage. It was about the size of a rhino on all fours (but often walked on its hind legs, making it much taller) and weighed about as much as an African bull elephant. In fact, there were only a few animals at that time, such as the woolly mammoth, that were bigger. The point I'm making is that *Megatherium* was big.

Do you know what else is big? The stone inside an avocado. There aren't many animals alive today that could swallow one of those bad boys whole, pass it down the oesophagus, through the stomach and intestines and out the other end without doing some major damage. I certainly wouldn't want to try it. Some animals may be able to chew the stone, but that would destroy the seed and defeat the purpose, plus it has some nasty, bitter chemicals that are released to prevent this from happening. The avocado tree and megafauna (really big animals) such as *Megatherium* co-evolved; as the animals got bigger, so could the seeds. Larger seeds provide the potential sapling with more energy to get a head-start when dropped to the ground in dense forest where little sunlight reaches the floor. It was a harmonious relationship, and worked perfectly in the warm forests where they existed together, but as the Ice Age ended, the climate became too hot and humans got hungry for giant mammal meat. The disappearance of the weakest link in the chain would usually spell disaster for both co-evolved life forms. But that didn't happen with our creamy, guacamole-making, delicious-on-toast-with-a-poached-egg-on-top avocado. So what did? Humans happened.

As it happens, we are always hungry, and not only did we have a taste for big avocado-eating animals, we also enjoyed the fruits themselves. Obviously, we couldn't eat the stone, but we enjoyed the flesh and were smart enough to work out how to eat one without the other. We were also smart enough to discover that if we planted seeds, more trees would grow, and we started to cultivate them. In fact, it's entirely possible that we even improved upon them by planting the seeds that gave a fruit with more flesh or a better taste or a skin that was easier to penetrate, therefore passing on those traits to future avocado trees. It would appear that we're not all bad, after all. Giant sloths clearly aren't our best friends, but avocados are big fans.

Even though I love dinosaurs and megafauna, I'm nearly certain if I saw either in real life, my wonder would turn pretty quickly to terror. I'm fascinated by the things people are scared of; when you're scared of something it feels perfectly logical to you, but totally bonkers to others. I also know, from the variety of things that my followers said they were afraid of when I asked them, that we all spend a large part of our time thinking about what frightens us. Let's confront our fears together!

FEARS

Thing 80:
A belly-button phobia is a
real thing

Some people are scared of snakes and some people are scared of heights – I'm scared of belly buttons. I don't like to see people poke theirs, I can't prod yours and if you attempt to force me to touch my own, one of us is going to get hurt.

Here's the thing: when somebody tells you they are scared of spiders, you don't throw a spider at them (unless you're a horrible moron). But when I tell people I hate navels, the first thing they do is either get their own out and start fingering it or come at mine with a digit extended. Watching somebody put something in their belly button is toe-curling for me, but having somebody threaten to put something in mine is enough to hurtle me well over the edge of being a calm, civilized man into becoming a full-blown irrational maniac.

I once threw my niece across the room when she was little more than a toddler. My sister (her mother) whispered in her ear to 'go touch Uncle Jim's belly button', so she innocently trotted over and plunged her chunky little baby finger knuckle-deep into my tummy hole. Instinct took over, I protected what was mine and launched her across the room. She touched down in a heap and stayed there for a few seconds while we all panicked that I had killed her. Then the tears came. Served her right.

It turns out that my fear of belly buttons is an actual diagnosable condition: it's called omphalophobia. I'm not sure what it is about them that makes me squirm, but upon doing some research it seems that my fellow omphalophobics agree that watching people touch belly buttons, or touching their own, is a big no-no. The scale of phobia depends on the shape and size of the button. I can control myself around a big, deep innie, but come at me with your outie or one where I can see the bulbous detail of the offending nubbin and your ass is grass.

I'm aware that it's completely irrational and I wish I could muster the strength to overcome it, but whenever I discover belly-button fluff or some other foreign object in there, everything stops. I develop a cold sweat, my breath comes short and shallow and my whole world comes crumbling down. It'd make my life so much easier if I was scared of something I could explain. A fear of heights would most likely be because I would worry about what would happen if I were to plunge to an early death. Snakes might scare me because of the way they move and the fact that many of them can kill you. What did a navel ever do to anyone?

As it turns out, omphalophobia is relatively rare. I couldn't find any literature with reference to its prevalence, so I took to the streets to conduct my own research. I wanted to ask strangers what their relationship with their belly buttons was like and it would seem that, on any given sunny Thursday afternoon on Charlotte Street in London, only one other person will report any button-related queasiness. Even this person won't experience the phobia in the same way I do, with only a 'mild discomfort' being reported. It's certainly not concrete evidence, but it does lead me to the belief that less than 2 per cent of the population can empathize with my plight and, based on my own experiences, a similarly low amount can be bothered to even sympathize.

It's hard to pinpoint exactly what it is about belly buttons that sends me into crazy town, but it's definitely something to do with the fact that there is just a tiny bit of scar tissue between the outside world and your internal organs. The placenta was joined to you via the umbilical cord, which sent nutrients directly to your body when you were in the womb. That's gross. Why can't humans hatch from eggs like any self-respecting fish, lizard or bird?

Here are some other genuine phobias:

- Allodoxaphobia – fear of opinions
- Xanthophobia – fear of the colour yellow
- Turophobia – fear of cheese
- Genuphobia – fear of knees
- Somniphobia – fear of falling asleep
- Coulrophobia – fear of clowns
- Octophobia – fear of the number eight
- Hylophobia – fear of wood or trees
- Venustraphobia – fear of beautiful women
- Aulophobia – fear of flutes
- Chirophobia – fear of hands
- Nomophobia – fear of being without mobile phone coverage
- Ombrophobia – fear of rain
- Velumiphobia – fear of umbrellas
- Uranophobia – fear of heaven
- Pogonophobia – fear of beards
- Trypophobia – fear of small holes (think sponges or honeycomb or woodworm)
- Triskaidekaphobia – fear of the number thirteen
- Phobophobia – fear of phobias

Thing 81:
The reason we haven't seen aliens is because they're biding their time before killing us

There is a terrifying thing called the Fermi Paradox which asks why, in an almost infinite universe, in which there are likely to be hundreds of millions of worlds capable of supporting life and in which the odds of them being much more developed civilizations than us are massive, we haven't seen definitive evidence of intelligent life out there. It goes into all sorts of fascinating permutations, including the fact that intelligent life really is just exceptionally rare and the vast distances of space are just impossible to deal with, but my personal favourite one to freak myself out with is that there is one race of aliens who got there first and developed the technology to travel across the vast distances of space. They're out there monitoring everyone else. Right now, only able to live on our planet, or just about get to the Moon, we're no threat to anyone. But the minute we develop technology that provides them with competition, that'll be another matter. Imagine the inaugural test flight in 2087 of the first antimatter space ship. At which point, the aliens appear and vaporize the entire planet because we got too big for our boots.

Thing 82:
We've almost certainly already killed the only allies who would help us fight off the aliens

I was playing on my Xbox the other day, shooting aliens, and it occurred to me that the extraterrestrials that I was murdering came in many shapes and sizes. I guess for variety's sake game developers design multiple intelligent life forms originating from the same planet, organized into an army for you to destroy. Although they all have different attributes – some may be light-weight and nimble, while others are smashy brutes – it would appear that there is no single dominant species among what-ever planet they come from. It leaves you with the impression that, back on their homeland, they all cooperate with one another and live happily, plotting how to overthrow that distant blue and green planet with the semi-intelligent, ugly weaklings and use its resources to further their reign of tyranny across the galaxy. It's amazing what a little cooperation can achieve. On Earth though, it's only us. We are the dominant species and the only ones intelligent enough to know it. Can you imagine trying to organize an army of cats to try and see off an alien army? But it wasn't always like that. We did have comparably intelligent company, before we (probably) killed them.

About 2.8 million years ago, early humans split from pri-mates, but it wasn't as simple as one day being a monkey, the next being us. It was a slow process, there were many hiccups along the way and we had a bunch of cousins that looked and acted a bit like us. In the same way there are many variations of frog or ant or deer, there were different species of people. In fact, humans as we know us only appeared on the scene around 200,000 years back and there were at least six other species of human-like hominid (the animal family we belong to) that we know of living at the same time. It seems that we cohabited alongside them for quite some time too, as there is evidence that suggests the last of our relatives were still with us as recently as 10,000 years ago.

We know for sure that within us there is a small amount of DNA found from other human-like species, such as Neanderthals, which means that we definitely cross-bred with them, yet still, for some reason, they died out and we kicked butt. It may be that they weren't as efficient at manipulating their environment as us, and so, as our species grew and used up resources, theirs couldn't cope and effectively starved. Or it may be that we killed them to get rid of the competition. Either way, when aliens play games where they shoot the Earthlings, we aren't going to have any backup unless the spiders make a surprise appearance and induce enough skin-crawling to send the invaders back on their ships so they leave us alone. (Also, I like to imagine that octopuses would take part in fighting off the bad guys, because they are much more intelligent than we give them credit for.)

Thing 83:
I'm pretty sure ghosts are real

You may find this strange given that the nature of this book is quite sciency and at least a little based-on-evidence, but I believe in ghosts. Kind of. I think. I'm not entirely sure what I believe but I know there's something that goes bump in the night.

If I hadn't experienced the tale I'm about to tell and you were to ask me if I believe in an afterlife, I would tell you that I think that we are biological machines and that when we die we leave nothing behind but a good meal for bacteria and beetles, and the memories held in the ones who love us. But then there was that room in my childhood house that was definitely, without a shadow of a doubt, unequivocally, terrifyingly haunted.

I'm still not convinced that I accept something happens after we die, but surely believing in spirits and not believing in a soul that continues after death are mutually exclusive; you can't have a ghost living in your house if all that happens when you die is nothing, right? Yet, to me, both have a basis and I have found myself at something of a stalemate, so I chose to ignore the subject when questioned because it hurts my head. Until I decided to ignore the pain in my brain and write about it in my book.

The house I lived in from birth until the age of seven was in a tiny hamlet called Wilby that consisted of a handful of houses. Apparently, before I was born, my home was built around a small, pre-existing building. I loved that house – it was large and warm and welcoming – but I would try to avoid going into the room that was there before the rest of it existed, because it was entirely terrifying. Nobody went in there much, not even my parents, and they were adults and adults aren't scared of anything.

Whenever I would have to fetch something from there, I would open the door as wide as it would go, grab what I needed, turn and run back out again before the door had a chance to close itself and leave me in there for those few extra seconds while I was forced to reach for the handle once more. It was always cold and, even going into the bathroom next door, the hairs on my arms would stand on end. There was simply something off about it. It just made everyone feel very uneasy. Even guests.

I remember that one night we had someone to stay who refused to sleep in that room, so they were given the one that my brother and I shared and we were relegated to spend the night in the scary chamber. We didn't sleep a wink; we clung to each other all night, shivering through fear and through cold, and we could hear someone outside the window. At one point, and for a very long time, in the absence of anyone else present, we felt a person sit on the end of the bed. We were too scared to peer out from under the blanket but we were both absolutely adamant, even though we couldn't have been older than five, that nobody entered or exited while we had been there.

Of course, all the adults told us that we were just being pathetic, but a few years later my mum told me that she had a remarkably similar experience when she had once stayed in there and that she wouldn't go back for all the tea in China (she loves tea, too). Everyone in the family, and anyone who came to visit, found something unsettling about that room and nobody went in there through anything other than necessity. To this day, I am convinced that it was haunted.

The trouble with it being haunted is twofold. Firstly, it means that ghosts exist and I'd rather live in a world where they didn't, and secondly, why? How? Who? What? Where? When? I don't like things that I can't explain or can't be explained to me and I certainly don't like this. How did that thing get there? Is it trapped? Is it still there now? Is it sad? Did it need our help? Did it want to kill us? Who was it? What happened to them? When did it happen to them? Why was it so spooky? I want to know the answers but, to get them, I would probably have to go back to that room and I haven't lived in that house for twenty-two years and I'm probably more scared of it now than I was when I lived there. I'll leave it.

Thing 84:
We'd best not make anything smarter than us

If you've ever seen any of the Terminator movies, or *The Matrix*, or *Transcendence*, or *Avengers: Age of Ultron*, or any other film where machines outsmart us, you'll know that creating artificial intelligence might not be such a sterling idea.

Obviously, we already have tons of artificial things in the world helping us live our lives in a more and more efficient manner. They can perform complex tasks in a fraction of the time it takes us humans to do the same things, but they have rules. They can only function on the challenges they are designed for and nothing else. This type of artificial intelligence is great. We love it; it's safe, it's helpful and can tell you the weather in Outer Mongolia in a matter of moments.

Our brains are super-duper complicated and it's totally possible that we will never have the ability to make a digital replication. And that's almost certainly a good thing. If (and when) true artificial intelligence, or the 'singularity' (dun dun duuuuuuun), is born/created, it could spell the end for the puny humans (as it will no doubt refer to us).

Seeing as it will be omniscient and have access to the internet, it will have no problem quickly upgrading itself and far outstripping even the brightest of human sparks. Once it has made itself into something our tiny brains can't fathom, it could create copies, meaning that it will not only know everything, but also be everywhere. Assuming it's a logical being, which I imagine it would be, because machines work on logic and 'emotions are for the weak' (as it would probably say to you as you begged it not to kill your family and turn them into the organic goop it uses to feed the enslaved humans), it would see us as its biggest threat.

The world has never seen more dramatic changes in climate, animal habitat and species numbers in such a short amount of time than since we learned how to make stuff and kill things. In fact, scientists believe that there have been five extinction events – when 50 per cent or more of all species go extinct in a relatively short period – in the history of our planet. They include the meteor that wiped out the dinosaurs and 'the great dying' that wiped out 95 per cent of all known life at the time. Then you have the sixth mass extinction – the Holocene Extinction, otherwise known as the Anthropocene Extinction. On the off chance that your Greek is a little rusty, *Anthropocene* derives from *Anthropos*, which means 'human'. It's our fault. We have changed the climate and made the oceans more acidic, we force creatures to find new areas to live that they cannot adapt to when we destroy their old spot, we accidently take rats and other invasive animals with us when we go places, and they, in turn, alter delicate ecosystems and, of course, we kill without discretion.

Any artificial intelligence would most likely recognize us as the biggest threat to the planet it calls home (on the assumption that it hasn't transcended our little globe and decided to spread its consciousness on Jupiter or something) and its largest competitor for energy resources. In the same way that we most likely wiped out the Neanderthals, this singularity would quickly lose patience with us and simply poison the water, or set off all our nuclear warheads, or create a Matrix (if it's feeling adventurous), or humanoid robots like the T-800 from *The Terminator* (if it's feeling ironic), or make itself into a supervillain with laser hands (if it likes superhero movies), or kill us in any other way it sees fit. And there would probably be nothing we could do about it. Of course, it could also be totally chill and let us do our thing, but let's not risk it, hey?

Tell you what, to the future brainiac who may invent AI, if you're reading this book: either don't do it, or make sure that humanity is above reproach and won't do anything to piss it off (and send us all some knee pads so we can bow to our new overlord without unnecessary discomfort).

Thing 85:
Water is terrifying and people should never go in deeper than their nose

Most babies are born with the innate ability to hold their breath, slow their heart rate and seal the path to their lungs to make it watertight when submerged. They can't swim, but if they go underwater for a short period of time, when they break the surface again, they should be unscathed. This usually lasts until around the six-month mark, when the instinct wears off and the child must start learning to consciously control their breath when around water. Most kids can do this. We tend to learn fairly young and carry the ability throughout our lives.

After all, we go underwater all the time. But it's something that I was never able to accomplish.

I can't swim. Well, technically I can swim, but it's ugly. I can get from one side of a pool to the other but it takes me much longer, requires a lot more energy and costs a ton more dignity than it does most people. I make a lot of splashes and some very odd noises.

On paper, I should be brilliant at it. My body looks as though it was built to swim; I have long limbs, broad shoulders and big hands and feet. On paper, I should also be an Olympic javelin thrower and the Wimbledon champion, but paper doesn't account for sheer lack of talent and a fear of putting your face in the water.

I'm genuinely scared. Not so scared that I will never get in it, but scared enough to make a really overdramatic noise every time I hold my breath. I screw my face up so tight that my own mother wouldn't recognize me, I dunk and then I panic. Within seconds I come up, wheezing, coughing, spluttering and burping almost immediately (I'll explain the burping in a moment).

I can't even look up in the shower without counting myself down from three and making a ridiculous song and dance about it. It's a bit of a secret shame that I have tried not to share with anyone (until I decided to mention it in a book) because it feels like a real weakness.

I put this all down to a near-drowning experience in Australia when I was white-water rafting. Tan fell in and I could see the panic on her face, so I jumped in after her without thinking and managed to push her to safety before getting swept away myself. I was told that, if you go in the water, the current will take you under and that you must hold your breath and simply wait for an opportunity to gasp when your head bobs up before it takes you under again. Simple. That opportunity took an age to come. Then the next took an age. And the next one. It takes a lot to rattle me; I'm usually pretty chill about most things and don't scare easily, but that definitely did the trick.

It's not like I have a flashback every time I submerge myself.

I've been snorkelling since and swam in open water from the side of a boat on a few occasions. Although I can always feel the panic under the surface of my skin, I keep it together. It's not an immediate or acute fear, it's more that my body has learned that too much water is not good for me.

My friends (and this includes my wife) have a tendency to lead me into the deep end, like a sheepdog herding its quarry, where they'll prod me until I sink. Once they're satisfied that I have gone down deep enough, they will drag me back to the surface, give me a second to catch my breath and burp (burp explanation imminent), and start again. It seems to provide them with hours of entertainment, while I constantly feel on the brink of death.

If I can touch the floor, I'm fine. I can go past my mouth to midway up my philtrum. When I start treading water or, worse, when I have to adopt the swimming position and lie on the surface, that's when it gets dicey. The point when you take that extra step and realize that you are on the very tips of your toes is when real panic hits. The momentum of the water has you and it's very difficult to turn around because you are nearly weightless and moving in a substance that is much thicker than air. When I have no choice but to give up on the solid ground beneath my feet and accept the fact that I am now swimming, my entire body goes to DEFCON 1.

I don't know if I'm a medical miracle or something, but on calm water most human bodies are supposed to float with minimal effort. Not my body. I go rigid and I go under. Usually feet first, which is something to be thankful for, I suppose. When it comes to actually swimming, my technique is appalling, mostly because a lot of different strokes require that your face enter the water. This leads to a socially unacceptable amount of splashing for anyone who does not require arm bands or is above the age of six.

One of the worst things about my swimming is the breathing technique I adopt. There isn't one. I panic, so I gulp air in, often along with an alarming amount of water. Some of the air goes into my lungs (although not as much as I'd like), and some of it goes into my stomach. Within a minute or two, the gas that went down the wrong hole begins to come back up in the form of belches. Sexy, I know. It's OK though, I've come to terms with the fact that I'm never going to look sleek or streamlined. I'm never going to emulate James Bond's aquatic exits. I'm never even going to impress the other holidaymakers who share the pool. For me, swimming is not a leisure activity, it's an exercise in putting my life in the hands of fate or Poseidon or anyone who has a floatation device.

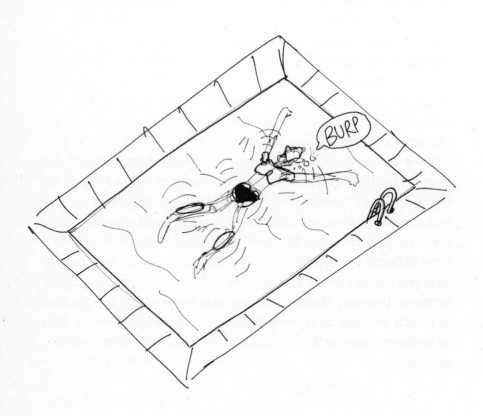

Thing 86:
If you own a gun and something good happens, don't fire it into the air to celebrate

You've probably heard that if you dropped a penny from the top of the Empire State Building, it would pick up enough speed to go through somebody's skull and enter their brain. Fortunately for those clumsy coin collectors with a head for heights, the terminal velocity (top speed under its own force) of a penny is enough to draw blood and sting a lot, but not sufficient to pierce a human cranium.

So a penny being hurtled at you from the heavens will not do any major harm, but what about all those bullets that are shot into the air in celebration? They can't just keep going up; air resistance and gravity will slow them down. Then what? Well, they definitely would do some damage. Depending on the power of the gun, a shot sent vertically could reach a mile into the sky before it meets its apex and heads back to Earth. It will be going a little slower on the descent because the energy from being fired will have been spent on the way up. However, bullets are aerodynamic and designed to kill, so even with the force of gravity alone, from that height it will have plenty of time to reach its terminal velocity and kill an unlucky stranger. In some major cities there is even a law against celebratory air firing for this very reason. The more densely populated the area in which you fire your weapon, the higher the chances of accidentally murdering some poor sod. Probably best not to have a gun at all.

Thing 87:
Don't read this if you fear getting buried alive

Getting buried alive would be no fun, right? During Victorian times, the fear was so intense that some people chose to be buried in a coffin with a bell they could ring if they happened to wake up while six feet under.

Guess what? It's extremely rare, with only thirty-eight cases being reported since 1982, but some people do come back from the dead. Scientists still don't understand how it happens, but it happens. It's known as Lazarus syndrome and, unfortunately, in most cases the once-dead person is left with severe brain damage. But not always. A few individuals have been known to wake up, after what I imagine is about as good a rest as one can manage, and live a perfectly normal life thereafter. In one such instance, in 2008, in the US, Velma Thomas's heart ceased to beat three times, which led to the pronouncement that she was clinically brain dead. All the current technology agreed; she was dead and there was nothing more to be done. There she stayed for seventeen hours until her son, after making the awful decision to switch off her life-support machine, left to make funeral arrangements. Ten minutes later, once her body was being prepared for organ donation, it transpired that apparently she wasn't as dead as the doctors had thought, because she woke up.

Thing 88:
If you are caught in space wearing only your Speedos, you are 100 per cent going to die in less than a minute

I know what you're thinking right now. You're thinking, *I wonder what would happen if an impromptu visit to space came about and I packed in a hurry, remembering my swimming trunks but forgetting my spacesuit. What if, for some reason, while only wearing swimwear, I didn't wear my seatbelt and, through a freak set of circumstances, I found myself exposed to the vacuum of space in my Speedos/bikini/on-trend retro one-piece? Would I die?*

Well, there's good news and bad news. The good news is that a lot of the things that you might assume would take place, the things that you see in sci-fi films, won't. The scene in *Total Recall* is the most graphic representation that comes to mind – with the eye-bulging and grotesque body contortions – but to be fair that bit happens on the surface of Mars, not in outer space. Regardless, those things wouldn't happen. The bad news is that you will still die, and it won't even be epic – although it may involve faecal matter in your trunks. Here are some more things that won't happen (just to put your mind at rest):

Thing That Won't Happen Number 1: Your blood will not boil

Physics dictates that the lower the air pressure, the lower the boiling point of most liquids. Air pressure is essentially the weight of the air that is pressing down on any spot. You may have heard that if you were to turn on a kettle at the top of Mount Everest, you wouldn't need to reach the standard 100°C necessary to enjoy your cup of tea. In fact, a mere 71°C will do the trick, which is handy because it's bloody freezing up there and I imagine you wouldn't want to wait around for a cup of tea. The reason for this is that at the 29,029-foot summit there is less air pressure, which basically means that it is much easier for gas bubbles to form and escape the liquid in question. So it boils more quickly.

Space is a vacuum: there is no air and so no air pressure, therefore it stands to reason that any liquid exposed to this would turn to its gaseous form instantaneously. Physics hits the nail on the head when it comes to exposed liquids. But your blood is not exposed, it's safe and sound in its own pressurized circulatory system, tucked away under your skin and entwined in the rest of the bits and bobs that keep you alive. Therefore, your blood will not boil. Good news. (Unless you happened to have cut yourself on your way out of the spaceship, in which case, you're totally screwed.)

Thing That Won't Happen Number 2:
Your head and/or body will not explode

Back to pressure: our bodies are designed with their own internal pressure systems that counteract the atmospheric pressure found on Earth. It keeps our blood circulating around our bodies and makes gas exchange, such as breathing and flatulating, much easier. Take us away from Earth, though, and the sudden drop in pressure would surely mean that all of our internal systems would be fighting against nothing. With no external forces keeping our internal ones in equilibrium, we would explode, right?

Unfortunately, it wouldn't be that cool. It turns out that our skin and connective tissue is plenty strong enough to keep us together, even in the vacuum of deep, dark space. More good news.

Thing That Won't Happen Number 3: You won't freeze to death

Space is about -270°C, which is more than a little chilly. Being exposed to that kind of extreme cold would usually lead to a pretty speedy demise. But not in space.

Physics is back to knock another cool potential way to die in space off our list. The rule of thermal conduction states that in order for something to lose heat, there needs to be something else for this heat to be transferred to. On Earth, this 'something else' is usually air. But guess what? There's no air in space. Your body will remain the same temperature it was when you were sucked out of your spaceship, leaving the rest of your crew behind you. Also good news.

So, your blood won't boil, you won't explode, you won't even get cold. How will you die? The answer is actually fairly dull. It turns out that you'll just suffocate very quickly.

One thing that the movies did get right is that 'in space, no one can hear you scream'. You need air to scream and you won't have any – sound needs something to travel through and, as you're aware by now, there is nothing in space. No matter how hard you clench your various sphincters, the vacuum would instantly pull all of the air from your lungs, your bowels, your stomach, your ears, everything, all of it. The pull of the air would be immediate and pretty violent, so when it leaves your intestines, it might be taking some other stuff with it. To be honest though, soiling your Speedos would be the least of your worries. Very shortly after, just ten to fifteen seconds in fact, you'd black out, as there would be no oxygen getting to your brain. And then you would suffocate. Any liquids not enclosed in their own system, such as on your eyes or in your mouth, would boil instantly. And without the protection of our atmosphere, it doesn't matter how much SPF you have on – the UV radiation will give you a pretty horrific sunburn. But hey, you'll be dead, so what do you care?

SPEEDOS IN SPACE

Thing 89:
Biting your nails could lead to an excruciating death

You know when you're suspected of murder and the police do a scraping of all the stuff under your nails to ascertain if there's any incriminating evidence? Well, the victim's skin cells (assuming you're guilty) are not the only thing they'll find under there. Think of where your hands go on any given day: in the bin; on public transport; in the bathroom; on raw meat; on your dog; in the gym; up your nose. The amount of filth your fingers accumulate is stomach turning, and the little bit of space under your nails is the perfect nook for a disgusting cocktale of vomit, diarrhoea, worms and death to breed.

My nan always told me that I'd get intestinal worms if I bit my nails and, as it turns out, this is not entirely an old wives' tale. Under your nails is usually twice as dirty as your actual fingers, and nail biting (or 'onychophagia') is the best way to get those germs, viruses and, indeed, worm eggs inside your body.

To be honest, having a worm in your gut seems like a treat compared to some of the other possible outcomes. Bacterial infections in your mouth, gums and throat are fairly common, as are colds, flus and other viruses. If you have gel nails, ingesting enough over a prolonged period of time can lead to toxic poisoning. Microorganisms like yeast and fungi can take hold around the nail, leading to pretty nasty infections. Teeth are harder than nails, but nails grow faster and the more you nibble, the more you wear your gnashers down. On top of this is the fact that salmonella and E. coli can knock around in the refuge of your nails and would love nothing more than to kill you in an extremely painful, runny manner.

My point is, there is a lot in this world that is just waiting for an opportunity to see you on your way to kicking the bucket. So why, knowing that it's wretched, continue to bite your nails? That is a question I've been asking myself since I was a kid. Yet I still do it. I haven't come down with E. coli yet, and as far as I'm aware, I don't have worms – but I am acutely aware of how utterly disgusting I am.

Clearly, I'm not the only person with this habit. You might not expect it, but it's actually really quite common, especially in teenagers, with around 45 per cent chewing chunks off their hands. It's not as simple as biting your nails to keep them short and groomed in the absence of clippers or scissors, either; there is something rewarding about it. In general, people are most likely to do it when they're bored, stressed, anxious, or working on something challenging, but much less likely when they're happy or in social situations. I know I do it most when I'm anxious, bored, chilling out in front of the TV or performing a menial task that doesn't take up a lot of brain power and where my hands are relatively free – like driving, for example. Sometimes I'll get out of my seat after a long journey and find myself covered in bits of nail and dead skin. It's foul.

It's not new information that, for a lot of people, nail biting reflects a particular emotional state and it's the first thing many people turn to to relieve that state. It has even been classified in severe cases as a symptom of psychological disorders like OCD, where impulse control is a problem. I'm not quite at that level, but still, just being told to stop or using a bitter-tasting deterrent has proven itself time and time again to be ineffective. For many, the root of the problem has to be tackled before you can cease the action. I feel that the same is true for me. The issue I have, though, is that I have no idea what is driving the behaviour.

I find it interesting that putting our fingers to our mouths is something we do so frequently (mostly when eating), that it's almost an automatic action. It's fairly fundamental to keeping ourselves fed, and it doesn't take a genius to see that this movement clearly has its perks. When putting food in your mouth from your hand in order to eat, the food rewards the behaviour and it is reinforced. Clearly it's a little more complicated than that because I tend to engage in nail biting when I'm absent-minded or anxious, but with such a fundamental movement at the heart of it all, it does seem little wonder that so many people fall into the habit.

Thing 90:
Jumping out of a plane
– why wind is a thing[*]

I went skydiving once and it was brilliant, despite going in early January a few miles inland from Southwold beach. It was freezing and the visibility was shocking, but still, the feeling of free-falling is something I'll never forget. Something else I won't forget is the panic that hit me when I realized that I couldn't breathe; it was like sticking your head out of a moving car going 125mph as you feel the air rush past you. From what I understand, most people can breathe fine – after all, you have more air rushing towards your face than in nearly any other circumstance – it's just that, for some reason, it triggered my gag reflex and closed my windpipe. Anyway, I know that technically it wasn't the wind that did this to me – the air was relatively still that day – it was more that I was rushing through it at high speed, which gave the impression of wind. Regardless, it got me thinking about why wind is a thing, so when I got my feet back on solid ground, I went straight on the internet to find out how it comes about.

---

[*] Actual wind. Not flatulence.

Earth is a very lucky hunk of rock; it's just the right distance from the Sun to allow liquid water on its surface, it has just the right mass to allow gravity to keep its atmosphere where it should be and its iron core creates a magnetic field that protects it from the Sun's solar wind, which would otherwise strip it bare and leave it barren. It also rotates on an axis of 23.5 degrees, which provides us with seasons and gives our weather system something of a kick.

If you've ever been outside, I'm willing to bet my mortgage that you've experienced wind (if you haven't, it's like when you blow, but on a much bigger scale and sometimes it can even knock your hat off). But have you thought about how that wind got there? There must be something that makes it happen. I mean, it's not like there's a giant fan over the Atlantic Ocean, constantly churning out turbulence.

It's actually really simple; as the Sun heats Earth's surface, it also warms the air around it. Warm air is less dense and so it rises, but seeing as the laws of physics don't allow a vacuum to occur under normal circumstances, cooler air rushes in to fill its space. The new air then begins to warm up in the same way its predecessor did and eventually it too will rise. As the hot air travels higher and leaves the warm surface below, it begins to cool, becoming more dense and dropping to fill the spot the cool air left when it travelled to fill the spot the warm air left when it became less dense and ascended in the first place.

It's a bit of a mouthful to explain, and for that reason I don't recommend bringing this fact out at parties. It won't help you make friends; trust me, I've tried.

Thing 91:
Being afraid of the dark
makes sense

A lot of the things with big teeth and claws like to use the cover of darkness to hunt for their prey for the simple reason that they are much less likely to get spotted on approach. We don't have big teeth and claws and it wasn't all that long ago that we were quite a distance from the top of the food chain, so fearing whatever noise you heard in the pitch of night was a good thing. It keeps us alert and is usually associated with behaviours that are more to do with survival when being hunted, such as hiding or running. Now, of course, we live in houses with walls that have greatly reduced the chances of a wolf eating you while you sleep (plus we've killed all the dire wolves because we don't like things that want to eat us), but we have maintained our fear of the dark. Although you probably won't get devoured anymore, our fear of the dark is still a good thing and you should probably listen to it when your mates try to get you to play silly games once the sun has gone down.

It makes sense to me that if you can't see where you're going it's best to exercise caution. The number of times I've whacked my shin when clambering in or out of my bed in the dead of night for the wee that I just couldn't ignore anymore is evidence enough of this. But apparently I'm a slow learner.

At the age of thirteen or so, I was a scout. Not a particularly good one; I didn't do many activities to earn badges and I spent most of my time shoving things on the end of sticks and dangling them in the campfire to see how they would burn.

Being a scout, I went camping quite a bit, where I quickly learned that the inside of a tent is uncomfortable, cramped and often damp, while the outside is a death trap. Everything is a tripping hazard; there are sticks and twigs to get your feet caught on, leaves hide dips in the ground and, with guy ropes tied around trees and stuck into the ground with pegs, I can't fathom how the death toll at these things is so low.

It's made much worse when it's a camping trip for scout groups from across the county. Suddenly there are twenty-five groups in one location, with fires and ropes and sticks everywhere. It's a good time to make friends, but sometimes new people, camping and ropes don't mix well. Especially when it's dark.

My scout group decided to challenge our neighbouring groups to a game of fox and hound. I have actually completely forgotten the rules to this game, but it involves a lot of running from people. It seemed like a good idea at the time, despite the fact that it was already pitch black. I was with a boy from my group called Jake, who was the same age as me but was much cooler and a lot bigger. As it turned out, Jake suffered from quite severe asthma, but seeing as I had never really spoken to him before, I was completely unaware of this. Until we both ran into a particularly taught guy rope attached to a tree about six camps over from our own.

Running at full speed, the rope caught me right on the philtrum, between my nose and top lip; it knocked me straight off my feet and onto my head, where there was more tree waiting to greet me. Feeling more than a little discombobulated, I got to my feet to find that Jake had also run into the same rope. Being taller than me, he took the brunt of the impact to his neck, which restricted the airflow down his oesophagus and led to a full-blown asthma attack. His inhaler was back at our camp, which suddenly seemed like a million miles away, but I managed to drag him to his feet and half carry him back, where we got his inhaler and controlled his breathing. We both had pretty nasty rope burn and, Jake's medical emergency notwithstanding, I still maintain that I came off worse. He had a mark on his neck, while I was left with a nasty scab crust where the rest of my friends were starting to grow moustaches.

I also have the scar to prove that you should never willingly blindfold yourself and let your older siblings lead you around the house, because they will definitely direct you into a huge earthen vase that you will definitely headbutt and your eyebrow will definitely have a gap in it for the rest of your life.

If I ever find myself in the darkness now, I do not rush. I don't care if the murderer from *Scream* is behind me, I squat down a little, stick my butt out for balance, extend my arms and pat anything I can find in an attempt to identify and avoid it. I'm not rushing for anyone.

With all that in mind though, there are exceptions to every rule and, if you're brave enough, you probably don't need to see at all. When I was taking part in the London marathon, I had to stop running and start walking after ten miles because my knee stopped working like a knee should. Of course, going slowly meant that a lot of people started to overtake me; at first it was the able-bodied runners, then the fancy-dressers, followed by those in much heavier costumes of horses and rhinos and drag-ons, and, finally, the less able-bodied runners. I was particularly surprised to be overtaken by one man who was blind. I can't even make it from my bedroom to my bathroom without inflict-ing serious damage to myself but this chap chose to run 26.2 miles in complete darkness and breezed past me.

Still, unless you're that guy, if it's dark, slow down.

Thing 92:
Without the Moon, Earth wouldn't be doing so great

The theory goes that, during Earth's infancy, about 4.5 billion years ago, there were many more 'protoplanets' knocking around in the Sun's gravitational pull than the eight still orbiting today. A protoplanet is a big old chunk of rock, dust and gas orbiting a star that is not quite a planet yet, but is more than just the sum of its parts. Anyway, note the use of the term 'knocking around' because evidence suggests that a Mars-sized hunk of rock (a protoplanet known as Theia) had a little bump with baby Earth and made a bit of a mess. By 'little bump', I mean 'planet-destroying catastrophe'.

When Theia's game of 'knock planet run' backfired, it was destroyed while Earth was left intact, if a little bruised. Bits of both planets were ejected into space, where gravity did its thing, making our planet spherical again, and bunching up all the debris into a new celestial blob, known as the Moon.

The jury is still out on whether this was the exact sequence of events or not, but it was a fairly long time ago, so I'm happy to go with the consensus. Either way, our neighbour, 384,400 km away in the sky, has been pretty important to the way life has adapted on our planet, and without it, things would take a turn for the worse.

Of most immediate concern would probably be the fact that we'd get hit by many more meteorites than we'd like. The Moon, you may have noticed, is covered in craters. Granted it doesn't have the wind, water, geological processes or life forms that the Earth does to resurface itself, so any impression left on its exterior will remain until something overwrites it – in fact, Neil Armstrong's footprint is still up there and it will be there until someone with a bigger foot replaces it, or a meteorite smashes it into another planetary pimple. Even with that taken into consideration, size for size, it still gets hit way more frequently than we do because it plays a brilliant game of gravitational defence and has been taking one for the team for billions of years. Yes, it may have let a few whoppers slip through here and there, and yes, the dinosaurs would probably have been a bit miffed that they went extinct because the Moon was napping when they got pummelled, but overall, it does a sterling job at being our space umbrella.

The Sun is obviously much more massive than the Moon,

but it's also much further away and thus, although the Sun does its part, the Moon's gravity plays the lead role when it comes to the oceans' tides. Water is drawn to its pull, so, as the Earth rotates, water shifts on the surface towards the Moon. When the tide is high, you know the Moon is overhead, when it's low, the Moon is over the other side of the planet, dragging the seas with it. Without the Moon, the Sun would be in charge of water and our tides would only be about half as strong as they currently are. Calmer seas don't sound like such a bad thing, but when you consider that currents and flows controlled by tides circulate nutrients and animals across great distances, it wouldn't take that long for wildlife to start to suffer.

Sticking with the theme of tides, before the Moon came along, our planet was rotating much faster than it does today. In fact, it's thought that, rather than the twenty-four-hour day we're used to, a pre-Moon day was only about eight hours long. The Moon provides something of a rotational break, due to a thing called 'tidal friction'. All of the world's water moving backwards, forwards and crashing into itself over the surface of the planet literally slows down the speed at which it spins. Every 100,000 years or so, our days get about two seconds longer, so in 200 million years, one Earth day will be twenty-five hours long.* If the Moon was to disappear, the Earth would speed up and our days would start to get shorter again. Have you ever heard anyone say, 'There're just not enough hours in the day'? Well, there actually wouldn't be enough hours in the day without our friend, the Moon.

Currently, our lovely little world spins on an axis of about 23.5° (an angle which varies between 22.1° to 24.5° every 40,000 years or so) and it's this tilt that provides us with seasons. Once

---

* An interesting and extremely mind-blowing aside is the Three Gorges Dam in China, which holds 42 billion tonnes of water, 175 m above sea level and, according to NASA, has slowed the Earth's rotation by 0.06 milliseconds since it was filled. This happens in the same way an ice skater pulls their arms closer to their body to speed up a spin and pushes them further away to slow down. Having that volume of water so far from the centre of mass slows the planet's rotation.

again, we have the Moon to thank; its gravity acts as a kind of anchor, keeping the imaginary line that runs between our poles relatively stable. Without it, we would be wobbling all over the place whenever another large object came close by. With the effects of massive planets like Jupiter having their wicked way with us, our axial tilt could vary drastically between 0° and 85°.

With an axial tilt of 0°, there would be no seasons because there would be no fluctuation in how much of any part of the world faced the Sun. We would have a permanent hot, dry band around the equator, a freezing cold zone around the poles and a temperate band in between. This is less than ideal and big parts of our planet would be no fun to live in, but we would survive.

It's a very different story for the Earth that's tilted at 85°, though. The equator and the poles would essentially switch; seeing as we would be orbiting at a near right-angle, what are now the North and South Poles would see tropical conditions, while things would be getting mighty chilly around the middle. Our day–night cycle would be the equivalent of the seasonal cycle, with one side of the Earth facing the Sun continuously for summer and then being plunged into total darkness through-out all of winter. As you can imagine, the temperature would be fairly extreme, as one side freezes in a night-time that lasts six months, while the other cooks during an equally long day.

Having no seasons at all is bad enough. Having seasons as extreme as those we would see with an 85° tilt is worse, but fluctuating between the two due to being pulled hither and thither by all of the celestial objects with gravity strong enough to affect us would really suck.

Considering the slightly bumpy start to our relationship, the Moon has proven itself invaluable and so, on behalf of every living thing (except the dinosaurs, who are still miffed about being dead), we thank you.

Thing 93:
Falling into lava would definitely kill you, just not in the way you may think

Have you ever melted a rock? Probably not. In order to heat stone to its melting point, you'd have to exceed temperatures of somewhere between 600°C and 1,300°C (depending on the type of rock), but our planet does it all the time. The enormous heat and pressure under the crust of our globe takes solid rock and turns it to liquid. When it's safely encapsulated below our feet, it's known as magma, but as soon as it breaks the surface, it becomes a massive diva and insists we start calling it 'lava'.

We all know that volcanoes have plenty of destructive power and if liquid rock starts exploding, hurtling or oozing out of the planet and making its way towards you, I hope you're sensible enough to run. If for some reason your instinct is not to escape but to reach for your swimwear, then, I hate to break it to you, but you will die. However, much to the surprise of everyone who came to witness your demise (and I guess, also to you, but you chose to jump in, so we'll stick with the by-standers), probably not in the manner they may have assumed.

Rock is pretty solid; all of our buildings are on top of it, as well as everything else on the surface of the planet and, unlike with water, if you decided to high dive into it, the only thing that would make a splash would be your body as it impacts the surface below. Our bog-standard water has a very similar den-sity to us humans and that's why we have some ability to control whether we sink or float by changing the amount of air in our lungs or moving our bodies. On the other hand, liquid rock, while less dense than its solid counterpart, is still at least three times more dense than you are. Therefore, unless you were coming at it with a decent velocity, you wouldn't break the surface. Instead, you'd linger and burn to death in agony. Not only that, the liquid in your skin would boil as it cooks and the layer of gas that arises would have you skittering across the outer skin of the molten rock.

If you were moving with sufficient speed to submerge yourself, your bones would most likely break under the impact before your body sank. But seeing as you are more buoyant

than lava, your body would try to float again. If you were lucky, you'd come back to the top, where you would burn to death in agony. However, lava is very viscous and it's not easy to move through, so escaping the body of liquid to reach fresh air might be more of a challenge than you'd expect, and the longer you were under, the more you would burn. Your skin would burn off and gases in your body would probably expand very quickly as they heated, causing mini explosions when they broke the surface. That is, unless you were fortunate enough to land in a pocket of superheated gas just under the exterior. In this instance you would sink, but rather than either popping straight back up to the surface or being stuck roughly where you were due to the viscosity of the molten substance, you'd just incinerate your lungs as you tried to breathe.

To be honest, in most instances you would be dead before you even touched the lava; the heat simply radiating from it would be so intense that once again any air that you tried to breathe would scorch your lungs, all the nerve endings in your skin would burn off and you would combust. It's probably best to avoid it.

Thing 94:
Australia is wider than the Moon

It is, however, also full of venomous spiders, lizards, snakes and mammals (the duck-billed platypus is one of the only venomous mammals in existence). Literally everything wants to kill you there; kangaroos will kick you in the face, koala bears carry chlamydia and if you get a flat tyre in the outback, you'll almost definitely die of thirst (or get the juices sucked out of you by a huntsman spider). I fancy my chances on the Moon.

Thing 95:
Spiders are gross and I hate them with a fiery passion

I don't like to admit it, but I truly detest spiders. I don't want to be just another statistic, just another person who has fallen victim to the most clichéd fear out there, so I've told myself for a long time that it's not arachnophobia, that I'm just not a big fan of them, but I think that it's time to confess that I might have a problem.

On occasion, I can muster some inner strength and deal with them, but it takes a lot of mustering and my inner strength feels much more like outer bullshit than inner strength. Also, this 'strength' only emerges when it's me, the spider and a third party. If no one else is present to judge me, I'll happily lose my shit and run out of the room, but I don't like to demonstrate my cowardice to others, so if anyone else is around, I'll take a deep breath and assess the situation with as much objectivity as I can pull out of my panic-stricken head.

Often this leads to trapping the creeps under pint glasses, and once they're secure in their transparent prisons, I'm tempted to face my fears and take a closer look. This is invariably a huge mistake. Have you ever seen a spider's face? It's like looking Beelzebub right in the eyes.

For me, size is the main factor in eliciting terror; the bigger the arachnid, the damper my cold sweat. Money spiders and things smaller than my thumbnail are no big deal. I wouldn't pick them up but I'm quite content to let them be, and as long as it doesn't bother me, I won't freak out and squash it with a magazine.

This brings me on to the story of how I met the biggest spider I have ever seen that wasn't safely on the inside of a glass tank. This one was in my fridge. The place I keep all the food that I want to eat. It probably touched everything. Anyway, there I was, going to my fridge to get a little snack, when I noticed something move on the bottom shelf as I opened the door. It's important to point out that, although this was the bottom shelf of my fridge, the fridge is very tall and the freezer section lives below it. At first, I thought it was a berry rolling to the back or something, so I lifted the vegetable drawer out of the way to find not a berry, but the hairiest, thick-legiest, most terrifying arachnid of all time.

At this point, had I been a little less petrified, I would have shut the fridge door again, forgotten about my snack (I would never be hungry again after seeing that anyway) and refused to open it for as long as I lived, but that's not what happened. Upon seeing the huge spider, I pulled in a sharp intake of breath, and then I froze. Seizing its opportunity, the spider charged me, only to fall from the fridge onto my tiled floor. It was such a weighty bastard that, when it hit the ground, it landed with an audible thud.

Now I had a real problem; at least when it was in the fridge it had limited stomping ground and I had the option of closing the door and living on takeaway for the foreseeable future, but with it being on the ground it could scuttle anywhere. It could go under the oven, where it would stay, sucking the juice out of unsuspecting insects, growing larger and larger until it was big enough to kill my dog; maybe up my leg, where it would climb under my T-shirt and further up until it ended up on my face and burrowed into my nostril; or off into the distance, where it would wait for me to fall asleep before making its way across my pillow and into my mouth. I was entirely convinced that all of these alternatives were 100 per cent going to happen, but none of them was acceptable to me, so I grabbed a pint glass from the side and prepared myself for a fight that I was sure I was going to lose.

Luckily for me, the fall must have knocked some sense out if it because the spider just sat there, dazed. My dog, hearing it hit the ground moments earlier and thinking it must be food, came trotting over to eat whatever I had dropped. Upon realizing that it was most definitely not food, she thought, *Hell, no; you're on your own, human; good luck,* and quickly went off in the direction she had just come from. I braced myself and placed the glass (which was only just big enough) over the bug and stopped to have a think.

I don't enjoy killing things, even if they are the spawn of Satan, and at this point I would usually get a piece of paper, slide it under the pint glass and transport the spider to the garden, where I would wash my hands of it and let nature do its thing. In this instance though, that wasn't going to cut it. I had a few concerns: what if, when I put the paper under the glass and picked it up, the arthropod was so heavy that it made a dent in the paper that then left an opening between the glass and paper that it would take advantage of and run up my arm and onto my face? What if it could bite through a sheet of paper and into my skin? What if it remembered me and would seek revenge?

The only option I could think of was to kill it. I could have stood on it, but I wasn't wearing any shoes and I certainly didn't want spider gunk on my bare feet, so I scanned the kitchen until I spotted one of those disposable tinfoil trays that you cook food in. I picked it up, lifted the pint glass and smacked the tray onto the spider. It dented where the bug had just been, but I figured that was that. Until the tray started moving. The spider had clearly refused to die and instead had decided to take a stroll with a kitchen tray on its back. That's when, horrified, I stamped on the tray repeatedly. That did the trick.

I wouldn't argue with you if you said I was overreacting a teensy bit. At six foot three inches, I'm a pretty big guy, and although the spider was very large, it was nowhere near as big, strong, fast or smart as I am. So, where did this irrational feeling come from?

In truth, nobody is really sure, so they assume one of two things:

- You can learn arachnophobia from witnessing other individuals have a meltdown around a spider
- It's in some people's genes and gets passed down the generations

I don't buy either of these explanations; I don't recall anybody close to me having such a disdain for spiders that their reaction rubbed off on me. Plus, my issue with them has been a slow, gradual unease that has built up as I've got older. It's not like I saw my mother get eaten by a huntsman and have been scared ever since.

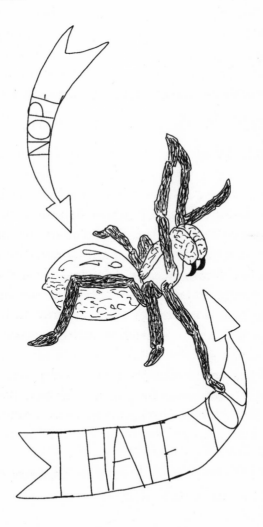

A genetic element does make sense at face value, if you consider that some spiders are venomous and those humans that were creeped out avoided them more efficiently and therefore lived to fight another day. But then you have to consider that the majority of spiders don't pose much threat to humans, but pretty much every crocodile could tear you apart, so if the genetic theory holds true, why are we not scared of everything with teeth or a sting?

The jury is out as to why I hate spiders, but the truth remains that I really do hate them.

Thing 96:
When the zombies come, the odds don't look good for humanity's survival

In *The Walking Dead* (which is my favourite TV show), zombies outnumber humans by a long way. But surely that wouldn't be the case in real life, surely we could fight them off and regain control as the dominant species, surely we're resilient enough to stamp out the undead. Nope. When that specific shit hits the fan, humanity is done for. It's simple maths.

There's a branch of science called epidemiology which studies the spread of viruses and uses statistical models to measure how long it could take for a certain bug to reach epidemic or even pandemic proportions. In most of these models, the basic factors to be accounted for are:

- The number of susceptible human beings likely to contract the illness if they encountered it
- Those that are infected

- Those that are removed from the model (either because they got it and died, or got it, survived and are now immune so won't pass it on)

However, with zombies, there are a few key differences that ruin everything:

- To my limited knowledge of the undead, nobody is immune; the virus is passed on 100 per cent of the time, if a bite occurs
- Humans will fight back, reducing the number of zombies (usually we don't kill people suffering from a virus)
- And the biggie: the *removed* category must be split into two – *undead* and *actually, properly dead*. The thing with zombies is they don't tend to die unless you smash their brains in, so people that would usually be removed from the equation are very much still a threat

Everyone likes to think that they would be brilliant in a zombie apocalypse: great at hiding and an expert at taking names with headshots and baseball bats, but the reality is that when an outbreak starts, the odds are that healthy humans won't even know what they are dealing with and will try to avoid killing the zombies, thinking they are just unwell. We will quarantine them first, but of course that will do nothing and they'll keep biting the people looking after them. Depending on how long the virus takes to turn a healthy person into a flesh-eating, dead-eyed, virus-spreading corpse, the newly infected people could be at home with their family when they get the munchies.

When we do eventually start firing our weapons, we will probably be unlikely to aim for the head to start with because, for the most, people trained with firearms aim for the body, as it's a bigger target. All of this means that, according to the maths, only one zombie could wipe out an entire city in less than a few days. As the number of humans drops, the number of infected rises and, unless someone nukes that city at this point, the future is looking very bleak indeed for *Homo sapiens sapiens*. Of course, you have to consider those that may not be aware that they are infected getting in their cars or on planes and spreading the virus across the country or the world.

Statistical models from some physics students at the University of Leicester show that if we weren't all that adaptive and didn't learn fast how to survive or run, there would be only 300 of us left after 100 days, but even if we were pretty adept at eliminating the undead, unless we did it pronto (and I'm talking killing-your-own-mother-because-she-looked-at-you-funny pronto), the outlook wouldn't look a great deal better.

When it comes to *The Walking Dead*, there's another variable at play which really screws the pooch. Everybody is infected. Being bitten by a zombie speeds up the process, but you're going to turn regardless. Even if you die of natural causes at the age of 102, you would still turn into a walker when your heart stopped. In this scenario, the number of zombies grows exponentially as we turn (or die) at the same rate and, just three days after the initial bite, there will be the same number of zombies as there are humans. According to the maths, being a living, breathing person is not a good thing when there are zombies on the loose. Unless we act aggressively and act quickly from the first instance, we're all doomed.

Thing 97:
Death by erection is another reason to hate spiders

Remember me telling you how much I hate spiders? Well, they suck, and as if they weren't already despicable enough, there's a wretched arachnid known as the Brazilian wandering spider which is not only the third most venomous in the world, it also causes a condition called priapism. Priapism only affects males, because only males have penises. If, somehow, you end up with an erection that doesn't deflate after the four-hour mark, you, my friend, have priapism.

It doesn't sound all that bad, right? A little inconvenient maybe and pretty uncomfortable to keep a stiffy tucked into your waistband for all that time, but worse things could happen, surely? Nope. If you have priapism (whether you've been bitten by the spider from Hades or not), get yourself to the hospital immediately, unless you want your willy to drop off.

A normal erection occurs when the arteries to the penis relax, allowing more blood to flow in, while the veins restrict to prevent it from escaping again. As the blood pressure increases, two cylindrical chambers full of blood vessels, called the corpora cavernosa, inflate like a couple of balloons and you're ready for action. When you've finished with it, blood flow slows again, the arteries close up and the veins remove the excess blood, leaving it small and disappointing, once again.

It's important to keep the blood moving in and out because the longer it stays stagnant in your member, the less oxygen it carries. Your cells need a constant supply of oxygen to function and without it they start to die. With deoxygenated blood lingering in the same area for so long, the penis can be left with permanent erectile dysfunction, disfigurement or even gangrene, when it will rot and fall off. On behalf of the segment of the population to carry a penis, I can tell you that none of these things is ideal.

Now, when the wandering spider (also known as the banana spider, because it likes to hang out on fruit, waiting to attack people who fancy a snack) bites, its victims get an unhealthy dose of a neurotoxin that will lead to loss of muscle control and eventual suffocation, as well as intense pain and, of course, the aforementioned big old boner. Fortunately, we have an anti-venom that is readily available in the areas these bastards frequent, so deaths are rare despite their aggression. They're bloody huge though and you could really do without hanging around with one, regardless of whether it's going to bite you or not.

If you are bitten by the wandering spider, or you happen to suffer from priapism via some other means, once you see the doctor they will most likely suggest you take a cold shower. If that doesn't work, you'll be given some medication. If neither of these work, you're going to have to endure a prick in your prick as the doctor sticks a needle in to manually remove the excess blood, which incidentally will be about as thick as tomato ketchup due to the lack of oxygen. This can take a little while and may require the needle to be inserted many times if the blood is particularly clotted. Sometimes sterile water will actually have to be injected in to irrigate the shaft and flush the viscous blood free before being sucked back out again.

Of course, this only solves the effect of the erection, not the cause, and if your body isn't done with the erection yet, once the blood has been removed, more can flood in, filling it right back up again. At this point, it's time to put down the needle and pick up the scalpel, and guess where that goes? Yep, in the head of your penis. The scalpel goes in, is twisted 90° and leaves a wound big enough to allow the blood to escape the winkle quicker than it can fill up. Quite frankly, if you still have an erection after a cold shower, medicine, multiple needles and a scalpel, you deserve a very phallic medal. Just writing this is enough to make me squirm and cross my legs.

Thing 98:
You can drink most venoms without feeling even a little under the weather

Poisons and venoms are very different things. They both suck and are desperate to kill you, but in different ways. Some creatures are poisonous, some are venomous (a few are both). Poisons must enter the body via coming in contact with the skin, being ingested or being inhaled. Once inside you from one of these methods, the poison will work all manner of mischief and, if the dose is right, kill you in a variety of excruciating, hallucinatory, haemorrhage-y ways. If it somehow gets inside your body under different circumstances though, you'll be fit as a fiddle.

The distinction is that venom, on the other hand, requires injection into your bloodstream, usually via a bite or a sting. Ingesting it, in most cases, will not do you any damage. I'm sure you're sensible enough not to go bothering your local black mamba to try this out and I'm also sure you have much better pastimes, but if you do find yourself a little thirsty and surrounded by venomous animals, arachnids, fish and insects, I still wouldn't advise milking them into your mouth (it's also worth noting that if you have even a tiny cut in your mouth, the venom will enter your bloodstream and you will die unless you seek help).

Thing 99:
You won't get sucked out of an aeroplane window, but you will stink after a flight

If you're scared of flying, I'm guessing that it doesn't matter how many times some wise guy tells you that 'it's actually the safest mode of transport on offer'. If being confined in a 450-tonne metal tube at 30,000 feet above sea level for hours on end isn't your thing, I can completely understand that, and although I'm not scared of flying myself, I can totally see why some people are. It's worth considering the pros and cons before setting foot on an aircraft, because if you forgo taking to the sky, you will find that it takes you much, much, much longer to travel long distances, but you'll also almost definitely discover that you'll smell better than the rest of us.

First things first, I want to make you aware that I'm writing this while flying home from South Africa and I'm not sure that overthinking this twelve-hour journey in such a way was the best idea in the world. I am now more acutely aware of the risks and stinks involved with aviation. If you happen to be reading what I am writing while on a plane yourself, it may be a small consolation to know that, yes, flying is indeed the safest way to get around; for every billion consumer miles travelled there will be only 0.07 deaths, while if you decided to go via a motorcycle over the same distance, you could expect to die 212.57 times over (fingers crossed you're not reading this while on two wheels).

Some of the most common fears associated with flying are entirely mythical; for example, you won't get sucked out of a tiny gap in the fuselage if there is a rupture, because aeroplanes are pressurized. There is very little oxygen at the cruising altitude of most jets, so passengers would suffocate pretty rapidly if it weren't for the clever engineers pumping the plane with more air on the inside than there is outside of it. Of course, that means that if the hull is breached, the air is going to rush outside to match the pressure of its surroundings. The dread is that this change in pressure could be so violent that anyone caught between the differing air pressures on their quest for equilibrium would get forced through the same gap the air is escaping through, no matter how small. The truth is that, unless the damage to the plane is pretty catastrophic and results in rapid enough decompression, nobody is getting sucked out of any holes. On the extremely rare occasion that the fuselage is damaged, the pilot will usually drop the plane to a lower altitude, reducing the pressure differential and preventing anyone from suffocating or getting squished through a minuscule crack.

You will also definitely not get sucked down the toilet, even if it does make the most terrifying noise you've ever heard. Unless your rump is the exact shape of the seat and it forms a perfect seal, you have nothing to worry about. Yes, if your butt does perfectly fill the gap, it is theoretically possibly to get stuck (although not sucked down), but most humans don't share the same circumference or dimensions as a loo seat. Besides, you'd have to be crazy to still be sitting on that toilet when you flush it. I'm usually halfway out of the collapsible door before I press the button. They're loud and scary.

If you're worried that there will be someone on your flight who fancies a bit of fresh air and decides to open the cabin door, exposing everyone to a sudden pressure drop and a mighty chill, don't be. Unless that person happens to be Clark Kent, who felt like slumming it and decided to take a sixteen-hour flight rather than donning his Superman costume and getting to his destination faster than a speeding bullet, it's not going to happen. The same pressurization that keeps passengers breathing while at cruising altitude makes that door impossible to open without invoking the power of Grayskull, and if you're a child of the Eighties you'll know that only He-Man has that power (for those of you that aren't children of the Eighties, He-Man was a cartoon superhero who could summon the power of Grayskull by simply yelling 'I HAVE THE POWER' while lofting his sword above his blond man-bob, allowing him to defeat his nemesis, the evil Skeletor). Prerequisites to summoning the power of Grayskull are that:

1   You must be Adam (no surname, as far as I'm aware), Prince of Eternia and defender of the secrets of Castle Grayskull

2   You need the special sword

Without a surname, he'll be lucky to get a passport, regardless of his royal connections, and there is no way he'd be getting a magical sword through security in his hand luggage. Therefore, you have nothing to worry about.

Your main concern should be germs and viruses. You'd think that, with a bunch of breathing, sweating, sneezing, sometimes oozing people in such a confined space, the air on a plane would be saturated with all sorts of putrid evil, but it's actually much cleaner than most other indoor public places. Filters remove up to 99.9 per cent of microbes and there is a total changeover of air every few minutes or so. But it's very dry up in the sky and humidity is often around 12 per cent, which is more parched than most deserts. As a result, it's very dehydrating and the mucus barriers in your nose that keep nasty things out don't do their job at all well, leaving you much more vulnerable to catching whatever is around. Plus, filters will remove a lot of the airborne scum, but humans are gross and they touch everything. Arm rests, toilet door handles, the little screen things, the luggage compartments, other humans. If you don't take alcohol gel to disinfect your hands after touching everything, it's very likely that you'll reach your destination with the black plague.

Now, we move on to the stench. I am writing this in the knowledge that (even though I can't smell it now due to the fact that your sense of smell is dulled at altitude), when I land after my twelve-hour stint of soaking it all up, there will be a layer of stink on me that is not easy to shift. It's a pretty hefty cocktail of all the food and drink on board, people's faecal matter and flatulence, as well as all of the years of general torpid pong that has settled into the leather seats and the carpeted floor. Then there's the dehydrated breath of your fellow passengers, your own breath, everybody's sweat, their attempts to cover their sweat with perfume or deodorant, and fumes from other planes when waiting in line for take-off or coming in to land.

It all combines to form a stagnant whiff that penetrates your clothes, sits on your skin and lives in your hair. It's grim and I'm very upset that I have to sit through the remainder of this flight before landing, going through passport control, collecting my luggage, getting into a car and going home, where I can wash it off. It's ruined my holiday, to be honest.

Thing 100:
Sawney Bean and his family ate lots and lots of people

People shouldn't eat other people. It's kind of an unwritten rule. Weirdly, in many countries it's not an actual written rule, although both murder and defiling a corpse are, so you might find yourself in something of a catch-22 situation if you were thinking about eating a person (unless you just carve little bits off a living human and they choose not to press charges for the harm you cause them).

In the fifteenth century, an incestuous Scottish family of forty-eight members (wow), headed by one Sawney Bean, preyed upon travellers and gobbled them up. Records indicate that they may have devoured up to 1,000 fellow humans. The Beans were found in a cave, surrounded by bits of body and loot taken from the dead, and were captured. As punishment, the men were burnt alive while the women bled to death from having their hands and feet cut off.

When I asked my followers what they were afraid of, not one of them said 'incestuous Scottish cannibal family', but maybe they should have.*

---

* While writing this book I learned that this isn't real. It's a mixture of various different folk tales and some true stories. I wish someone had told me this when I was a kid; it would have saved all sorts of bad dreams.

Thing 101:
It's best not to eat yourself,
if you can avoid it

Here's the scenario: you're stranded in the desert but miraculously have found yourself in an oasis with fresh water and some palm trees to provide shade. Water and sun exposure aren't a problem, but unfortunately the palm trees are barren and provide no coconuts. You're very hungry. You're actually starving to death. Help is on the way but it's going to take a few days to get to you. Then a thought crosses your mind and you contemplate eating your own arm as sustenance.

You're an idiot and you're definitely going to die, but you do get brownie points for thinking outside the box. In a way, it kind of makes sense for you to consider it (even before delirium kicks in) – you get to take in the calories that an arm provides while having fewer body parts that require calories to function. That said, in reality, if you were already on death's door, adding blood loss and infection isn't going to do you any favours.

But you're a wise guy – before you found yourself in the desert you were a surgeon, and you know how to amputate a limb without risk of infection and with minimal blood loss. Well, it turns out that you're still an idiot and, as a surgeon, you should know better. Your body is actually more efficient at using its energy reserves from the fat stored in it than generating new energy via digestion. In fact, people who lose limbs under more 'normal' circumstances where food is not an issue will probably find themselves eating a little more so their body can repair itself, as well as doing all the normal jobs a body does.

The average human, if kept hydrated, can survive between thirty and forty days without food, and by eating your own arm, you're only reducing the days you have left. It's better for you to let it wither and die during the process of starvation and wait it out. Basically, if you decided to self-nibble, you'd be an arm short, in a lot of pain, you'd still be really hungry and you'd almost certainly die before help reached you.

ANNOYANCES AND GRIEVANCES

People can be irritating, life can be annoying, but it's important to keep your chin up. Even if your chin happens to be much closer to faecal matter than you'd prefer. I like to think the first story makes this clear.

Thing 102:
Other people's poo can really put life into perspective

I live on a quiet little street in London and recently discovered that my tiny garden sits a bit lower than my neighbours' when all their faeces filled it up and lapped at the threshold of my back door.

My garden is no stranger to poo; after all, it's my dog's toilet. She frequents it multiple times a day, but she is about the size of a fat squirrel and her plops are miniature and adorable. An accumulation of an entire street's worth of human waste does pose a slightly more challenging conundrum. And a conundrum it was. My wife, myself and my dog arrived home from a few days away to find that our little suntrap had been transformed into the stinkiest swimming pool imaginable. When the plumbers arrived, they got their galoshes on, their rods out and had a good old slosh around. After four hours they were no closer to discovering the origin of the problem than when they started. The best they could do was to pump it all out (through my house and out the front door).

Of course, without discovering the route of the issue, the

problem persisted and our garden required pumping twice daily. Interestingly, I could tell when my neighbours were at home or not via the volume of sewage that made its way out of my manhole. The plumber would return once in the morning and again in the evening, when he would suck out what was there and try to establish a cause. This went on for five days and, although the pong permeated my house and I had to give my dog to a friend to avoid her getting sick and so she had somewhere to do her business without risk of drowning in faecal matter, the circumstances did provide me with some perspective. The reason I was away and missed the initial up-fill of my garden was because I was at my stepfather's funeral. Arriving home to any quantity of poo after that seemed inconsequential. Not because I was too distraught with grief to pay it any mind, but because it was simply no big deal. It wasn't going to kill me, I would get it fixed and worse things happen all the time. It was merely an inconvenience that came with the upside of the necessity to eat out every night due to the fact that my garden attaches to my kitchen and the stench was not conducive to an appetite. The situation was also a great icebreaker that allowed me to bond with some neighbours that I hadn't even spoken to since moving in.

As it happened, after talking to John from number one, the plumber had a look down his manhole and discovered the source of the block and fixed it within a few minutes. It's hard not to be friends with someone when the first conversation you have with them is about what comes out of their bottom. Obviously, nobody wishes for a garden full of poo, but shit happens and you can't let it get you down.

Thing 103:
Water freezes at zero, OK,
America?

America does a lot of things better than us Brits: their parking spaces are angled so they are easier to get into, they top-up your drink for free at dinner and their Netflix selection is far superior. But I cannot get my head around the way they measure stuff, particularly temperature.

Since learning it in school, I've known that water freezes at 0°C and boils at 100°C. These are easy figures to remember and mean that I know how warm it'll be just by looking at a number. No mental maths required. Freezing is too cold, boiling is too hot, 50°C is smack bang in the middle and somewhere around 18–22°C is exactly where I like it. Go across the pond, though, and I can never work it out, and according to my (somewhat limited) pool of American friends, I'm not the only one. They use Fahrenheit rather than Celsius and I've asked a number of Americans to explain to me where their freezing and boiling points are, and they rarely seem to know. I just googled it and found out that, in the United States of America, water freezes at 32°F and it boils at 212°F. Brilliant.

Apparently, the reason to favour Fahrenheit is that it has smaller integers between points, which gives you a more accurate measurement. There is less of a gap between 1°F and 2°F than there is in the Celsius equivalent. But still, it makes the maths of it all very hard and I refuse to even try to understand it, out of principle.

Thing 104:
While your sorting out your units of temperature, have a look at weight, too

I work in kilograms and, in my world, 1,000 kg is equal to a tonne. But in America, pounds are used and a ton is different to a tonne. One ton is 2,000 lbs, or 907.185 kg, whereas one tonne is 2,204.62 lbs, or 1,000 kg. Then, of course, you have the imperial ton, because obviously having two units of measurement with the same name and differing weights is too simple. The imperial ton weighs 2,240 lbs, or 1,016.05 kg. I still don't even know what a pound is.

Thing 105:
Trampolines can burn in hell

Trampolines are fun, right?

Sure, if you count getting your leg trapped down the gap between the springs that then pinch the skin of your upper thigh, while your face comes down and strikes the knee of the leg that is still up on the tarpaulin and splits your lip open.

Or if you count misjudging the bounce by a tiny fraction of a second and awkwardly jarring your knee or your spine.

Or if you count trying to do a front flip and landing on your neck.

Or if you count accidentally jumping clean off the bouncy surface and having just enough airtime for your brain to consider how much it's going to hurt when you land but be completely unable to do anything about it.

If you count those things as fun, trampolines are my favourite.

Thing 106:
Hair doesn't dissolve

Dear wife,

Your hair is not special. Like everyone else's hair, it does not dissolve in water. Therefore, I would greatly appreciate it if, every once in a while, you would empty out the sink trap in the shower. As much as I love you, I will not hesitate to file for divorce if I have to plunge my hand into the plughole to extract your grotty, discarded clumps of cold, dank, matted locks, congealed with old conditioner and mildew, one more time.

Love you to the moon and back,
Jim

Thing 107:
You're not 'double-checking', you're just 'checking'

You know when you're in a restaurant and decide to play fast and loose with the menu? When you request to swap the chips for veg and the waiter says, 'I'll just double-check on that for you'? He's not *double*-checking. He's just *checking*. He didn't already check for you. It's a singular check. Unless he has some Professor Charles Xavier-level mind-reading capabilities, knows what you want to eat before you've even looked at the menu, has already asked the chef once if it's possible (if this is the case, he should be working for MI5, not the Horse and Plough) and is going to now check again once you've officially asked him, he'll be checking for the first time. Single. Check.

I know it's not a big deal but it's a stupid turn of phrase that has no place in my life, it's factually incorrect and it stresses me out.

Thing 108:
I know that 8 a.m. is in the morning, you don't have to tell me

This is a completely irrational pet hate and I dislike myself for mentioning it, but, for me, the turn-of-phrase equivalent of scraping fingernails down a blackboard is when someone says a time, followed by one of the qualifiers a.m. or p.m., followed again by another qualifier – 'in the morning' or 'in the evening'. Everyone does it and it makes me unreasonably mad.

By telling me that it's a.m. or p.m., I know if it's in the morning or the evening and you're repeating yourself. Save the brain power, save the oxygen, save our friendship, save our time and just pick one way of informing me about what part of the day you are referring to.

Thing 109:
Never put anything thicker than water down the sink

Liquids that are more viscous than water, or that have a very low boiling point, should never be disposed of down the sink. I'm aware that this leaves you with an odd conundrum: it's too wet to put in the bin, but too thick to pour down the plughole, so where does it go? I've yet to find an adequate solution to this, so my usual plan is to take it into the garden and water the plants with it. Less than ideal, I know. But it always seems to be the best or only option when the situation arises. Every time, I tell myself, 'Jim, you must think of a better resolution for next time,' but as soon as the offending object has been discarded I forget about it and move on with my life.

Examples of these liquids include, but are not limited to: leftover cereal; runny porridge; any type of oil; gel; paste (toothpaste is acceptable, on the condition that you have used it in your mouth and it's combined with sufficient saliva); chunky soup; gravy; fat; and hot candle wax.

I draw particular attention to that latter liquid. Candle wax is solid at room temperature. It's not until it's exposed to heat that its state alters to liquid. So why on earth did my wife think it appropriate to pour hot wax down the sink? Sinks are usually colder than room temperature – her disregard for basic physics dumbfounds me. As soon as it hit the plughole, the wax solidified and blocked the pipe, good and proper.

I learned this lesson while I was still living with my mum. Tan, on the other hand, did not. She had decided that the glass her nice scented candle came in would make a lovely make-up brush holder, so in her infinite wisdom chose to pour the wax away. This was all happening in the bathroom while I was in the bedroom, playing on my Xbox. I thought she'd been gone for a while but figured that she was shaving her legs or something, so I left her to it. Shortly after I had this thought, she came back into the bedroom, looking a little sheepish, and confessed her wicked, candle-wax ways.

Now, my mum is lovely and brilliant, but she's also quite particular; she's not a big fan of mess and, when things don't do what they're supposed to (e.g. when a sink doesn't drain), she has a tendency to overreact. At this point in my life, I had been with Tan for about a year and, although they got along fine, she was still not entirely comfortable around my mum. She was certainly nowhere near ready to handle one of Mum's flared-nostriled, angry-eyed, pointy-fingered, disappointed, 'expected more' tell-offs. They take years of practice and an iron will to withstand, which Tanya was a long way from mastering. Knowing this, I became acutely aware that I was at risk of having to take a side, which was almost more concerning than the solid wax that had ceased to cascade down the sink the way Tan had anticipated. Being in the middle of my mother and the girl I love didn't seem like a pleasant prospect, so I rushed to the bathroom – wire coat-hanger in hand. I deconstructed the hanger and shoved it down the sink in an attempt to dislodge the blockage while running the hot tap to re-melt the wax.

Nothing happened. The water wasn't hot enough. I went down to the kitchen to boil the kettle and, after the third or fourth kettle load, my mum began to get suspicious. Why would a person possibly need to keep going up and down the stairs with boiling water? The game was up. She burst into the bathroom and had a meltdown, telling me (in her calm voice, which is even more scary than her shouty voice) to call an emergency plumber. Bearing in mind it was 10 p.m. and I didn't have any money, I told her that I would sort it.

Two hours, four gallons of boiling water, three wire coat-hangers and all the cleaning products I could muster later, the pipe was still blocked.

Before retiring to bed, deflated and defeated, I decided to have one last stab and went for it with new-found gusto and palpable desperation. I think some divine entity must have taken pity on me because all of a sudden the cocktail of water and various cleaning fluids that were filling the basin began to drain through.

I rushed into the bedroom to tell Tan about my great victory and to reassure her of the condition of our drainage system, but she was already fast asleep. Cheers, Tan.

As it turns out, this problem is not just restricted to my wife, nor to my mother's house. In 2015, sewage workers had to remove a ten-tonne 'fatberg' from deep beneath London. As I'm sure you can picture, a fatberg is the grease, faeces and sanitary waste equivalent of its iceberg cousins, only I imagine fatbergs smell about 780,000 times worse and you probably won't find any sea lions basking on them. This hunk of congealed lard had collected over the course of years, combining from all the lumpy filth that Londoners had been sloshing down their

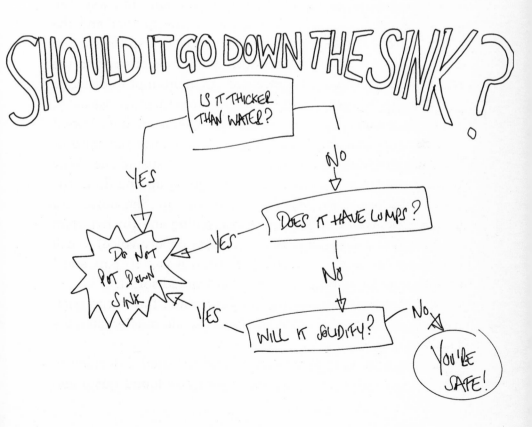

drains. It was so engorged that it ended up at forty metres long and took workers ten days to break up and move down the line.

From this day on, I want you to remember this rule: nothing thicker than water goes down the sink.

Thing 110:
Smell it before you eat it

Sometimes food looks like one thing but tastes like something else. Case in point: I once ate a little bit of potpourri thinking it was a sweet. If you've never tried potpourri, don't – it tastes like soap. If you've never tried soap and so can't empathize, don't – it's not worth it.

To be fair, I was a plonker; it was dark and I was hungry and I didn't have the sense to check what was going in my mouth. But one thing you'd think would always be reliable would be the macaroon. Not so. In fact, they're reliability has been seriously called into question by some maniac who decided to make a savoury version. I believe they're still in circulation, somewhere in the world, at this very moment, and they are rancid. I was at a swanky event once and little brown macaroons were being handed out from a slate tile carried by a waiter dressed in black tie; I figured, 'Great; brown baked goods are nearly always chocolate flavour; at the very least they'll be caramel or hazelnut.' These ones were duck liver. Usually I'm pretty decent at controlling my face and hiding emotions such as disgust in a public environment, but I was so utterly shocked by the meaty treat that my face basically turned inside out and I nearly dribbled the half chewed-up brown gloop down my tuxedo.

If only I had given both of these things a whiff before diving in, gullet first, I would have saved myself a considerable amount of displeasure and a couple of horrendous aftertastes. Heed my warning.

Thing 111:
Blisters on your ears are no fun

Have you ever had blisters on your ears? If not, you won't know this, but they really suck. I've always tended to get sunburnt quite quickly so I became wary of the sun from a young age and usually seek the shade on hot days. During the school summer holidays, I would be one of the only kids to apply SPF to avoid the blotchy, red agony that would undoubtedly follow (the only other boy in my friendship group to douse himself was called Craig Widowson; he was very ginger of hair and extremely fair of skin and would burst into flames almost immediately if the Sun decided to poke its head out from behind a cloud).

It is hard to keep track of which bits you've covered and which still need a little TLC though, and who remembers to put sun cream on their ears? I do, now at least. All because of this one occasion: the time they got so burnt that they blistered, then oozed, then scabbed over, then oozed again, then bled a bit (I picked), then dried up, then peeled, then went leathery for a little while. I was skateboarding with my friends on an uncharacteristically hot day in Attleborough (the little town I did half of my growing up in), but before I headed out, my mum did her due diligence and made sure that I had applied my SPF. I assured her that I already had and that I was even wearing a peaked cap to keep the sun off my head and out of my eyes. The trouble with caps such as that one is that your ears don't go inside them; they stick out like protruding flaps on the side of your face, and with no hair to cover them, they just collect the Sun's rays and cook.

The basic mechanism of being burnt by the big ball of burning gas in the sky is that the ultraviolet (UV) radiation actually damages some of the DNA in any skin cells that are exposed and unprotected. Your skin is the biggest organ on your body and it's very important; after all, without it, you'd have nothing to keep your insides inside. So, as a defence mechanism, a dark pigment called melanin is produced to absorb some of the UV radiation and you now officially have a tan. Congratulations. If you let your tan go too far, however, it causes damage to your tissue, so your immune system kicks in and blood rushes to the area to clean up the dead cells before they can become cancerous (cancer occurs when mutated cells multiply out of control and UV radiation is the perfect catalyst to begin this mutation). The extra blood here accounts for why the affected area becomes a telltale shade of red and why it gets so much warmer to the touch than the rest of your skin. In the short-term it's painful, unsightly, it can blister and it peels, which is gross, but the long-term damage can be far worse; premature aging, saggy, leathery, dry, wrinkled skin, pigment issues, and of course cancer, can all occur if you don't protect yourself.

SPF products work by reflecting or scattering the UV rays and/or absorbing them before your skin can. It can save you from an embarrassing sunburn, keep you looking younger for longer and can even save your life. Just don't forget to do your ears.

Thing 112:
Be careful of stray hairs; they may enter your skin and cause all sorts of mischief

It happens to hairdressers all the time: cutting hair can leave strands with a sharp edge that can easily pierce and enter your skin like a splinter. I'm not a hairdresser but I do have a tale to tell about this phenomenon. A tale that has left me vary wary of stray hairs on bare skin. A tale of pain and discomfort and a shrivelled winkle.

Before I tell this story, I just want to point out that I am aware that I've already mentioned my own penis in this book a few times and I nearly didn't include this fable for fear that you'd think me obsessed. I'm not obsessed, but the truth is, a lot of odd (mostly unfortunate) things have happened to my willy and it has a lot of stories to tell. Plus, this is interesting, embarrassing, mysterious and tense: everything a good anecdote needs (also, I promise to express this account exceptionally well and I swear that I won't talk about my genitals anymore after this one. It'll be worth it). Perhaps, once you've read what I have to say, you may even have an idea of how it happened in the first place, because I still have no idea.

I'm a morning showerer; I struggle to start my day without a good, long rinse. Partly because I feel like it's more hygienic to wash off the night's sleep, partly because if I showered before bed I would always hit the hay with wet hair (I usually let it dry naturally), which would result in me having serious bedhead and – according to my mum – getting more colds (more on this later), and partly because I use my morning wash as a chance to think about the day ahead, muse on life and think up brilliant chapters for a book that was a pipe dream until I started writing it. It was during one of these morning showers that I noticed a long hair clinging to my nether region. I didn't think anything of it; it wasn't unusual for me to find long hairs on my body. It still isn't unusual now; after all, I share my bed with my wife, who has long hair. I seriously regret the vigour with which I attempted to remove this hair from my intimate area, though.

I'm sure that everyone has found a long hair clinging to their wet body while in the bath or shower and I'm sure you are aware that they can be tricky to remove; sometimes they get a little stuck by the water or vacuum or static electricity (I don't know, I've never looked into it; perhaps I will and include it a little further along in this book) and you need to use much more force to dislodge them than is required for a dry equivalent. Previous experience had also taught me that the faster you pull the hair away from your body and the quicker you get it under the running water from the shower-head, the less chance it will have to adhere to your fingers and hand while you flail it around like a sodden lunatic, splashing your entire bathroom.

Well, I pulled at this hair relatively sharply and felt the tension run through it as it got caught on something, before I felt the pain and realized that the thing it had got caught on was the underside of my penis. Somehow, in my sleep I presume, this hair had thread itself in and back out of the skin about two thirds of the way up and had managed to tie itself into a loose knot. When I pulled at it, the knot tightened and cut into the skin like cheese wire. It's amazing how such a tiny thing could cause such acute discomfort in such a short amount of time. I was a little panicked, but before I let it get out of hand, I took a deep breath, braced myself and gave an altogether more tentative tug. More pain. It was at this point that I knew I had an issue. I tilted my head down to investigate, but this was before I had laser eye surgery – I couldn't shower in my spectacles and I hadn't put contact lenses in yet and my eyesight was equivalent to an earthworm's. Also, when you have running water landing on your head and you look down, it all goes in your eyes, up your nose and in your mouth, which is exactly what you don't need when your penis is sore and could, for all you know, have fallen off entirely.

I turned off the shower but didn't want to run out of the room to get my glasses or upset the status quo of the situation by leaving the shower to find my contacts, so I crouched down as close as I could get and squinted hard. It was a struggle to make out, but I could assess the damage; there was no blood, thank God, but the hair had been tied into a tight knot that closed around where it had somehow sewn itself through my skin. The areas either side of the hair were a little bulbous, pink and sore. I had a little fiddle to see if I could loosen it at all and quickly discovered that loosening it was not an option at this stage, so I composed myself and decided to trim the hair, in case it got caught on anything and caused me any more misery.

I went to the bedroom to find my glasses and have a closer look, but it's quite hard to see the underside of an unhappy penis, even with corrected vision, without contorting into shapes that a body won't allow. So, I called Tanya, who was overjoyed to get involved once I had confided in her about what had occurred (she loves to be part of things, especially secret things, and this was a secret). She had a good long look that left me feeling very exposed, and attempted a few prods. Upon realizing that she couldn't loosen the hair and that, every time she touched it, I would wince in pain, she suggested I call the doctor. I don't go to the doctor's for much; if I'm bleeding, it'll scab over and stop, eventually. If I'm sick, soon enough there will be nothing left to throw up and the bug will have run its course. If I have a fever, I'll sleep and sweat it out. However, I will rush to see my GP if I have anything wrong with my eyes or my tallywhacker; they are my favourite parts of my body and I refuse to take chances with them.

To get an appointment at that doctor's surgery, you had to call at 8 a.m. and stay on the line until somebody answered and gave you a slot. The only other way to get seen on the same day was with an emergency appointment, but by the time Tan and I had reached the decision to call the doctor, it was 9.45 and the receptionist (who asked me to explain in detail) came to the conclusion that this didn't count as an emergency and that I would have to wait until the next day. I spent the rest of the day uncomfortable and worried about the risks involved with leaving it any longer. I phoned at eight o'clock sharp the following morning, and after an agonizing wait on hold was told that I could go in that afternoon. When the afternoon came, I couldn't wait to flash myself to the doctor. It was looking worse than the day before and more swollen around the hair, kind of like when a tree grows around a fence. I explained the situation and told him that I had no idea how the hair had actually got there but that it seemed to be fairly stuck. He asked me if I had done it to myself as a joke or a dare. I guess he couldn't see any other explanation as to how such a thing could occur. When he asked me this, of course I said, 'No, I did not sew a hair into my own knob as a joke,' but I must admit that, for a second, I did wonder if Tan had done it to me while I slept, as an experiment.

The doctor then proceeded to get out a magnifying glass and a pair of tweezers (not a flattering move) and went to work. I didn't watch what he was doing but it was uncomfortable and took longer than I anticipated. When he was done, he matter-of-factly lifted the hair in front of his face, gave it an inquisitive look, put it down and exited the room. Apparently, that was also my cue to leave, but I was unaware of this and lay there on the bed until he walked back in with a mother, father and small child, who all looked as horrified and shocked as I felt. The doctor said, 'Oh, you can go now.' I didn't reply – I was too crippled with shock – so I simply pulled up my underwear in front of a small child, her parents and a nonchalant doctor, and left. My penis recovered but my dignity has never been the same since.

MYTHS, LIES AND URBAN LEGENDS

Thing 113:
Coffee doesn't sober you up but it does make poop happen

I'm not really a big fan of coffee – it tastes a bit like dirt – but it does wake me up in the morning so I will often have an espresso to kick things off when I'm slow to rise. This early beverage can lead to near-immediate, borderline-emergency bowel movement. And I'm not alone when I say that a skinny cappuccino wakes up more than just my brain; it's a common side effect of drinking the black stuff and, according to a study carried out by some scientists called Brown, Cann and Read in 1990, 29 per cent of coffee drinkers also feel the need to poop shortly after that first sip.* The thing is, nobody is entirely sure why. It's not just the caffeine, because decaf coffee has the same effect and there are many other caffeinated drinks out there that don't send you running to the bathroom.

What we do know is that something in the coffee stimulates bile excretion, which readies the intestines for food. It also encourages the release of stomach acid by bringing a hormone called gastrin into the mix, while rousing contractions in the stomach and further down the digestive tract, including the colon. This is known as the gastrocolic reflex and, although we're not sure how coffee triggers it, we've been drinking it for about a thousand years and it hasn't killed us off yet, so let's not worry too much about the science. Also, one thing's for sure: it can certainly clean you right out.

---

* Seriously. One of the scientists researching whether coffee makes you poop is called Brown.

Thing 114:
Baby pigeons exist

You just don't see them because pigeons are just rock doves who escaped and are extremely secretive with their nests. I've seen pictures of baby pigeons and, believe me, the secrecy's a blessing. Those things are scary-looking.*

---

* And, thinking about it, how many baby birds do you see generally? Ducklings, sure. Cygnets, sometimes. It's not like you see *every* other sort of baby bird apart from this one. But it's only pigeons that have this reputation for being somehow secretive. As if somewhere, just out of sight, there are hundreds of thousands of baby pigeons ready to take over the world.

Thing 115:
The five-second rule is total fiction. Don't eat from the floor

For anybody reading this who has never dropped any food on the floor, the five-second rule states that, whatever it is and wherever it landed (within reason; I certainly wouldn't eat a Tic Tac that landed in a puddle of dog vomit), you have five seconds to pick it up and eat it without any negative consequences. The idea behind this lunacy is that bacteria doesn't have enough time to get onto your morsel and contaminate it, so you are free to ingest it without a care in the world. However, you'll certainly have a few cares when you come down with staphylococcus food poisoning.

It may seem common sense to some people that bacteria can't make a dash for the bagel you just fumbled because bacteria don't have legs and can't get anywhere fast. But they are everywhere, covering nearly all the surfaces on the planet, and although you can't see them, if you drop something, bacteria will likely transfer from the surface of the floor to the surface of your food. However, what you drop and where you drop it does make a difference.

There has been actual research into this by a clever clogs by the name of Robyn C. Miranda, and she found that, typically, the longer food is left, the more bacteria it picks up, but that even after one second, there would likely be enough to give you a nasty case of the runs (and maybe death) if the germs were particularly nasty. It was also found that the spot which you clumsily hold your food over plays a big role; Robyn unleashed four foods (bread, buttered bread, gummy sweets and watermelon) onto four surfaces (carpet, tile, wood and stainless steel) and found that the carpet was actually the slowest at contaminating, while the flat surfaces shared germs much faster. Also, the wetter your snack, the quicker the nasties get onto it, with the watermelon consistently picking up the most.

If I were being responsible, I would say something along the lines of, 'Whatever you drop, wherever you drop it, regardless of how long ago you dropped it, don't eat it. If it's watermelon from a flat surface, definitely don't eat it,' but I like to live life on the edge and if I drop something tasty, nine times out of ten I will still eat it, and I have a little dog running around and making mess. My house probably has more bacteria in it than most, but I'm still around, so screw it – you do you, and adhere to the five-second rule if you like, just don't say I didn't warn you when your tummy explodes.

Thing 116:
Toast falls butter-side down from the height we have breakfast

According to actual scientific studies, the toast falls butter-side down something like 62 per cent of the time, but only if dropped from the height of an averagely high breakfast table. Obviously, your toast is butter-side up on the plate, and with the average amount of force knocking it from the table, it only has time for half a revolution before landing butter-side down. You could always butter both sides, that way you're guaranteed to have at least one side with butter but without hair and dust bunnies.

Thing 117:
You don't see rats milking dogs

I understand why we drink the milk from other animals; it's calorific, easy to come by and provides plenty of nutrients, but that doesn't make me OK with it. Don't misunderstand; I drink milk and eat dairy, but I do find it very odd that we steal it from other mammals. You don't see rats milking dogs, yet we are happy as Larry to go hell for leather on any teat we can get our hands on.

In the case of the cow, milk is used to make a calf grow into a big, strong adult, quick smart. I don't know if you've ever seen a cow, but they don't look a great deal like us humans and they clearly have a different diet and need very different nutrition to develop to independence. I guess, technically (and, to be clear, I'm not saying I think this should happen), if we were going to continue drinking milk into our adulthood, it would make much more sense for that milk to come from a human breast. Yet, for some reason, despite the fact that this variety of the white stuff is much more fitting for our consumption (our babies love it and grow very fast when they drink it), this idea is more repugnant. Regardless of whose milk we choose to drink past the necessary period of infancy, the ability to digest it is a fairly new thing among humans. In fact, only 30 per cent of us can do it properly.

Lactose is the sugar found in milk and it's tough to digest. During infancy, we produce an abundance of the enzyme known as lactase, which breaks it down and allows us to reap all the milky goodness it has to offer. And, for 70 per cent of us, that's where our love affair with milk ends; shortly before we reach double digits in age, we stop making lactase and the ability to digest milk leaves us forever. A life of lactose intolerance beckons. I'm not lactose intolerant myself but, from second-hand experience, I can tell you that it's not pleasant. If you find yourself on the blunt end of it, you have stomach bloating, pain and cramps to look forward to, along with nausea or vomiting and lots of farts, some of which may come loaded with diarrhoea.

We started domesticating animals around 11,000 years ago and, although at that time it's thought that none of us could digest milk, it seemed silly to waste all of that potential food, so we came up with clever little ways to get it into our bodies without the nasty side effects that come with intolerance. We discovered the joys of yoghurt and cheese. Both of these are made by fermenting milk and I imagine that the first time this was done, it was an accident. The question that springs to my mind immediately when pondering the first person that made and ate cheese (and I have given it a lot of thought) is this: why? What drove that individual to put it in his or her mouth? Cheese is made when microorganisms eat the lactose in milk and turn it into lactic acid. Less lactose means less lactose intolerance, but of course this person didn't know that. All they will have known is that the milk smelt off, tasted sour and had separated into lumps floating in a watery liquid (what are known as curds and whey, respectively). Still, something possessed that person to clump all the solids together, discard the liquid (probably) and tuck in. I'm glad that person took one for the team and committed, because I love cheese, but I certainly would not have been the first guy to put a mouldy chunk of smelly milk in my mush.

Anyway, I digress. Cheese and yoghurt reduced the lactose in dairy produce, which allowed people to enjoy it without burping, farting and dribbling its half-digested remnants down their legs, but they still couldn't enjoy a nice chug straight from the teat. That is until someone came along with the random genetic mutation that meant they continued to produce lactase throughout their life. Obviously, this was a real bonus, and this person's genes can now be found in 30 per cent of the population. Interestingly, the highest concentration of people that can digest milk are found in areas where milk is consumed more:

further north. About 90 per cent of those that live in the UK or further north can drink it without a problem, while that number drops dramatically nearer the equator. There are some communities where fewer than one in ten can digest it. It all makes sense when you think about it; milk keeps better in colder climates (and is more enjoyable – who wants a glass of milk on a hot day?) and it also has a lot of vitamin D. Vitamin D is typically produced by the body in response to the sun, and I can tell you that, in the UK, the sun can be a rare commodity. We'll take our vitamin D where we can find it.

I find it so satisfying when questions like, 'Why did we start drinking milk?' and, 'How come some people can't drink it?' and, 'Why are the majority of those people located in an area where it is drunk less?' have such a well-rounded, simple answer. Still, it doesn't explain why someone ate cheese for the first time.

Back to the original point: milking other animals is weird, milking humans is weirder, and it took a chance mutation to allow us to digest either kind into adulthood. And eating cheese is the weirdest.

Thing 118:
Going out with wet hair

Having damp hair when outside means your head will feel cold, but sorry, mums of the world, it doesn't increase your chances of catching a cold, however much you say it. Colds are viruses and they don't care what state of dampness your hair is in. Being cold and catching a cold are very different things. Of course, letting yourself get too cold can add stress to the body which can have negative effects on your immune system, making you easy pickings for the cold virus. But there are much quicker ways to get chilly than damp hair, so pick your battles, mums.

Thing 119:
It's bad luck to not look someone in the eyes when you say 'cheers'

When you think about it, banging drinks together is an odd thing to do, but then handshakes are an odd way of saying hello. Why not touch elbows, or blink twice, or just give a thumbs up?

Let's consider, for a moment, that you decided to use one of these methods of greeting, and let's also consider that the person you were greeting was concealing a dagger. Touching elbows, blinking or giving them an enthusiastic thumb would leave you none the wiser and you'd probably end up getting stabbed in the brain. Essentially, a handshake is a friendly and welcoming way of saying, 'Hi, I don't trust you and I'm concerned that you're trying to kill me, but I'm lonely and want a friend, so, by grabbing your hand, I am making sure that you're not clasping anything that could kill me, and, by shaking it, I aim to dislodge anything that may be up your sleeve. I also hope that you're not left-handed.' I like this theory because it adds a little mystery and suspense to a common gesture that we still use today. I like to believe it's much less likely that anyone I shake hands with will be waiting for a chance to murder me, but you never know.

Some people think the reason we 'cheers' stems from a 'trust no one' train of thought; by bashing cups, we slosh some of our drink in each other's cup and prove we're not poisoning anyone.

Thing 120:
Do carrots help you see in the dark?

The answer here is 'sort of'. Carrots are full of vitamin A and this is good for your eye health generally – a deficiency of vitamin A is certainly bad for your vision. Therefore, if carrots were your only source of vitamin A and you chose not to eat them, your eyes would likely suffer, but eating them won't improve your eyesight, just keep your peepers in optimum condition. Interestingly, it's thought this rumour began during the Second World War; to stop the Germans realizing we had a specific technology that let us target their bombers during the night, we put about the rumour that we could see in the dark because we ate lots of carrots.

Thing 121:
Banana-flavoured things taste like a species of near-extinct bananas

One of my wife's favourite morsels from any pick 'n' mix selection is the humble foam banana (and the fried egg, the little shrimp things, the occasional cherry and the candy letters), but I hate them because they don't taste like banana.* Only, they do.

Up until the 1950s, the world's most popular fruit was called the Gros Michel Banana ('Big Mike' to its mates, the apple and

---

* An interesting aside: human beings share half their DNA with bananas.

the apricot).* It was a little larger and sweeter than today's choice, the Cavendish, and it tasted much more like the banana-flavoured food stuffs that we are still familiar with in our sweets, our synthetic milkshakes and our ice cream.

Most of the bananas that were exported were grown in Central America, until poor old Big Mike suffered from a nasty case of Panama disease, a fungus that destroyed vast swathes of the crop and left inadequate supplies to feed the masses. In fact, it nearly went extinct in this region of the world, save for a few plantations that were lucky enough to exist on non-infected land.

The Gros Michel's downfall was its lack of seed; you may have noticed that, when you eat most fruits, there are little pips, bigger stones or tiny seeds within them. As we've discussed, typically, an animal will eat the fruit, go for a wander and poop the seeds out in a different part of the land, where, if the conditions are right, a new fruit-bearing plant will grow. This kind of plant reproduction ensures genetic diversity, as evolved characteristics (such as resilience to certain fungal diseases) are passed on and mutations allow new characteristics to appear.

There are hundreds of different kinds of banana in the world and the majority of them have seeds within them, but apparently they're a little too bitty for us fussy humans, so we selectively bred them out. Those little tiny brown specks in the centre of your Cavendish – they're the remnants of what used to be seeds. The trouble with having smooth fruit with no lumps is that, in order to grow more of them, you must remove part of the mother plant's stem and re-embed it, making all of the bananas from every plant after this initial generation genetically identical. Having sterile clones makes for tasty, seedless fruit, but it isn't good when a pesky fungus comes a-knocking,

---

* The kiwi uses the literal translation of 'Fat Michael', as it's always been jealous of Mikey B's popularity.

because if the mother plant is susceptible to the disease, so is every single other one. Such was the plight of the Gros Michel.

Very quickly, the entire banana trade system had to be restructured around the Cavendish, which was immune to Panama disease. However, we clearly didn't learn our lesson because we are still using the same method of reproduction, and while our bananas haven't been developing new defences from fungi, the fungi have been working on a way to get to the Cavendish. Now there is a new kid on the block that can infect the fruit and has started picking off crops. Luckily, we know more now about fungi, genetics and pathogens than we did when the Gros Michel took a turn for the worse, and some scientists are even genetically engineering Cavendish bananas with immunity to Panama disease. We were also quicker to react this time and managed to isolate the affected areas before too much damage was caused. Or so we thought. As it turns out, even with all of our knowhow, we're still a bunch of idiots, and the Cavendish is on the decline. This new strain of the disease has made its way from Australia to Africa via South-East Asia, and seeing as it lives in the soil, it is very hard to destroy. It can lie dormant for years, so even if you burn the infected crop to the ground and start again, it will be lying in wait.

I suggest that, if you are a fan of the Cavendish banana, you make the most of them, because before long we may be forced to turn to yet another variety. Unless we can get very clever, very quickly (or if we hadn't been so clever in the first place and just accepted that fruits have seeds in them and dealt with it), it looks like we might once again be saying goodbye to the world's most popular fruit.

Thing 122:
Everybody likes the colour blue

There's a huge conversation around making toys for girls pink and toys for boys blue. The interesting thing here is that studies have shown that, before a certain age, all children prefer blue. Past a certain point, there is a tendency for girls to score pink highly, but that's almost certainly because there's so much out there in society saying they should.

Thing 123:
But is your colour blue the same as my colour blue?

What if I saw a different colour to you? I'd have grown up seeing that colour, with people pointing at it, telling me it was called blue. Things with blue in them would look a bit different to me, but consistently so. How do we know that's not the case? I'd love to be able to give you a definitive answer to this, but the simple truth is that we have no way of knowing how another person perceives colour. My blue might be your red. When we both look at the same blue sky, you could be witnessing what I would call red, but because we both label the colour 'blue', we will never know if our experiences are different.* And it's at

---

* Not to mention the fact that the words you use for colour actually do have an impact on your ability to see colour. In Russian, there is no such thing as 'light blue' and 'dark blue' – they are separate colours.

right about this point that my head can't cope with how unique the human condition is.

Thing 124:
Is there such a thing as a
good egg?

You know when you hear people say, 'He's a good egg,' when talking about someone? Well, thank goodness that person being talked about isn't an actual egg, because they would sink and drown, if submerged. I don't know about you, but I do find it tricky to keep track of my eggs – you may have had some from a previous visit to the supermarket that didn't get eaten, but now you've gone and bought some more and somewhere along the line they've been mixed up, so you're not sure which are which and how old each egg is. In this instance, the old saying 'eggs is eggs' is completely wrong, and could potentially lead to a very runny tummy. Eating an off egg is not a pleasant experience and, although you will probably realize your mistake before too much damage is done (due to the terrible taste and smell), it's one that can linger in your stomach and bowels for longer than you'd like.

Fortunately, the way to establish an egg's worth is simple: place your chosen one in a bowl of cold water. Good eggs will sink, while horrible bastard eggs that would ruin your day four hours or so after eating them will float to the top.

The shell and membrane of eggs are slightly porous, allowing air to seep in over time, which creates extra buoyancy in bad eggs. Fresher eggs haven't had the chance to collect this extra gas and so they head to the bottom. This makes perfect sense, but I still get confused and have to google it. When I think of good eggs vs bad eggs, I think of winners and losers. For me, winners should be at the top and losers at the bottom, but with eggs, that's not the case. When in doubt, just remember that good eggs do the opposite of what Jim thinks.

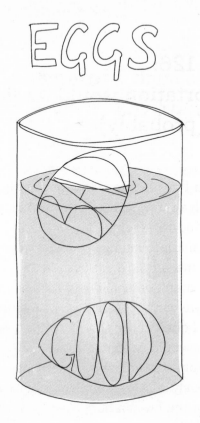

Thing 125:
Ebenezer Scrooge was wrong

When he's trying to convince himself there's a rational explanation for him seeing ghosts, Ebenezer Scrooge wonders if it was cheese before bed that did it. And people still wonder if there's a connection. There's absolutely no evidence that this is the case. In fact, cheese contains something called tryptophan, which in some people actually reduces stress and helps stabilize sleep.

Thing 126:
Teleportation would be the death of us (probably)

Sometimes, when I'm stuck in traffic or my flight is delayed, or I'm going through a tunnel on the train and I lose my 4G signal, I long for someone to invent a teleportation device so I can travel to my destination instantaneously. But then I remember that it would kill me, and I reconsider.

Living things aren't data, like a text message, a video file or a phone call, so we can't be sent to new locations in the same way. To send, oh, I don't know, a human to a new destination via teleportation, you would need to disassemble that human while scanning their atomic structure so they can be reformed at the other end. Obviously, disassembling someone atom by atom is less than ideal for the human body, because being torn to base matter will definitely result in death. But don't panic; they'll be brought back to life when they are reassembled at the other end, right? Well, yeah, no, kind of, but not really.

This mass of vaporized human data is sent to the destination and reconstructed into a person that looks and feels and thinks and remembers and senses just like the now-dead person from the previous location. And of course, the resulting human doesn't feel like it has just died because it has been assembled in exactly the same set-up (assuming everything goes according to plan) as before, but the old human is definitely dead and a new one is standing in a new spot.

It's all a bit of a grey area, to be honest, because if the new person thinks they are the old person and so does everyone else, then what does it matter? Well, it matters to me; murder is murder and ripping someone down to particulate matter is certainly murder, despite that matter being reassembled into a mega-clone at a new destination. Still, it'll get you from A to B much faster, and maybe that's worth quasi-dying for.

Thing 127:
Don't eat a suckling pig in the pool, but apart from that you'll be fine

Generations of kids have grown up being told they have to wait half an hour after eating before they go back in the swimming pool, to avoid cramp.

This is, non-negotiably, just something parents say to have a relaxing time after lunch. I'd recommend not eating so much that you feel sick diving in the water, but apart from that there is no real reason to watch the clock.

Thing 128:
If you really squashed me, I would become a black hole

Everything has the potential to become a black hole if its entire mass gets so utterly squashed it reaches what is called the 'Schwarzschild radius' (otherwise known as 'gravitational radius'). Everything: a star, a potato, a grain of sand, my tiny dog, me.[*]

It's a complicated bit of algebra that I don't understand, but the principle is that, in theory, if you were to compress an object into a sphere, for that sphere to become a black hole, the radius of that sphere would need an escape velocity that is equal to the speed of light, blah blah blah. All of the mass of the object would have to get so tiny that the gravity becomes so great that light can't escape it.

So, in order to turn the Earth into an all-consuming black hole, you would have to squish all 5,972,000,000,000,000,000,000 tonnes of it into roughly the size of a Brazil nut. I weigh about 80 kilograms at the moment (although I'm bulking and looking to get to 82 kilograms, lean, but that's beside the point), and doing the maths (I didn't do it; it's too confusing; I typed 'Schwarzschild radius calculator' into Google), I would need to be condensed down to a sphere that is 4.678×10^{-24} inches in radius; that's 0.000,000,000,000,000,000,000,046, 780 inches. Clearly that's small, but I had no concept of just how minuscule until I found out that a human sperm cell (the smallest cell in the human body) comes in at a comparatively leviathan 0.002 inches. Every atom of my being would have to be crushed down into a sphere that is 427,533,130,000,000, 000,000 times smaller than the single cell I originated from. I like a challenge. Let's make me into a black hole.

---

[*] My editor wants to make it clear that, legally, 'I was trying to make a black hole' is not a valid defence for crushing anything.

Thing 129:
Get ready to yawn

We've all had that experience of watching someone yawn and then immediately needing to yawn ourselves. Studies have shown that 50 per cent of people yawn when shown an image of someone yawning. For some people, even seeing the word yawn makes them want to yawn. No one knows why yet, although there are theories that it links to our sense of empathy, but it's definitely a thing. I might even have made you yawn as you read this. My power is immense.

Thing 130:
It takes three minutes to boil the perfect egg

I had what escalated into a substantial argument with my brother-in-law while up a mountain once. We were snowboarding and he made a passing comment that went something along the lines of, 'We're in a rush to hit the slopes tomorrow, so we'd better not have boiled eggs for breakfast because they take an eternity to cook at this altitude.' Being the smart-arse that I am, I took objection to this and told him that this cannot be the case because water boils at a lower temperature at higher altitudes and so eggs must cook quicker.

I'm an idiot.

I explained earlier in this book that, when there is less air pressure, water boils at a lower threshold and that, at the top of Mount Everest (not that the ski resort of Chamonix is quite that high), you only need to reach 71°C. To me, that obviously meant that an egg would cook quicker, simply because the water it is in reaches a boil sooner than it would at sea level. I forgot to factor in that 71°C is a full 29°C cooler than the temperature you would usually cook an egg in and that I was totally wrong. Basically, if water boils at a cooler temperature, just because it's boiling, it doesn't mean it's hot enough to cook an egg. Something my brother-in-law and eight other friends I was with would not let me forget. Thankfully this happened on my last night, so I only had to endure their ridicule for a night, a day, a trip to the airport and a flight. When I got back to London, they were all dead to me.

Thing 131:
Nobody likes a smart-arse

See previous.

Thing 132:
If you want to show your historical knowledge, order a glass of shaddock juice with your boiled egg

A lot of people want to know why there is a fruit called a grapefruit when there's already a fruit called a grape. There is actually very little in common between grapes and grapefruit. Grapefruit is a citrus fruit, while grapes are a berry.

Up until the nineteenth century, the grapefruit was known as the shaddock or shattuck. In about 1830 there was a rebrand, and it got a new Latin name – 'Citrus Paradisi', meaning 'Garden Citrus'. It appears that the public thought the Latin was all a bit poncy, but they had noticed the fruit grew on the tree in clusters, just like grapes. And the name stuck.

Thing 133:
Great, you can time travel; that doesn't give you an excuse to go stealing children

Let's say you've made a time machine and, rather than using it to prevent plague, famine or war, rather than going back to catch a *Velociraptor* and teach it to play fetch, rather than saving JFK, you decide to steal a baby from an early human and raise it as you own. The question you've asked yourself is, 'How far back in time could you go and still steal a child that could be raised like a modern human, showing no differences to a baby born today?' You won't be winning the Nobel Prize any time soon, but it's your invention so you can do what you want with it, even if you do decide to be a dick.

We know that our species (*Homo sapiens sapiens*) has existed for 200,000 years, but although a baby from this time would be anatomically modern, you'd be out of luck if you went back all that way looking for an infant that is behaviourally modern. We've evolved since then and the child most likely wouldn't have crucial gene mutations that allow for our complex language and higher thought processes. We know this because it wasn't until around 50,000 years ago that we really got into our stride in regards to making stuff and killing things.

We got better at creating tools and our cultures grew richer as we were able to problem-solve and speak more efficiently.

If you do manage to invent a time machine, I implore you to use it for humanity's greater good (or at least to bring me a baby dinosaur); however, if your decision is to kidnap a newborn, you'll be looking at going back around 50,000 years or less to be sure you can raise it to modern standards. Of course, then you have the issue of the child's timeline, had you not been a monster and ripped it from its mother's arms. What if it happened to be one of your ancestors and, by pilfering it before it had the chance to reproduce, once you get back in your time machine and head home, you never existed in the first place? What if this child would go on to invent something great, like the wheel, and when you arrived home, we were all still living in caves, dragging things uphill? What if this kid carried a gene that would make it immune to some virus that was previously killing humans and it never got a chance to pass that immunity on? You would end up killing the entire race, you arse.

Thing 134:
Things happen to people

People often ask, 'Why do bad things happen to good people?' At one level, the answer to this is that there is no such thing as a bad thing or a good person, just things and people. No one has yet found a moral particle, so as far as the universe is concerned, we're all just matter going about its business.

However, there may be an interesting scientific reason we remember bad things happening to good people. It all has to do with the bit of the brain we use to store memories, the amygdala: negative experiences are stored separately to positive ones and they seem to form stronger connections. This makes sense, as a positive memory can make you feel tingly, but you may only get one chance to learn from something that was really awful, so our brains try to make the negative stuff particularly strong. The likelihood is that bad things happen to bad people and good things to good people just as much, but we just don't recall those instances as well. It's actually worth remembering this more generally, as studies have shown repeatedly that we tend to pay more attention to negative memories than positive ones. Although, as I said, it makes sense, in terms of our mental health, it can also make things feel pretty gloomy.

Though it might not feel like it a lot of the time, there are lots of things that are going pretty well. There are bad things happening, but we hear plenty about them. Here are the ones I like to concentrate on. So, in order to finish this book on a high, I want to tell you some things that cheer me up.

REASONS
TO BE
CHEERFUL

Thing 135:
We're not as bad as you
might think

It's easy to believe, with the news sharing the worst of our behaviours and our inventions of increasingly efficient ways of killing one another, that we have reached the pinnacle of violence, but, however contrary to popular opinion it may be, this just isn't the case. The rather uplifting news is that we are actually more peaceful now than we have been since well before records began.

World-renowned psychologist and all-round smart guy Steven Pinker gave a brilliant TED Talk in 2007, suggesting that we have actually got increasingly less violent as time has gone by. Way back, 10,000 years ago, when we were all hunter-gatherers with no set places to live, evidence suggests that anywhere up to 60 per cent of men were killed by other men. If this had been the death-rate of the First and Second World Wars, there would have been 2 billion deaths, rather than the 100 million actually sustained. If the Bible can be taken as gospel, mass murder and rape were just part of everyday life before the birth of Jesus, and the death sentence was handed out willy-nilly for all sorts of minor indiscretions. Straight-up murder has dropped by two orders of magnitude since the sixteenth century, and although our media is now much more efficient at broadcasting the atrocities that do happen, we are experiencing significantly fewer wars (with significantly fewer deaths), genocides and homicides than ever before.

Nobody is entirely sure why this is, but one theory that makes sense to me is simply that lives mean more now. We live longer and are exposed to less death and disease than in previous periods of time, and so we place a higher value on life. That, combined with the fact that the world is getting smaller due to better modes of transport, communication and the internet, allows us to recognize that, regardless of where we come from, what we believe in or the colour of our skin, we are all fundamentally the same. This empathy for people we have never met may be a big factor in maintaining peace.

Thing 136:
You're a born winner

When you existed in your father's testicles and made a break for the safety of your mother's egg, you were the fastest of the 300 million other sperm that would have ended up as only half you (same egg, different sperm). Congratulations, little single-celled you – with that sort of can-do attitude, you'll go far!

Thing 137:
The world seems to be repairing itself

There was a very clever man called Thomas Midgley Jr. who, in the 1920s and 30s, invented two substances that caused more damage to the world than anything else before or since.

The first was 'tetraethyl lead', otherwise known as TEL, or leaded petrol, which cars loved because it made engines run more smoothly. Human beings were not so keen on it though; lead is a neurotoxin that lingers in your bone marrow and accumulates over time. It can lead to all sorts of neurological ailments, such as hallucinations and convulsions, as well as organ failure and eventually a rather nasty death. Despite the side effects, it was easy to produce and hugely profitable, so cars chugged along on the stuff until it was banned in 1986. Good news, but as I mentioned before, lead accumulates, and there are still many people around today from the generation just before mine that still have up to 625 times the amount of lead in their system than they would have, had leaded petrol not been created. The other good news is that the amount of this harmful substance in the air has dropped dramatically since the ban and we're on the road to recovery (a road where more and more people are driving electric cars, which is a good thing).

The other thing Midgley invented was chlorofluorocarbons, or CFCs. In his defence, unlike with the petrol, he had no idea how much damage these little bastards could do and he did have good intentions when he invented them. In the 1920s, refrigerators were chilly deathtraps. The gases used as coolants were flammable and poisonous and they often leaked out. Dodgy fridges were responsible for many a calamity at the time. CFCs solved this problem; they were safe to breathe and non-flammable. Hooray. The wondrous gas didn't take long to catch on and was soon everywhere: in household appliances, our deodorant cans and our air-conditioning units.

This is where our ozone layer comes into the equation – it consists of a thin smattering of special oxygen molecules that soak up harmful radiation from the Sun and prevent our lovely little planet from overheating. CFCs, although not hugely abundant, have a voracious appetite and every one molecule of them can destroy 700 of our ozone. Thus, a big old hole ripped open, the ice caps started melting, the world got hotter and global warming went bananas.

It's not all doom and gloom though; our planet is a resilient little ball of rock and, since the ban on CFCs in 1974 (despite some being legally produced in parts of the world until quite recently), there has been evidence that our ozone layer is repairing itself, with estimates stating the hole shrunk by 1.5 million square miles between 2000 and 2015. Global warming is still a huge concern and we are pumping out a ton of other greenhouse gases that keep the world too warm, but banning things like TEL and CFCs mean we're giving Earth a chance. Good job, humans (apart from Thomas Midgley, who was very naughty).

Thing 138:
Suck it, global warming

This might come as a surprise to you, but we're actually getting better at using renewable energy sources. Some countries are really leading the way: Germany has gone from using 6 per cent renewables in the year 2000 to 32.6 per cent in 2015. *Gute arbeit, Deutschland* (Google Translate told me that means 'Good job, Germany'). In 2016, all of Portugal was run solely on renewable energy for four days straight. *Caminho a percorrer, Portugal* ('Way to go, Portugal', according to Google Translate). But even they were beaten by Costa Rica, who managed 100 days!*

Obviously, switching to solar, hydroelectric and wind energy isn't going to happen overnight – we have all the infrastructure in place for fossil fuels and it takes time to recalibrate the world's set-up, but it is definitely happening. Pollution and global warming aside, we will eventually run out of oil and gas, and the limited stock pushes the price up. Also, reserves are

---

* And it's not just faraway places. From 23–26 December 2016, Scotland's wind turbines provided more electricity than Scotland used.

often found in specific locations around the globe, which makes some countries very rich, as they own the world's most valuable commodity. But the Sun will be shining for at least a billion more years, there is always wind, our water isn't going anywhere and these resources can be found wherever you look. The fact that renewable energy is endless and found everywhere should mean that it is also very cheap and the money it does cost needn't be funnelled into a few wealthy countries, so global economies should level out, a little at least. Our air will be cleaner, the climate will be more stable and the more that powerful countries like Germany lead by example, the faster the rest of the world should follow suit.

Thing 139:
Versova beach got cleaned

In less than a year, a group of concerned citizens in Mumbai, India, cleared more than 4,000 tonnes of rubbish: the largest beach clean-up in human history. It began with two concerned neighbours, but using social media they were able to expand to 200 volunteers. We need to stop plastic before it gets into the ocean, but people standing up and making a positive difference should always be celebrated.

Thing 140:
The Netherlands is running out of criminals

Apparently, everybody is bloody lovely in the Netherlands – they don't have enough criminals to make all their jails financially viable. In 2009, they closed eight prisons; in 2014, they closed a further nineteen; in 2015, they borrowed some inmates from Norway to fill up unoccupied space (and because Norway ran out of room) and, in 2016, it was announced that they will be closing a further five.

Part of the reason the Netherlands seems like the kind of place you would feel comfortable leaving your bike unlocked is because punishments are becoming a little less severe for relatively minor crimes, such as drug use and the like. This is brilliant news and when coupled with the justice system opting to focus on rehabilitating offenders with the use of ankle bracelets, and other community-based techniques, the rates of recidivism have been shown to reduce by up to 50 per cent compared to incarceration.

Let's all go to the Netherlands (but only if you promise to be on your best behaviour. I would hate for them to have to reopen correctional facilities for a bunch of no-good tourists).

Thing 141:
Next stop, Robocop

Previous generations of bionic appendages have been lacking in terms of degree of movement and how many actions can be carried out. They worked by attaching sensors to the site of the trauma and picking up on muscle twitches, but the issue is that usually the muscle is damaged, meaning the signals are incomplete. But there's a new method in development that's supercool and can actually pick up on the signals your brain (via your spine) gives off when you intend to perform an action. These prosthetics move when you think about moving, just like an actual limb. Now, some people who are unfortunate enough to lose a limb will be able to regain much more movement and control than previously possible. The best news is that it's early

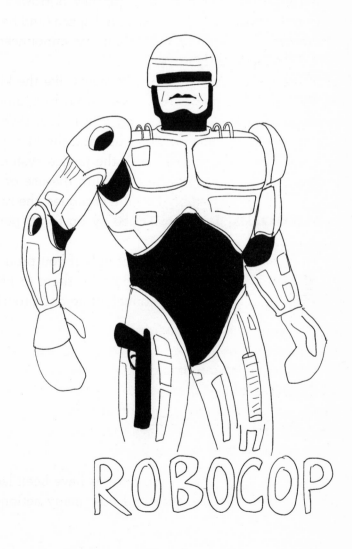

ROBOCOP

days for this technology and there is lots that's still to be achieved. With any luck, it won't be long until scientists can add little extras, like rocket fists and laser fingers.

Thing 142:
5p can make a big difference

Everyone moaned a bit when the 5p plastic bag became a thing, but it reduced the use of bags by about 6 billion, a reduction of close to 85 per cent. It's been so successful that other countries are beginning to do it, too.

Thing 143:
Throwing ice all over yourself is an excellent idea

Remember the ALS ice-bucket challenge from 2014? I took part in it and I imagine a lot of you did too. Well, it turns out that it was totally worth it, as it raised enough money and awareness that, in 2016, a gene that is at least partially responsible for the degenerative disease was discovered. Finding this gene is the first step towards treatment and eventually, hopefully, a cure.

ALS, or Amyotrophic Lateral Sclerosis, is a neurological illness that exhibits itself with the inability to control motor functions, and eventually leads to paralysis and death. It's an awful hand to be dealt and, up until the ice-bucket challenge, I had never even heard of it. I find it incredible that a simple game, harnessing the power of social media, has resulted in the biggest breakthrough in the disease's history. The internet is brilliant, science is brilliant, people are brilliant.

Thing 144:
Medicine is great

It's not just ALS; we have a vaccine for malaria that's testing 46 per cent effective, increasingly effective HIV medications, a new TB vaccine is under trial, and there have been recent reports that Alzheimer's researchers have started animal-trialling a cure. Even with cancer, where there is a massive way to go, in the UK you are twice as likely to survive today as you would have been forty years ago.

Thing 145:
Human beings aren't getting any less ingenious

Every year, Forbes releases its list of thirty scientists under thirty making a difference. In 2017, the projects they were involved in ranged from artificial tissue used for drug trials, targeted antibiotics and finding habitable planets, to recycling batteries for use in the developing world and scavenging wind power between buildings in cities. The world is anything but perfect, but if there's one thing that you can count on, it's that us hairless apes like to solve a problem.

Thing 146:
Someone has come up with a formula for happiness

A gifted individual by the name of Mo Gawdat, a former chief engineer from Google, has recently published a book, *Solve for Happy*, where he has worked out a formula for happiness. He's a really interesting guy and there are lots of variables, but ultimately, he says that happiness occurs when our perception of our life as it is matches up to how we think life should be.

There are all sorts of reasons why we are unable to look at our own lives properly, whether that's because we find it hard to look at ourselves with honesty, we are always worrying about the past or busy thinking about the future. But so many studies show that, regardless of disposable income, those that are less materialistic have a higher sense of life satisfaction. People that put value in acquisition of possessions over more enriching pursuits, however, tend to have lower levels of well-being. Professor David Myers reviewed loads of the studies in this area and discovered that, in recent years, there has been a definite correlation between the number of things we own and rates of depression and other psychological disorders. Of course, correlation just means that there is a relationship between the two variables, but it's hard to tell if materialism causes low self-worth, low self-worth causes materialism, they feed into each other in a more complex pattern or something totally different is affecting both. Maybe it's the cockroaches, in their bid for supremacy, who are releasing some sort of neurotoxin from their armpits that is making us buy more and feel worse, but I doubt it.

It's been suggested that, when striving for the next material object – whether it be a watch, a house, a car, or a handbag – it's possible for someone to value that object over and above more fulfilling activities, such as adventure, new experiences and nurturing one's relationships with other people. Some people have a value system that is focused on the social image that having material objects presents. A 2012 study by some psychologists called Bauer, Wilkie, Kim and Bodenhausen found that this belief system comes with the cost of higher rates of anxiety and depression, along with a diminished sense of social and self well-being and fewer personal relationships. Basically, people that tended to put value in 'things' over people and experiences ended up more lonely and more sad. It's common sense, when you think about it.

Professor Tim Kasser gives an explanation that, to me, sums it up quite well; he says that, as a species, us humans are good at acquiring and using stuff. We had to be good at collecting, creating and applying items because, hundreds of thousands of years ago, we would have starved to death or been eaten by the things with big teeth and claws if we weren't. Our ingenuity is what has made us so successful as a species, but ingenuity is useless without the raw materials. A long time ago, those materials could have meant life or death, but not only that; those that had lots of resources would likely have been con-sidered more attractive by potential mates, because they could be prepared for when times got tough. Having things was a form of showcasing your social status, and this is a trait that is still within us. It's much less a case of life and death, and much more a case of constantly working to gather more and more material things to exhibit social standing. What was healthy when we had little more than sticks, stones and animal hides to collect has become something worrying when you consider the sheer quantity of things available today.

I've tried not to be driven by money or material things, but it's easy to get caught up in the luxuries my job has to offer. However, losing my stepdad in the process of writing this book has really hammered it home: you can't take the money and the stuff you've bought with you when you pass away. Brian invested his time in people and relationships and, in the end, what really matters is that he was loved. He was so loved, in fact, that he had the busiest room in the hospital, full of friends, family, well-wishers and even extra nurses who had taken a liking to him. In a ward that was all too full of patients who had nobody, Brian had a small army of people, all by his side when he passed. You can't buy that.

What I wanted to do with this book was to give everyone as many different ways as possible to think about life and about their own existence, whether that's in time or space, or just seeing that we don't have it all worked out. I hope you enjoyed it. If you did, come and let me know. If you didn't, well, just keep that to yourself in honourable silence, or better still, lie to every-one you meet and tell them it's bloody excellent. See you later.

Oh, I nearly forgot.

Thing 147:
There is an answer to, 'What came first, the chicken or the egg?'

This was the number one question you wanted answered.

People have been asking this question for thousands of years as a kind of philosophical brain teaser. If you mean eggs full stop, not specifically chicken eggs, then it's definitely the

egg. We have fossilized dinosaur eggs that are almost 50 million years older than the first birds, let alone the first chicken.

If you mean chicken eggs, then, luckily, now we have science and evolutionary theory, we can definitively answer it: it's still the egg.

Because of how evolution works, at some point, deep in the mists of time, a creature that was not quite a chicken, but a very close ancestor of it, gave birth to an egg containing a creature that would later become the first chicken. I'd love to be able to tell you which mutation made that chicken more likely to survive, but I don't really understand how they survive now. Seriously, have you ever spent time around chickens? They haven't even come up with a good excuse for all that road-crossing people like to joke about so much.

One final thing for luck (and irony)...

Thing 148:
147 is the highest score possible in snooker

So, we've established that I know 147 things, but there is much more out there that I am completely oblivious to. For example, as I was informed by nearly everyone I told about this book while writing it, 147 is the highest score you can achieve in snooker. I think. I looked it up and I still don't really understand it. What I can confirm is that the number 147 definitely has some import in the world of cues and balls and green felt.

Further Reading

Bullying

www.bulliesout.com

www.kidscape.org.uk

Bereavement

www.rainbowtrust.com

www.muchloved.com

www.cruse.org.uk

Abusive Relationships

www.womensaid.org

www.lovedon'tfeelbad.co.uk

Mental Health

www.mind.com

www.rethink.org

www.sane.org.uk

Body Image

www.bodycharity.co.uk

www.bodygossip.org

Sexual Health

www.brook.org.uk

www.fpa.org.uk

LGBTQ Charities

www.stonewall.org.uk

www.itgetsbetter.org

www.glaad.org

Science

www.newscientist.com

www.howstuffworks.com

www.waitbutwhy.com

www.livescience.com

www.wired.co.uk

Animals and Conservation

www.greenpeace.org.uk

www.nationalgeographic.com

Nutrition and Fitness

www.nutrition.org.uk

Internet Issues

www.bbc.co.uk/webwise

Acknowledgements

As I quickly discovered while on this journey, it takes an army to write a book and I am forever grateful to every single person who has helped me on the way.

Big love, huge respect and mammoth thanks to my team at Gleam: Lucy, Georgia, Milly and Abi. To Daisy, who has persevered with my daily panics and all-too-regular stressy episodes. To Dom, who has been with me since the very start of my career and has become a cherished friend.

To the entire team at my publishing house, Pan Macmillan, some of whom I am yet to meet, but have all worked on this venture nonetheless. My editor, Jamie, for his excellent feedback, generous deadlines and for giving me the freedom to do basically whatever I wanted. To Alex and Jess for doing the book things I still don't fully understand, but doing them better than anyone else.

To my excellent family for their unconditional love and for providing me with all the material I could ever need since the day I was born.

To my audience on the various platforms I have found myself on, who have chosen me to be this voice for them and watched me grow up.

And, of course, to my beautifully souled, endlessly patient and brutally honest wife, Tanya, who has tolerated me throwing random facts at her since very soon after we met and still, despite that, seems to be quite fond of me.

(Oh, and a canine shout-out to my dog, Martha, who sat on my lap for at least 138 of the 147 Things.)

Elizabeth Ashcroft | Gyda Elgseter | Dinika Sharma | Éabha McNally | Lauren Drake | Abigail Warren | Sara Hassoune | Rebecca Eriksson | Chloe Gudgin | Lucy Welford | James Redmond | Gerardo Piña | Francine Nuñez | Imelda Tran | Michelle Callaway | Gabrielle Andrus | Sofie Johansen | Suzanne Kirchner | Mariam Hussain | Laura Mckittrick | Ava Wallace | Ceryn Seivwright | Olivia Farley | Sofía Olivar | Rachel Rothnie | Faye Boucher | Chloe Webber | Kayleigh Black | Abbie Collins | Olivia Tompkins | Daphne Argyropoulos | Faizah Rabbye | Kendra Maquina | Jen Lask | Natalya-Victoria Botham | Ami Beverley | Meghan Kelsey Andrew | Arwa Stone | Janine Faber | Maddy Gannaway | Sarah Freier | Kayleigh Dowty | Georgia Wakeley | Hugh Sloane | Toby Berryman | Katrína Skidmore | Clare Rabbitt | Honor Buxton | Emily Sullivan | Katie Clements | Caley Starbuck | Delilah McIntyre | Jessica Mander | Sara Stockholm | Zara Ahmed | Jessica Spratt | Abigail O'condell | Tegan Norman | Mario González | Chloe Ryan | Chloe Ratten | Emma Walters | Phoebe Mansford | Hannah Hyde | Hannah Holm | Alice Hann | Holly Mccluskey | Karolina Bulisova | Gemma Hutchinson | Lucy Bromley | Ellie Rice | Meredith Koh | Chloe Fixter | Gesa Bresch | Georgina Harden | Lucy Cade Inês Rodrigues | Hannah Walshaw | John Tzanis | Hannah Lindsay | Owen Rees | Jane Carr | Kalvin Croucher | Isobel Hulland | Charlotte Osborn | Victoria Man | Maria Emelyanova | Courtney Stevenson | Imogen Watson | Caitlin Grafton | Carmina Policarpio | Kirstie Bryce | Christopher Tilley | Chloe Morgan | Baxter Bradford | Holly Todd | Holly Charlton | Krystal Moore | Marijn van Engelen | Amelia Fitzsimons | Alice Ullyart | Georgia Levington | Poppy George | Minaal Meer | Hana Stastna | Sophie Lorentzen | Andreea Botea | Isha Arora | Kiara Blanche | Nikoletta Slusarz | Georgie Edwards | Nicole Therese | Aoife Doogan | Natasha Soper | Nicolai Harning | Hazel Reid | Olivia Gribble | Amy Slade | Amy Giles | Jaay Hussey | Megan Weilersbacher | Lucy Dawes | Kira Donald | Caitlyn Dinsdale | Ellie Harber | Taylor O'Grady | Alice Guilbot | Jaslyn Kan | Paige Bajus | Tereza Vacurová | Eleanor Kimber | Audrey Farina | Amy Predgen | Emily Saba | Charlotte Booth | Sonja Reiter | Georgia Hankin | Emma Ikonen | Belinder Kaur | Bethany Hurst | Meghann Cleary | Olga O' Meara | Marion Raboisson | Samantha Morton | Emmaleigh Ough | Céline Scholte | Heather Prentice | Ryan Suarez | Emilia Hawthorne | Hannah Vincent | Kerry Mee | Ellie Marsh | Nia Borsey | Isabel Manders | Miroslava Glassova | Alexa MacLaren | Tanika Naidoo | Davina Ralph | Olivia Fox | Rachel Alex Marie | Phoebe Ashmore | Pien Bos | Polina Bogomolova | Bhargavi Iyer | Johanna Weitbrecht | Maria Brimah | Anahita Keer | Nancy Reagan-Wallin | Salma Essid | Sophie Temperley-Guest | Eva Hargrove | Cajsa Marquardt | Moona Shafiq | Alice Sausman | Aimee Mayer | Ellie Fanning | Caroline Maria | Carina C. | Sabrine Abdelli | Libby Cross | Manish Thakrani | Jade Milton | Sarah Machado | Erin Waddilove | Alex Corrigan | Kayleigh McCarthy | Katie Hopper | Aline Willi | Vanessa Simão | Mélanie Chédotal | Nadezhda Popova | Courtney Palmer-Jones | Shannon O'Connor | Olivia Gough | Libby Cosford | Charlotte Young | Eline Dotinga | James Patterson | Amelia Inman | Taya Xiao Skaaning | Julia Weymann | Maria Renteria | Karien Venter | Madison Tharnish | Kate Rooney | Jesse Ebenal | Anika Mody | Mackenzie LaCourse | Danielle Hong | Alexa Vassos | Bonnie Eberhart | Carlos Gomez | Jessica Laden | Brielle Tilley | Adriana Valdez | Rhianna Hiom | Rachael Leong | Hailey Grotkowski | Marie Deshays | Hadiya A. | Bethan Streatfield | Lacey Littman | Lauren Quebral | Amrutha Lakshmi Gadamsetti | Amy Sugden | Kalisha Bhanabhai | Jasmine Chong | Adrienn Jurkovics | Ammara Talati | Corina Brändle | Demi McMonagle | Klara Eul | Melissa Breedveld | Alex Conry | Emma Blachford | Olivia Neadle | Louise Szeto | Ellen Campbell-Gaskell | Gemma Gooch | Monika Leon | Elli Brooke-Smith | Katie Pearcy | Jessica Azzopardi | Lili Souch | Kevin Mckinlay | Livvy Sayers | Meg Howat | Niamh Long | Dionne Gledhill | Ella Bennetts | Romy van Dijk | Victoria Wrathall | Flora Caia | Bryan Hariadi | Shannon Buergne | Rachel Cohan | Steff Torres | Vinny Littlemissstyleguru | Melissa Dipp | Demarco Tunstill | Hmwe Thinn | Karen Díaz | Courtney Raleigh | Tanya Phanda | Kristina Vega | Samantha Boring | Katherine Mazzotta | Jessica Sim | Ximena Zuniga | Colleen Terra | Claire Vander Ploeg | Marissa Redden | Elizabeth Watters | William Turri | Juliann Guerra | Kaylynn Arsenault | Judith López | Kira Tabron | Sarah MacLean | Rachel Cheong | Jillian Burke | Cecilia Nguyen | Hannah Keeton | Adriana Deluis | Brandon Stevens | Sarah Shoa | Nerisha Reddy | Cydnie Safruik | Jaimee Troutt | Anjelica Arias | Rayanne Cardoso | Cormac Foley | Bonan Om | Hallie Meadows | Liana Meli | Meaghan McGrath | Andrew Ithurburn | Arista Alexander | Candice Lade | Olivia Gagnon | Katherine Burns | John Diether Barroga | Claire Volna | Kelci M. | Alicia Lynne Zinia Sultana | Megan Hanson | Sydney Brant | Tracy Atkinson | April Cobar | Terence T | Najla Redha Rachel Prowler | Emily Anderson | Makenna Woods | Sheridan Horne | Kira Weis | Julia Allsop | Pihla Pitko | Jasmine Aquino | Simi Newman | Chiara La Barbera | Matilda Thorén | Callum Parsons | Michaela Judson | Tori Resseguie | Amélie Levray | Grace Guthrie | Jenny Rine | Tayler Bulluck | Gabrielle Piloto | Sarah A | Jennifer McMullin | Anniina Puska | Rebecca Allison | Maria Shipovsky | Christina Purdon | Alicia Madore | Michaela Tutty | Danielle Shepherd | Melanie Bubevich | Karine Castonguay | Anna Furtado | Ana Bravo | Michaela Baker | Jessica Garrick | Francisco Romero | Caitlin Hunter | Lindsay Yates | Madison Holdaas | William Carter-Bertrans | Abby Shore | Eliza Bracey | Iris Antunez Villegas | Nathalie Venne | Sai Lyons | Sanjana Ravi | Tawny Louise Cortes | Hana Yamagishi | Dj Elzinga | Amado Villanueva | Angela Canonoy | Abu Zar Ahmad Buhari | Caitlin Meness | Sydney Ly | Antonia Rout | Teresa Huntington | Liv Borzi